INVENTION AND REINVENTION

Pete ... we will change
the world !

Mary Shadbolt

INNOVATION AND TECHNOLOGY IN THE WORLD ECONOMY

MARTIN KENNEY, EDITOR
University of California, Davis and Berkeley Roundtable on the International Economy

---

INVENTION AND REINVENTION

The Evolution of San Diego's Innovation Economy

MARY LINDENSTEIN WALSHOK
AND ABRAHAM J. SHRAGGE

STANFORD BUSINESS BOOKS
An Imprint of Stanford University Press
Stanford, California

Stanford University Press
Stanford, California

Special discounts for bulk quantities of Stanford Business Books are available to corporations, professional associations, and other organizations. For details and discount information, contact the special sales department of Stanford University Press. Tel: (650) 736-1782, Fax: (650) 736-1784

Printed in the United States of America on acid-free, archival-quality paper

Library of Congress Cataloging-in-Publication Data

Walshok, Mary Lindenstein, author.
   Invention and reinvention : the evolution of San Diego's innovation economy / Mary Lindenstein Walshok and Abraham J. Shragge.
      pages cm
   Includes bibliographical references and index.
   ISBN 978-0-8047-7519-9 (cloth : alk. paper)—ISBN 978-0-8047-7520-5 (pbk. : alk. paper)
   1. San Diego (Calif.)—Economic conditions. 2. Technological innovations—California—San Diego—History. I. Shragge, Abraham J., 1950– author. II. Title.
   HC108.S65W35 2014
   330.9794'985—dc23   2013021466

Typeset by Thompson Type in 10/13.5 Minion

This book is dedicated to
Marco Gary Walshok
Urban Political Scientist, colleague, friend, beloved husband
and father.

and to
Elaine S. and Harmon M. Shragge
Who during their lives constantly encouraged knowledge seeking,
excellence, and service to community.

CONTENTS

FIGURES AND TABLES

Figures

Tables

ACKNOWLEDGMENTS

Each of us has relationships and experiences that merit acknowledgement in this work. Let us begin by loosely tracing its development. Mary Walshok has spent most of her life as a full-time academic administrator at UC San Diego, leading a large and very community-engaged extension service. This has allowed her to participate for close to forty years in the economic and social life of the community, in particular, the growth of new industry clusters that are creating jobs for which "new economy" skills are needed. In a sense, San Diego has been her laboratory for learning.

She brings to this work nearly ten years of research and writing. It began to take shape in her mind during a sabbatical semester at Kellogg College, Oxford University, supported by the Bynum Tudor Fellowship in the fall of 2004.

In 2006, her team received a multimillion dollar contract from the U.S. Department of Labor through an evaluation research organization in Berkeley, Berkeley Policy Associates. This evaluation project, on which Mary was the principal investigator, allowed her to spend four years studying thirteen regions across America that were trying to turn their economies around, moving from old-economy industries in the direction of more innovative technology-based clusters and manufacturing. The regions in this study included places in Florida, North Carolina, Central California, upstate New York, and Central Michigan. It was an extraordinary opportunity to develop a comparative perspective on how civic culture varies from place to place and the differential effects of particular kinds of industrial legacies, migration patterns, and local history on the capacity for adaptation and change. Within two years, the same research team received another major grant from the National

Science Foundation to compare innovation outcomes in three major R&D hubs—Philadelphia, St. Louis, and San Diego, as well as support from the Lilly Endowment to work with Indiana-based BioCrossroads to document innovation efforts in the health and medical device sectors. These research opportunities resulted in Mary's understanding that there was much that needed to be known about the early history and distinctive character of a place to understand its contemporary capabilities. She is deeply indebted to the federal funders and foundations that have been willing to invest in her research and to her team at UC San Diego for providing such a wealth of comparative regional knowledge.

In Abe Shragge, Mary found the historical grounding that she sought. With a particular focus on the social history of San Diego and the important role the military and the federal government played in San Diego's birth as a major city in the twentieth century, he was the perfect match, made, in part, thanks to a friend and supportive colleague, Chandra Mukerji. Abe's mother Elaine S. Shragge encouraged his academic interest in history. His interest in investigating San Diego's unique heritage came from his late father, Harmon M. Shragge, whose experience in the U.S. Navy during World War II prompted questions about the role of the American military in civilian society. That there might be a special relationship between the service and the city of San Diego emerged in exchanges with Professor Steven Hahn; Abe found Steve's guidance and encouragement indispensible to his later study. The work, and later the advice and support, of Professor Roger Lotchin of the University North Carolina, Chapel Hill, proved to be of immeasurable value to his research and writing, as did the counsel of Michael Bernstein and Steven Erie. Abe must thank three hardworking individuals who suggested and found many a dusty archival box and otherwise opened up any number of obscure sources: Steve Coy in the Mandeville Department of Special Collections at UCSD's Geisel Library, Barry Zerbe in the Military Records Department of the National Archives and Records Administration, and Deborah Day, who for many years directed the archives at the Scripps Institution of Oceanography. Mr. Max Schetter, then executive director of the Greater San Diego Chamber of Commerce, gave Abe free rein to study that organization's voluminous records. And Robert Summers helped fill in a number of critical research issues from a long distance and on short notice; Bob also created the map of San Diego's military installations that appears later in the book. Abe also wishes to thank his colleagues, especially Professor Yong S. Lee and students at the Korea Development Institute of Public Policy and Management, who have been highly supportive since he began teaching there in 2010.

Together, we are extremely grateful to the team at UCSD Extension who has been so supportive of their multiple research and writing projects while Abe has taught in Korea and Mary serves as an associate vice chancellor at UC San Diego: Josh Shapiro and Nathan Owens, Mary's research team on multiple projects; and Brenda Macevicz and Jennifer Rowe for amazing help in manuscript preparation. Thanks also go to Margo Beth Fleming at Stanford University Press and Martin Kenney at UC Davis for simultaneously being our champions and critics. Finally, it is important to thank the many people who agreed to talk with us personally and to share books, papers, and connections as we developed this volume. They include such people as: Neil and Judith Morgan, Bob Witty, Pat Crowell, R. B. "Buzz" Woolley, John Davies, former Governor and San Diego Mayor Pete Wilson, Mike Madigan, Pete Garcia, Bob Hamburger, Peter Salk, Charles Cochrane, Stanley Chodorow, Harvey White, Ivor Royston, Tim Walleager, Pete Schultz, Richard Ulevich, and Richard C. Atkinson.

ACRONYMS USED

BRAC	Base Realignment and Closure
CIRM	California Institute for Regenerative Medicine
CTRI	Clinical and Translational Research Institute
DARPA	Defense Advanced Research Projects Agency
DOD	Department of Defense
D-Z	Day & Zimmermann Company
EDC	Economic Development Corporation
GA	General Atomic
GD	General Dynamics
HP	Hewlett Packard Corporation
IP	Intellectual property
IT	Information technology
JCVI	J. Craig Venter Institute
LEED	Leadership in Energy and Environmental Design
MCC	Microelectronics and Computer Technology Corporation
ONR	Office of Naval Research
R&D	Research and Development
S&L	Savings and Loan
SAIC	Science Applications International Corporation
SANDAG	San Diego Association of Governments
SBIR	Small Business Industry Research Program
SD-CAB	San Diego Center for Algae Biotechnology
SDSU	San Diego State University
SEAL	Sea Air Land Teams (US Navy)

SIO	Scripps Institution of Oceanography
SPAWAR	Space and Naval Warfare Systems
TSRI	The Scripps Research Institute
UC	University of California
UCDWR	University of California Division of War Research
UCSD	University of California San Diego
USD	University of San Diego
VA	Veterans Administration
VC	Venture Capital

INVENTION AND REINVENTION

PREFACE

More than a decade ago, the distinguished journalist James Fallows, who grew up in Redlands, California, in the 1950s, wrote a book entitled *More Like Us.*[1] Fallows's evocative book captured an idea about America, about California, and, we would argue, about communities like San Diego, that has shaped our thinking about the story of this place. Reflecting on literary treatments of the West, his book calls up images from the 1950s of women in shiny new convertibles, dressed to the nines with bouffant hairdos and high heels, arriving to do their family shopping at the local Safeway. With parents who were likely dirt-poor farmers from the Midwest who had migrated to California in the 1930s with the last few dollars they had, driving cross-country in an old jalopy, they still believed in and hoped for another chance, a new life, a better life—and they achieved it. Fallows argues that at the core of American culture is this belief in the possibility that no matter who we are or where we came from, we can reinvent ourselves. Those women in the Safeway parking lots no longer were the daughters of poor farmers from the Midwest; they were no longer "Okies," but rather prosperous, well-dressed middle-class housewives, shopping for their families in the California sunshine. This idea, so effectively presented by Fallows, resonates with our experience. However, as we will argue in the pages that follow, in America, not only do individuals reinvent themselves, but whole communities and economies do. The story of places like San Diego that shift and adapt over time is very much a story of reinvention.

The two of us came together around the writing of this book based on our shared history as Californians. We had engaged in earlier collaborative activities at UCSD as part of a Pew Charitable Trusts grant to launch a short-lived but meaningful UCSD Civic Collaborative; the book project grew out of our mutual interest in the interplay among civic culture, regional economic outcomes, and the natural advantages of specific places. Walshok is a sociologist, long interested in the ways that broader social dynamics shape individual opportunities and outcomes. Shragge is a historian who has investigated the specific ways that individuals and social organizations at the local level create opportunities that shape the character of their communities, especially their key economic activities.

We also share an abiding curiosity about the relatively unknown history of the community in which we have lived and worked for multiple decades: San Diego, California. What is available is not terribly helpful to understanding the nature of the place, particularly its urban development and its fascinating economic transformations over time. San Diego, like most communities, is rich in its early history—stories of individual families, photographs and archives about distinctive groups and neighborhoods, but little has been written about the evolution of the region over time. Walshok's lifelong interest in the social dynamics of innovative communities, in particular, what it is that communities do to develop new economic opportunities that result in new businesses and new jobs, strongly motivated her interest in doing a book about San Diego. Shragge's research in the historical evolution of the San Diego region, especially the city's unique relationship with the federal government, in particular the military, has helped elucidate the character of the contemporary civic culture; that was the inspiration for his involvement in this project.

The collaboration between an industrial sociologist and a social historian began to make a great deal of sense the more we talked about what we each wanted to do. Shragge's detailed work on the history of San Diego, while fascinating, could not take on its full meaning and implications without connecting it to the compelling contemporary social and economic dynamics of San Diego, which have captured the attention of civic leadership across the country and around the world, as communities grapple with how to turn their economies around. Walshok's ongoing interest in the contemporary dynamics of San Diego's innovation economy could not be fully elucidated without understanding the details of the full history of the place—who came here, what the early industries were, how a civic culture developed that enabled the growth of R&D in the region and gave rise to such an inclusive and opportunistic business community. It became clear that to understand the interplay of civic culture and the shifting economic and social outcomes that have characterized the San Diego region for more than 150 years, a great deal of attention to historical detail was required as well as a great deal of familiarity with contemporary stories that had yet to be written to document this evolution. Our partnership, we believe, has allowed us to do this.

We also share a healthy skepticism about this place we love so much. San Diego's history and contemporary character present sharp contradictions that we hope will be better understood because of the work we have done. We think of them as the "paradoxes of place." In the case of our place, San Diego, an overriding paradox that shapes all of its history and continues to frame economic growth issues moving forward is the desire of citizens in the region to build a world-class city with only minimal investments and/or costs in terms of taxes, environmental stewardship, labor conflicts, or infrastructure development. The history reveals to us that San Diegans have always wanted to have their cake and eat it, too. They want a great world city, but they don't want to spend; they don't want to invest; they don't want to be taxed. They want to avoid labor conflicts at all costs. Always, they want to preserve the beauty of the place, its pristine environment.

We will demonstrate other dramatic paradoxes throughout this book. One is the paradox of an essentially conservative political culture that has for more than a hundred years based its economy on feeding at the federal trough. San Diegans have sought the federal government as a funder and a customer more aggressively than possibly any city in the United States, and yet, until very recently, its core political culture has been, albeit an environmentally conscious one, conservative and Republican. Rather than build a truly sustainable political economy, the city has dealt with its growth in recent generations by borrowing from pension funds and short-changing many public institutions and infrastructure projects in the desire to avoid new taxes. No one seems to see the city's foundational paradox: Its prosperity comes from living off the federal taxation system, which pays for national defense, R&D, and many of the federally funded infrastructure projects from which the region has benefited over time. That simply does not match the community's antigovernment, antitax political culture.

An additional paradox of the place is the opportunism and boosterism as well as occasional corruption that has characterized its business culture over time. San Diego has a tendency to oversell itself, but, ironically, sometimes it actually works . . . it actually pays off. We talk at great length in the pages that follow about the importance of the 1915 Exposition, the post-World War II efforts to build R&D institutions in the region, the audacious strategies used by all the research institutions, and in particular UC San Diego, as they began to grow their R&D infrastructure throughout the 1960s and 1970s. Moreover, we present the continuing efforts among San Diegans to be a world leader in biotech, renewable energy, and stem cell research. In so doing, San Diego has swum repeatedly against the tide of more mature and well-resourced regions, reaching far beyond its grasp but in fact generating real success now and then, even spectacularly at times.

We hope as well that this book will help illuminate some contemporary paradoxes about the region. One is the belief among many that nothing important happened in San Diego until the UC San Diego campus was founded in 1960. We suggest that the region's civic culture always included a deep respect for science, technology, and higher education, including an understanding of their value to economic growth. The clusters of science and technology companies whose development has accelerated significantly since the 1980s clearly benefited from the parallel growth of the research institutions, most prominently UC San Diego, on what is known as the Torrey Pines Mesa. However, our research and data make clear that, as early as 1902, local citizens were investing in research enterprises; the federal government, particularly the military, was locating some of its most important technology development activities in the region by the 1910s, such as the largest radio tower in the United States being located on Chollas Heights, and that city boosters, in particular the Chamber of Commerce, since the 1920s actively promoted through marketing materials, advertising, and lobbying, the importance of San Diego to the nation's technological future.

A final paradox that we seek to illuminate is the unexpected growth in entrepreneurial high-tech business development from the 1980s onward in what was otherwise a defense contracting town. This transformation of the business culture is not well understood as a foundation for the region's economic success over the last few decades. Many other cities and regions across the United States and the world look to San Diego because of its impressive gains with few of the early advantages possessed by more robust centers of technology and entrepreneurship such as Boston and the San Francisco Bay area. The critical role played by an opportunistic and adaptable business culture in this transformation is an important part of this story.

In sum, as two individuals who were born and raised in California since the 1940s, we have witnessed the transformation of the entire state, but especially the community of San Diego, over a fifty-year period. It is a fascinating tale of invention and reinvention and one that we are delighted to place in the light of day in this volume you are about to read.

1 INVENTING SAN DIEGO

What is the matter with San Diego? Why is it not the metropolis and seaport that its geographical and other unique advantages entitle it to be? Why does San Diego always just miss the train, somehow?[1]

It was with some justice, back in 1923, that San Diego's preeminent business leader John D. Spreckels chided earlier generations of city builders for their sincere but ineffective efforts. Even a casual observer at the time, however, would have noted how dramatically circumstances had changed for the better in just the past few years. In fact, the city and its economy had grown prodigiously after 1913 as a new development strategy gradually gained traction. During the first two decades of the twentieth century, San Diego emerged as a player of note on multiple stages—California, the nation, and the Pacific Rim. After more than fifty years of frustration, indeed failure, to put their town "on the map," San Diegans had at last invented a means of urban development for themselves that worked. They had found a way to harness the limited, problematic resources endowing their region such that they could now attract investment, in-migration, industrialization (of a very peculiar kind, to be sure)—in short, most of the trappings of modern urban growth.

What San Diegans of the nineteen-teens and twenties had wrought remains largely visible today: an attractive seaport city well-appointed with desirable amenities for business and tourism; a large military presence; impressive institutions devoted to culture, the arts, and higher education; a beautiful outdoors-oriented environment that includes beaches, bluffs, mountains, and desert; and a sprawling, bustling urban/suburban presence. Beneath that surface, though, lies a complex process of successive reinventions: Contemporary San Diego is a product of a distinctive pattern of evolutionary development, the investigation, interpretation, and understanding of which might provide valuable insights for engaged citizens in cities across the United States in search of new opportunities for progress.

San Diego of course suffers from the same kinds of urban problems found almost anywhere, including economic inequality, ethnic and racial tensions, government corruption and fiscal mismanagement, decaying infrastructure, congestion, and pollution, to name the most prominent. Despite these, the city has still found a way to maintain its reputation as a relatively bright spot on the map, even in the face of major crises. Since the global economic downturn that began in 2008, for example, San Diego has managed to steer clear of many of the difficulties that have mired other cities in gloom. According to federal statistics, San Diego's overall economy "not only continued to grow in 2008, but the pace of expansion accelerated," even "as the rest of California and the nation significantly slowed."[2] The U.S. Department of Commerce's Bureau of Economic Analysis attributed this feat to three factors: First, federal military spending and defense procurement—longtime anchors of the local economy—increased; second, the rebuilding activities that followed a series of horrendous wildfires during the previous year generated considerable economic activity around the city and county; and third, professional and business service industry groups contributed greatly to the city's strong performance, offsetting declines in other sectors such as real estate and trade, both wholesale and retail.[3]

A closer look at two of those areas in particular reveals a great deal more about the invention and reinventions of San Diego's economy, political as well as otherwise. The federal component included not only increasing military payrolls, retirement benefits, and activities of the Veterans Administration, but also aerospace manufacturing and shipbuilding. Of greater significance was growth in the information sectors, which encompass "professional and business services, educational and health services, leisure and hospitality and government services." The public sector alone contributed 17 percent to the region's GDP (gross domestic product), a much higher percentage than anywhere else in either the state or the nation. A long history behind that is one of the themes this book will explore in greater detail in the pages that follow.

Before traveling back in time, it will be useful to examine today's San Diego and the pillars that support its civic culture and political economy. Although the statistics enumerated in the following discussion may at first appear to be nothing more than straightforward economic indicators, they demonstrate something more profound about the nature of the community and its identity—issues hard fought and won over generations.

Many people from outside the region identify San Diego first and foremost as a prime vacation destination. The beaches, world-famous Zoo and Safari Park, Sea World, resorts to accommodate any taste or budget, and myriad other attractions bring visitors to San Diego by the tens of millions each year.[4] Their economic impact on the city is tremendous: The "visitor industry" contributes nearly 10 percent of the gross regional product (GRP), or $17.1 billion in 2011, and employs 160,000 workers; the transient occupancy tax alone adds $177 million to the city's coffers. Tourism is in sum the city's third-largest source of income. Second largest, as already noted, is government, composed of activities and income derived from state, federal, local, and military agencies. San Diego is perhaps equally well known as a Navy town, a reputation that began to emerge during the World War I era and that, we will argue, became the city's predominant and most durable signifier ever after.[5] The total economic value of the military in the San Diego region amounted to $22.3 billion in fiscal year (FY) 2007, or 8.3 percent of GRP, which represents a combination of highly diversified direct and indirect spending. In and around the city reside fourteen major Navy and Marine Corps installations, dozens of tenant commands, 107,800 sailors and marines, and tens of thousands more military family members. The Department of Defense (DOD) employs 19,600 civilians in San Diego (down from 24,000 a few years earlier). Military retirement and disability benefits (267,000 veterans live in San Diego County) bring $1 billion a year to the region, plus another $1.1 billion from "direct payments to individual veterans; spending, salaries, and contracts to administer the VA; hospital, nursing care, and other grants; and guaranteed and insured home loan programs."[6] And all this comes before accounting for DOD-administered procurement contracts performed in San Diego by local businesses and other major defense contractors such as Northrop Grumman and Science Applications International Corporation (SAIC)—these amount to 52 percent of DOD revenues in San Diego County. Looking beneath the surface of the aggregate figures, however, reveals an issue that defines the heart of this book. As the *San Diego Economic Ledger* has noted,

> Professional, scientific and technical services now dominate San Diego's defense industries, supplanting aerospace and shipbuilding, which led the local defense industry for much of the past century. . . . The Defense Department is focusing more on high tech equipment and weaponry that can be used to fight insurgents in places such as Afghanistan, and spending less on fighter jets and other large weapon systems designed for more conventional wars. "Technical services" in San Diego with military applications are led by computer programming, engineering, and other scientific research and development.[7]

In other words, while the artifacts of San Diego's invention remain highly visible and essential to local identity and economy—the ubiquitous warships, fighter planes, uniformed servicemen and -women, and military bases—the real attributes of the city's reinventions have become even more important. And these facts refer only to the defense-related elements of San Diego's knowledge industries, while the nondefense technology sector endeavors, involving the life sciences, software, and communications, are nearly as important. San Diego hosts 6,023 technology companies (as of 2010), which generate 20.8 percent of the county's total payrolls, at remarkably high rates of pay. The *San Diego Economic Ledger* pointed out, moreover, that the 138,800 tech jobs produced a huge multiplier effect, which "indirectly accounted for 103,000 more jobs and induced another 120,400 local jobs."[8] Defense and civilian high-tech manufacturing have experienced astonishing advances during the past few years, in part a result of increasing value-added mechanization and fewer but more highly skilled workers, whose productivity has grown by $1.2 billion between 2009 and 2011.[9] And as they have engaged in the wars against cancer and other devastating illnesses, San Diego's health research institutions have gained world renown in their quest for cutting-edge treatments.

In a similar vein, the educational and health services component of the information sector has expanded recently despite the Great Recession, although local economists have noted its gains have "lagged the rest of California and the nation."[10] The city's great public institutions of higher education, San Diego State University (SDSU) and the University of California San Diego (UCSD), have suffered massive cuts in their share of the state budget; even so, UCSD in 2012 was ranked fifth in the nation for annual federal research and development spending, and its research faculty includes numerous Nobel and Pulitzer prizewinners, members of the National Academies, and recipients of MacArthur Foundation "genius grants." With regard to the health industry, San Diego's hospitals and health care providers rank among the county's largest employers—106,000 workers—and receipts from operations generated $10.9 billion in income in 2007, or 9.3 percent of the county's total economic activity.[11] San Diego during the past twenty-five years has built five new clusters of technology-based companies, which today include fifty research institutes, 600 action sports companies, 600 life sciences companies, 1,100 wireless and software companies, 250 energy and environmental companies, and 300 defense and security companies—an astounding record of growth in a very short span of time.

While these facts and figures present a picture of San Diego's economic endeavors that is both rosy and biased, some salient conclusions nevertheless emerge. First, all of these industries have deep and persistent sociocultural roots in the community, and all were present to a significant degree in the invention of modern San Diego that occurred at the turn of the twentieth century. With the exception of tourism, they may have appeared in a different form back then; for example, early experiments in aviation represented the high-tech sector, while the city's reputation as a health resort was once based on at least some notorious quackery. Institutions of higher education and scientific research were dreams that San Diego's turn-of-the-century leaders worked hard to conceive, gestate, and birth, although they didn't mature until decades later. Thus the military element was the one that really took off first and formed the core of the city's civic culture and political economy. Second, the role of the national government, in particular its capability and willingness to fund these endeavors in whole or in part, was always a key to San Diego's twentieth-century development. Third, given the nature of the undertakings in combination with federal underwriting, these activities were all at least to a degree immune to economic downturns, which meant that San Diego rode the nation's political/economic roller coaster somewhat securely during times of depression and recession as well as during war and peace. This is not to say that such security came comfortably or easily: It required several massive reinventions along the way, although more in the form of evolutionary change rather than Schumpeterian "creative destruction." Fourth, all the elements of San Diego's development depended on the natural capital of the region, as limiting as some of the region's natural assets always were. San Diegans, however, saw opportunity in the environment and found particular ways to modify it and harness it to their needs while protecting and preserving some of its most precious attributes. Finally, we must credit the city's lively human capital—its visionaries, its political and business leaders, its ordinary citizens. Some saw the region's potential, others engineered it and made it work, and others supported it with their votes, their tax dollars, their labors, and their enthusiasms. These ideas encompass precisely what we mean by the terms *civic culture* and *political economy*—how citizens identify their needs and wants, how they marshal the necessary resources, and how they generate the social capital and political will to make the pieces fall into place, over and over again.[12] That is the story of San Diego we propose to illuminate.

SAN DIEGO AND OTHER "PIONEER CITIES": EARLY ADVANTAGES OF PLACE

To bring San Diego's socioeconomic history into sharper focus, a brief look at three other pioneer cities that were founded during the same era as San Diego, but emerged as thriving centers of activity much earlier, will prove instructive. It will demonstrate how civic entrepreneurship has made creative use of natural resources to generate distinctive economic outcomes. St. Louis, Missouri; Detroit, Michigan; and Chicago, Illinois present valuable insights, whether in contrast or similarity to what occurred in Southern California during the latter half of the nineteenth century.

The four cities shared some remarkable similarities during the early period of their development. They all required copious boosterism to help them take off;[13] they all required significant alterations to the natural landscape for the sake of productivity and transportation infrastructure (often financed and executed by the state and/or federal government); they all rode the same boom–bust roller coaster that characterized the American economy during the nineteenth century; and they all took great advantage of technological progress to build their individual urban economies, undertaking major programs of innovation at strategic moments. Moreover, these cities' civic cultures during the early years were all imbued with what their boosters liked to call the frontier or pioneer spirit because they all perched at least for a time at the edge of American civilization as they sought to establish themselves as successful, permanent urban places. Their initial periods of urbanization occurred between the 1810s and 1830s, following the opening of the Northwest Territories after 1789 and Louisiana Purchase (1803) with the subsequent movement of American settlers into the Ohio and Mississippi River valleys. All three places had attracted the attention of colonial explorers and traders long before the onset of serious trans-Appalachian migration. Their town sites were all claimed or founded by French voyageurs: Chicago as early as 1673–1674, Detroit in 1701, and St. Louis in 1763. (Spanish explorers/conquistadors had visited San Diego in 1542 and 1602, but the first Spanish colonizers didn't arrive there until 1769.)

According to Robert Spinney, most of the several hundred newcomers to Chicago in the early 1830s were "Easterners looking for a fresh start and cheap land in the west," as was the case for a majority of the migrants during this period of intensifying westward movement.[14] They dreamt first of successful subsistence farming, but before long they began to eye the growing market economy of what by then had become known as the "Great West," an urban phenomenon inseparable from the agrarian experience. As Howard Chudacoff and Judith Smith have pointed out, though, "Cities accompanied and even preceded the western frontier, acting as commercial outposts and depots from which settlement radiated."[15]

For settlers, the commercial possibilities of early Chicago, Detroit, and St. Louis far outweighed the creature comforts available at the time. By all accounts, these places were physically inhospitable, especially in winter, and they lacked all the basic amenities of civilization. Their geographic locations, however, suggested bright futures for adventurous entrepreneurs who had the fortitude (and capital) to endure some substantial hardship. Indeed, all three settlements enjoyed strategic locations at natural breakpoints on centuries-old transit routes that positioned them well to generate and capitalize on future commercial development. Such was apparent to French explorers in the Chicago area in the 1670s and 1680s who, despite the lakeside area's cold marshiness, understood its value as a crossroads, soon to be exploited by European fur trappers and traders. As early as 1682, the French voyageur Robert Cavelier Sieur de la Salle predicted that the site would someday be "the gate of empire," and "the seat of commerce."[16]

Chicago's position on the southern shore of Lake Michigan and its proximity to a mini–continental divide connected it to the Mississippi River Valley and the great river's outlet at New Orleans as well as to the Great Lakes system, engendering a huge potential for waterborne commerce within a vast region of the continent; once the Erie Canal opened for business in 1825, it connected the lakes to the Hudson River and New York City and to the whole universe of Atlantic trade. Despite those advantages, the nonnative village that began to emerge at "Chigagou" (the "place of wild garlic") after 1750 seemed to have little to offer its pioneers for generations to come. A report prepared by mineralogist William H. Keating for the U.S. Army Corps of Engineers in 1823 noted the wretched condition of the climate, soil, scenery, commerce, and housing; in short, it was a place that offered "no inducement for the settler." Even its perch on the lake appeared to be of scant value, its potential as a harbor yet undeveloped and perhaps undevelopable. As such, "it must ever prove a serious obstacle to the increase of the commercial importance of Chicago."[17] In 1830, fewer than 100 people lived there.

Central to Chicago's evolution from frontier outpost to capital of the Great West, as William Cronon put it, were "the connections and disconnections between city and country, consumer and producer, humanity and nature," shaped by those who saw and seized the opportunities to build, inhabit, and benefit from the great gateway city. As agricultural productivity grew along with the settlements that supported them, Chicago's early city builders had to make huge, expensive alterations to the landscape for the city's merchants to take good economic advantage of the hinterland. This in turn depended on "cheap lake transportation to the east" as well as strong and extensive ties with the American northeast. Here, according to Cronon, emerged a winning combination of human and geographic determinism. Because they couldn't lower the troublesome water table to eliminate the ubiquitous swampiness, they raised the city above it. To connect the city with the countryside, they built roads and dug canals, all difficult and costly to finance, which "brought striking changes to the regional economy," in particular by expanding Chicago's economic backyard all the way to the Mississippi River just north of St. Louis.[18]

Chicago's boosters overcame enormous adversity to develop the city's first railroad connections in the late 1840s, thus setting the stage for exponential growth that lasted for much of the rest of the century. By virtue of the city's consciously crafted role as frontier gateway to the Great West, through the linkage of "its hinterland with the markets of much wealthier communities farther to the east" says Cronon, Chicago "drew trade to itself as no other city could do, becoming a metropolis second only to New York through its privileged relationship to the West."[19]

Much of Chicago's postrailroad success came at the expense of St. Louis, whose city builders had counted on the Mississippi River to create and maintain that city's position as "lion of the West." St. Louis originated during the colonial era as "an explicitly commercial enterprise . . . tied by royal charter to the interests of an expansionist government concerned with supporting global ventures." American settlers there after 1804 found hunting, trade with Native Americans in furs and other commodities, and river navigation to be more attractive occupations than agriculture. A prominent historian of the region notes that "St. Louis's future in the years following incorporation depended on equal parts luck, money, and geographic fortuity." Even so, settlers developed a highly productive agricultural hinterland by the 1860s, which in tandem with booming food-processing industries came to comprise a substantial fraction of the city's economy.[20]

The advent and proliferation of the steamboat enabled the business leaders of St. Louis to profit greatly from their central position in a commercial network that ran from New Orleans at the river's southern extremity to the Southwest, and all the way through the Ohio River Valley. Thus local boosters' claim that St. Louis was "by nature best point for the distribution of commerce, intelligence, and forces of the West" seemed believable by the 1830s and thereafter. As had been the case in Chicago, however, the landscape required significant work to make this so: Sandbars in the river approaches to the town constantly threatened the viability of the harbor. Local citizens attempted on their own to keep the channel open, but a more definitive solution didn't materialize until 1837 when Congress appropriated $50,000 for Army engineers (led by Robert E. Lee) to build dikes. This amount was one-third of what Lee said he needed; not until ten years later did Congress vote $75,000 for the task, but President Polk vetoed the bill. It was left to the city to finish the job, which it did early in 1854, at its own expense of about $250,000.[21]

Nearly four times Chicago's size (in terms of population) in 1840 and still more than twice as large a decade later, St. Louis's growth trajectory leveled off while Chicago's skyrocketed in the post–Civil War era. The 1870s was the crucial decade during which Chicago surged ahead decisively and permanently. Despite a strong pattern of industrialization during the middle 1800s that included brewing, distilling, meatpacking, textiles, brick making, and stove making, more capital-intensive manufacturing remained scarce in St. Louis as investors found commerce and real estate more attractive. One of Missouri's U.S. senators, archexpansionist Thomas Hart Benton, was instrumental—by convincing local investors and winning huge state and federal subsidies—in securing St. Louis's position as terminus of the Pacific Railroad, which started building westward from the city in 1851. Cost overruns, quality-control issues, competition from other cities and states, rampant insider trading and related malfeasance, a volatile national economy, and the coming of the Civil War all contributed to the railroad's problems.[22]

Despite the massive corruption that tainted such government–business partnerships, St. Louis continued to progress during the years following the Civil War. According to Eric Sandweiss, "A vast new tributary territory, shipping raw materials to St. Louis and consuming its commercial goods and industrial products, was created in the south, southwest and west; and railroad connections were established in all parts of the state. In the upper Mississippi Valley [, however,] St. Louis lost its dominant position to Chicago, but not for want of trying." The folklore of the time attributed this outcome to the energy, entrepreneurialism, and vision of Chicago's leaders as opposed to the conservatism and complacency found in St. Louis's business and political communities. But Chicago's natural advantages, coupled with its eastern financial connections, seem the more likely explanation. Chicago's strategic position on the Great Lakes—in effect the far western terminus of the Erie Canal—enabled it "to gather all traffic headed East from the upper Mississippi region." Moreover, Chicago's railroad connections, financed and built more than a decade earlier that St. Louis's railroads, were conceived and bankrolled by business leaders in New York and Boston, to which Chicago was much more closely tied than St. Louis, whose business leaders looked to New Orleans. And once John Deere's revolutionary steel plow broke the fabulously rich soil of Chicago's hinterland, the farmers of the region "yearned for quick access to the best markets in the industrial northeast; and St. Louis could not have reversed that fact if it had built a dozen railroads to Chicago's doorstep."[23]

The advantages of place—what scholars of urban America call the "doctrine of natural advantages"—did much to shape the comparative developmental trajectories of Chicago and St. Louis between the 1840s and 1870s. Both grew rapidly into major cities during this short period, anchoring the huge agricultural, industrial, and commercial productivity that characterized the outsized reality as well as the mythology of westward expansion before the closing of the frontier in 1890. Throughout these years, San Diego remained but a speck on the map of the United

States, if it indeed appeared on the map at all. In fact, its natural advantages were not to become manifest until after the turn of the twentieth century.

A brief history of Detroit during this same time will help to round out this part of the discussion. Antoine de la Mothe, Sieur de Cadillac, founder of the settlement that became Detroit, Michigan, was a French soldier whose military prowess earned him in 1688 a royal grant of territory in what today is the state of Maine. In 1701, Cadillac, as he is best known, established a trading post and fort on a site called "the strait" (*de troit* in French) on a river that connected Lake Erie with Lake Huron via Lake St. Clair. The original site of the settlement, which became Fort Pontchartrain and later Fort Detroit, occupies the center of the modern city. The company of fewer than 100 settlers planted a successful crop of winter wheat, built some essential structures—church, stockade, and storehouse—and sent to France for their wives and children.

Soldiers and settlers farmed, traded for furs, and fought a series of battles with Native Americans after 1706. During the French and Indian War (1754–1763), France ceded Fort Detroit to Britain, and in 1796 the settlement and surrounding area became part of the United States. According to the *Detroit Almanac*, approximately 500 people resided there at the time.[24] Incorporated as a municipality in 1802, Detroit burned to the ground three years later and was subsequently reincorporated in the Territory of Michigan. Thanks to the fortunate confluence of rapidly improving means and networks of transportation and "abundant cheap labor," Detroit thrived as a frontier city—"the metropolis of the territory and state," whose history and destiny were "inseparable from the ages-old story of the river," according to historians Frank and Arthur Woodford .[25]

The Detroit River—all twenty-six miles of it—along with its exceptional function connecting two of the Great Lakes, established the town's importance as a garrison, granary, workshop and way station that served "one of the most significant folk migrations in history."[26] After the Erie Canal opened in 1825, thus creating a direct passage between New York City and the Lakes, many thousands of settlers as well as countless tons of produce and cargo embarked or debarked at Detroit's waterfront. As the Woodfords point out, the canal opened a vast market for Michigan crops, making Detroit a natural, classic break-point in transportation routes (where people and goods disembarked from one mode of transportation, for example a ship, and boarded another, for example a train) that extended, directly, all the way to Europe by 1857.[27]

During the 1840s, primary industries, including copper and iron mining, emerged in the region, which benefited greatly from Detroit's transportation-related advantages. Heavy-metal refining enterprises soon appeared in Detroit itself. Although similar industrial development in the Chicago and Pittsburgh areas eclipsed Detroit's metallurgical productivity only a few years later, commercial activities grew apace, as did population both within the city and out in its hinterland. The local lumber industry extracted "more riches from Michigan's pine forests than were taken from California's gold fields," generating abundant "ready capital for venture enterprise, and developing industry attracted a labor force with highly specialized mechanical skills." The "frontier enthusiasm" persisted in Detroit beyond the 1870s, for the city "was a crossroad of opportunity and young men gravitated to it and achieved beyond their wildest expectation."[28] According to the Woodfords' history, "Detroit came of age as a city in the late 1880s and 1890s . . . having attained a state of metropolitan sophistication."[29] "It followed that when the world was ready for the automobile, Detroit was ready to become the Motor City."[30]

Despite the many similarities in the early development paths of San Diego, Chicago, St. Louis, and Detroit, the trajectories of the three inland cities differ from San Diego in at least three key areas, and thus the story of San Diego's distinctive past will illuminate the main claims we make in the rest of this book. First, although all four originated as colonial outposts long before their accession to the United States, Chicago, St. Louis, and Detroit each served and prospered as gateways to the West during a period of intensive westward movement, while at the same time they supplied vast markets in the older sections of the nation with the products of their regions' farms and factories. In contrast, San Diego existed at the far western end—geographically but not chronologically—of American continental expansion. To San Diego's mid-nineteenth-century settlers, regional growth meant filling in a much more limited hinterland in comparison to the territory that surrounded the cities of the Great West; moreover, San Diego would never be a gateway to San Francisco or the gold and silver mining districts in northern California and Nevada. It might *someday* emerge as a gateway to the Pacific Rim, but that reality remained only a dream for some time to come. Second, the three interior cities were blessed with abundant exploitable natural resources then and always in demand, while semiarid San Diego boasted no such extractable wealth. Third, city builders in Chicago, St. Louis, and Detroit succeeded early in establishing significant transportation infrastructure (river, lake, canal, rail, and road) connecting them to their hinterlands, the rest of the nation, and indeed, the world, while San Diego remained isolated for an embarrassingly long period of time. Fourth, at least in the cases of Chicago and St. Louis, within twenty years or so from the date of their incorporation as American cities, these places experienced tremendous demographic and economic growth. Although Detroit was slower to grow between 1800 and 1840, even its population numbered 116,340 by 1880. Much to the consternation of its boosters, though, San Diego had to endure a much longer period of painfully slow urban growth, refusing to take off until after the turn of the twentieth century.

Nevertheless, examining these cities' stages of birth and early growth brings to light the common factors that need to be addressed to understand how city builders create something from practically nothing. The chapters that follow address systematically certain near-universal issues relevant to the processes of sustained urbanization. These ideas have informed the way we have organized San Diego's story and what it might mean to the development and evolution of other regions.

WHY REGIONAL STORIES MATTER

Scholars offer many competing views about how economies grow and transform. We base the structure of this book on a documented history of a place and its economic transformations over time, as well as a deep understanding of its contemporary productivity and activities. The San Diego story suggests that there is much to be said for a more evolutionary approach to understanding how regions sustain their economic prosperity in spite of major shifts in global realities, technologies, and markets. Our narrative also makes clear that natural advantages become more or less valuable at different points in time, depending on shifting externalities. Local communities filter their understanding of these shifts and their implications for society through the lens of their own particular cultural values, social experiences, and familiarity with specific economic pursuits despite macrolevel changes such as technological revolutions or shifts in the global political economy. We will argue that this occurs in large part because of the early patterns that become established during the initial consolidation of a regional economy, what we call throughout the book the "invention" phase. The particular natural assets, technologies, and mix of talent, as well as the perceived needs and desires of the community, enable the invention process, thus invariably shaping how the future unfolds. A community's sustained response to these conditions will lead over time to the emergence of distinctive patterns of behavior, cultural grooves, and shared values—what we identify as the "civic culture." As a civic culture emerges from the kinds of behaviors and practices that enabled early industries, it also tends to shape the community's way of grasping its economic future.

Demographics, by which we mean the characteristics of people who settle in a community (for example, gender, ethnicity, age, socioeconomic status, place of origin, and so on), also affect the civic character of a place. Thus, even when dramatic technological shifts or changes occur in the global political economy, these local values intersect with larger events. They affect how readily individuals, as well as communities as a whole, understand, absorb, and ultimately integrate new realities into the ongoing economic life of their communities. We will argue that not only in the case of San Diego, but in virtually all communities, including iconic first-tier economies such as Boston and the Silicon Valley, understanding the historical, cultural, and sociological factors that shape and determine absorptive capacity and capacity for change are critical to any understanding of innovation and regional transformation.

San Diego, California, presents a fascinating example of this process. We therefore offer in this book an investigation of the ways by which the region's natural assets first gave rise to distinctive economic development strategies that shaped a civic infrastructure and a way of doing business that has carried it across more than a century of adaptation to constantly changing conditions. In our view, San Diego is a community that continuously repurposes its assets and realigns its economic development strategies and organizations to sustain prosperity over time. The city's early successes have framed this repurposing and realignment; perhaps unique to San Diego's case is the way the community mobilized its limited natural assets in response to its needs to compete for national—mainly military—resources, which the city began to win thanks to the dawning of the "Pacific Century."

FORCES SHAPING THE ECONOMIC HORIZONS OF PLACE

We suggest five distinct recurring factors that are relevant to the understanding of any economy as its actors create an initial path to economic growth; we further assert that these factors remain important and in play over time, even as the community attempts to accommodate itself to changing conditions. They include the issues discussed in the following subsections.

The Natural Advantages of Place

The history of all great cities begins with a set of economically leverageable assets that an early group of enterprising people sees as promising. Historically, communities with abundant natural resources such as timber, coal, or agricultural land, as well as communities well positioned with transportation links such as harbors, rivers, and eventually railroads, mobilized those assets to achieve economic growth. Many cities, such as Rochester, New York; St. Louis, Missouri; and Detroit, Michigan, became industrial and agricultural centers for the nation in the nineteenth century. Other cities, including San Diego, possessed less immediately exploitable resources and learned through trial and error how to take advantage of what they had, typically at much later times in history. San Diego's unique location and imperfect harbor were able to be developed for economic purposes in large part because of the decision by civic entrepreneurs to leverage gifts of vast expanses of publicly owned lands for complementary military and research and development (R&D) purposes.[31] San Diego's success began to emerge only after 1900 with the acquisition of an American overseas empire in the Western Pacific, which moment some historians have poetically called "the dawn of the Pacific Century." In contrast, Rochester, Detroit, and St. Louis took off well back in the nineteenth century.

The Core Values of Early Settlers

Demography matters. A dramatic example appears in the difference between the economic histories of two cities in Michigan that are today only two hours apart. Grand Rapids developed throughout the nineteenth century amid forested lands in the western part of the state. It attracted enterprising Dutch Reform furniture makers who saw an opportunity to manufacture products to serve the rising middle and upper middle classes in the industrial hubs of Chicago, Detroit, and St. Louis. In contrast, Detroit, long a center of mining, industry, and transshipment, was an early mover in automobile design and manufacturing and, with Henry Ford, the development of assembly line technologies. The ambitious individuals who initially built these opportunities in Detroit actively recruited non–English-speaking, uneducated workers from Europe and eventually poor Americans from the agrarian southern states for low-skilled assembly line jobs. The economic trajectories as well as the population characteristics, attitudes toward education, and entrepreneurship are quite different in the two cities today.[32]

In San Diego's case, the beauty- and health-giving characteristics of the natural environment from the beginning attracted many mature, better-educated, often affluent individuals, a large percentage of whom had respiratory and health issues. Although some came in part because of health problems, many also were no longer satisfied with the status quo in the places from which they came, and so they sought alternatives, in particular a place where they might shape the environment to their own tastes. San Diego's history is less about fortune hunters than it is about collectors, experimenters, utopians, and idealists, who migrated from the ravages of the industrial Midwest, hoping to build a different kind of city. This theme is echoed across the generations, well into the 1950s, 1980s, and even to 2010, as entrepreneurs, scientists, and engineers have been drawn to the region because they see it as a blank slate on which they can build something new and meaningful. The social, educational, religious, and ethnic characteristics of the early migrants to a region are important because such individuals carry values and social practices relevant not only to the early invention of a local economy but also to the capacity of that economy over time to adapt to new economic forces.

How Communities Organize to Achieve Economic Promise

We define the heart of civic culture as the ways in which citizens behave and organize their activities to realize economic growth compatible with the core values they bring to their place. The heroes in San Diego's history are not the captains of industry, such as a Ford or a Carnegie, but philanthropists, such as John D. Spreckels, E. W. and Ellen Scripps, George Marston, and Irwin Jacobs; government advocates such as William Kettner and Pete Wilson; and, eventually, government contractors, such as Reuben H. Fleet and John Jay Hopkins. San Diego, for example, has a long history of pooling resources among small players, of public votes supporting grants of land to institutions that promise economic return. The robber barons and the big landowners rarely appear in San Diego's history; rather, it is technocrats, scientists, and engineers, such as Roger Revelle and Edmund Keeney, Jonas Salk and Craig Venter, as well as successful technology entrepreneurs such as the aforementioned Fleet and Hopkins and later J. Robert Beyster.

In the industrial Northeast and Midwest, the early advantage of rivers, harbors, and rail connections as well as abundant resources such as coal and iron ore allowed for major industrial development that created massive cities and fabulous individual wealth throughout the nineteenth century. In contrast, in San Diego, abundant land and the power of the municipality to give it away represented the primary leverageable asset. Tens of thousands of acres of so-called pueblo lands were allocated to San Diego during the Spanish colonial era. From 1850 and throughout the twentieth century, San Diego leaders used this real estate, first to develop the city and then to lure the military, and subsequently during the Cold War and thereafter to bring defense contracting, manufacturing, R&D, and commercial enterprises to the region. This book will examine not only how San Diegans used land to achieve economic ends but also the sorts of distinctive strategies used to finance infrastructure and attract investment to the region, as well as approaches to building a competitive regional labor force.

What Resources and Talents a Community Cultivates

In their quest for development, communities seek to cultivate talent and resources according to community values, which can vary considerably over time. In the case of San Diego, there is a long history of attracting well-connected, well-educated, and technologically oriented talent to the region because of an enduring commitment to growth through "clean" industries. A century or so ago, San Diegans offered numerous entertainments and lavish public displays as they welcomed the Navy to the region—a defining element of the city's civic culture. In the postwar era, the city's leaders made significant efforts to attract R&D institutions, scientists, and engineers to the region in the interests of national security, and this continues today in the interests of global competitiveness.

We know from economic history that, in contrast, some communities actively recruited diverse, less-educated workers—the automobile industry stands out in this regard. Historical documents reveal the antagonism many of San Diego's early settlers had to the gritty industrial experiences of the nineteenth-century American northeastern and midwestern cities. They explicitly describe their move to the West and to San Diego in particular as a way to escape the poverty, the grime, and the unruly working classes that then characterized many of the nation's great industrial cities. San Diego's early settlers said they wanted a "clean city" and thus "clean" industries and a disciplined, orderly, and patriotic workforce. The military and most especially the Navy, with its supposedly closely controlled, courteous men in blue suits, seemed an attractive alternative to many. A compelling idea running throughout the book is the creative tension between these rather conservative values about clean industries, well-behaved workers, and disciplined and courteous social norms and the enterprising, opportunistic, and at times devious business culture that characterizes San Diego's history.

How Citizens Define and Promote Their Place

Marketing and branding serve to enhance a community's reputation and ensure its continuous economic prosperity along the path it has identified. In most communities tipping points occur, events or activities that by their magnitude reposition the place in the national consciousness; events such as the opening of the Erie Canal in 1825 or Chicago's World Columbian Exposition in 1893 serve as examples of such tipping points. San Diego's first great tipping point was the Panama–California Exposition of 1915. After the Spanish–American War and the acquisition of Hawai'i, Guam, and the Philippines (1898–1899) as American territories, San Diegans creatively exploited the unique geographic position of their harbor as the gateway to the Pacific. Citizens redoubled their efforts to position the town as a city for the Pacific century, a Navy town, a military town important to the nation's commercial and national security interests.

San Diegans' strategy has consistently sought to attract clean industry, first courting the Navy and then mounting the Exposition of 1915, but also in successive efforts through contributions of land to bring aviation, naval, and general defense contracting to the region. San Diego in the 1930s billed itself as the "air capital of the West" and became a Federal City throughout World War II; in subsequent decades it began to brand itself as "technology's perfect climate."

In sum, the chapters through which the social and economic history of San Diego unfolds emphasize how certain cultural values, social practices, and industrial legacies became established early in the community and eventually became the platform through which change and future opportunities, new ideas and economic horizons were filtered and understood. Understanding the interplay of these issues in dealing with changing externalities and macro forces can be an important lesson not only in understanding how cities are built but in understanding how they adapt, particularly in the age of knowledge.

DISTINCTIVE CHARACTERISTICS
OF THE SAN DIEGO EXPERIENCE

San Diego's evolution from a small isolated village at the tip of California on the border with Mexico was importantly shaped by a number of larger critical events and opportunities in response to which an initially small but soon growing number of individuals and civic alliances developed to harness them for city building. This book details how the intersection of these broader opportunities converged with the region's distinctive civic culture such that they represent critical moments, indeed the tipping points in the region's development.

In broad terms, the first of these was the dawn of the Pacific Century, which opened a tremendous window of opportunity for what was still a village in contrast to both Los Angeles and San Francisco at the turn of the last century. In specific terms, we describe the actions taken by San Diegans on the heels of the Spanish–American War in 1898 and most especially around the opening of the Panama Canal and subsequent buildup of naval and aviation forces as critical to setting the initial direction of the region's economy.

In broad terms once again, the mobilization of the nation around World War II stands as another tipping point for San Diego. However, specific to the San Diego experience was President Roosevelt's designation of San Diego as a Federal City and the University of California's decision to make Scripps Institution of Oceanography (SIO) its Southern California headquarters for the UC Division of War Research. Both of these positioned San Diego leaders and institutions in unique and important ways with federal agencies and priorities in a manner that substantially benefited the region in the 1950s and 1960s and continues to benefit the San Diego economy today.

On the heels of the war effort, the Cold War, along with the USSR's success at rocketing the Sputnik satellite into orbit and the growing interest in national security through science and technology, mobilized San Diegans to become early proponents for building R&D institutions of value to the nation in the service of national security. A new national outlook on health emerged as part of this movement, as exemplified by the war on cancer declared by President Richard Nixon in 1971. With the end of the Cold War in the late 1980s, global economic and technological competitiveness in a now much flatter world became the watchword. Again, San Diegans mobilized early and effectively to build clusters of science and technology companies as a path to expanded economic growth. Today, in the twenty-first century, with the restructuring of multinational corporations and the convergence of technologies in arenas such as renewable energy and health, the region's civic culture once again has mobilized to create interdisciplinary collaborative institutions that will assure the region's economic vitality moving forward.

The central purpose of this work of social history is to elucidate how the civic culture and specific actions occurring within a singular place, San Diego, allowed entrepreneurial responses to major challenges in the larger political economy over time, thereby enabling the region's invention and continuous reinvention of its core economic activities. San Diego continues to adapt, evolve, and expand its economy in ways that are surprising given its early undistinguished roots. All of this invention and reinvention, however, is occurring within a distinctively attractive but limiting geography that can best be understood by looking at the values and attitudes about community and place that early citizens and subsequent migrants to the region brought to its civic culture.

As the chapters in this book demonstrate, San Diego's early settlers and enterprising city builders earnestly valued two qualities essential to any approach to their city's development. First, they desired to preserve its beautiful natural environment and its many amenities of place, which provided a seemingly health-giving climate, potential for family-scale agriculture and a more healthful, relaxed lifestyle than could be found in the nation's older industrial cities. Their second primary concern, closely related to the first and particularly after 1900, was to find some economic path to greatness other than the industrial trajectory of the cities from which many of them had migrated—Chicago, Detroit, Cleveland, and St. Louis. Paradoxically, between environment and civic culture, these ideals precluded large-scale agricultural and industrial development, an irony that appeared repeatedly in San Diego's civic discourse.

Given the aggressiveness with which San Diego pursued the Department of the Navy, San Diego's story became a military story, in part because of new military opportunities that arose after the Spanish–American War in 1898. Up to and through the World War II era, the city's monocultural devotion to the militarization of the local economy caused San Diego to forgo opportunities for commercial and industrial development seized earlier by cities such as Los Angeles, San Francisco, and Seattle on the West Coast. Civic leaders in San Diego were both opportunistic and strategic in their pursuit of the military; opportunistic because with the dawn of the Pacific Century a new window, a new path for development opened up for which they could compete, and strategic because of the ways in which they mobilized regional resources and worked with the federal government to secure their desired ends.

The parallel growth in health as an industry was slower but no less opportunistic and strategic. As early as the 1880s San Diego business leaders, physicians, and philanthropists were investing in sanitariums, hospitals, and health research clinics. This occurred coincidental to the formation of a variety of utopian communities and what we would today call "alternative" health movements. Relocation for health and health tourism featured prominently in San Diego's early history, and we will show in this book how it transformed over time into hospitals, clinics, clinical research, and eventually basic research in the life sciences, which today represents one of San Diego's most distinctive global assets.

All the biographies of San Diego's early leaders, as well as the historical studies of early efforts to develop the city's economy and attract settlers, underscore the health-giving features of its natural environment—the arid climate, the warmth of the sun, the invigorating waters of the Pacific, and the year-round availability of fresh produce. In the late nineteenth and early twentieth centuries, when antimodernism swept through Europe and America, San Diego, a place largely unformed but with tremendous natural amenities, offered a new chapter for many already prosperous health seekers and people imbued with utopian ideals. Alonzo Horton in 1867, George P. Marston in 1870, and, most especially, the large and prosperous midwestern family of newspaperman Edward Willis (E. W.) Scripps in the 1890s: All saw the promising quality of life San Diego offered. On his initial encounter with the city, Scripps described it as "a busted, broken down, boom town . . . probably more difficult to access than any other spot in the whole country."[33] As historian Molly McClain points out, nonetheless, the embryonic character of the region at least partly enabled the Scripps family's San Diego "experiment." Many among the American landowning classes were seeking "regeneration and renewal in a variety of different ways; sojourns into the wilderness, shows of military virtue, exploration of native cultures, psychological study, aesthetic production and experimental urban planning," so well described in T. J. Jackson Lears's *No Place of Grace: Anti-Modernism and the Transformation of American Culture, 1880–1920.* Such ideas even emanated from the White House, with President Theodore Roosevelt (1901–1908) strongly advocating conservation of natural resources and enjoyment of the nation's natural wonders.

San Diego truly offered newcomers a chance to build a different kind of city. The role played by the large and philanthropic Scripps family from the 1890s well into the 1930s set the stage for many of San Diego's most impressive contemporary achievements, most especially in the medical, biological, and environmental sciences. McClain's careful reading of Scripps family letters of this period reveals a deep ambivalence about their roles as wealthy industrialists and their significant accumulation of wealth at a time when the life of the "masses," as described by Edward Bellamy, was characterized by "overwork, bad food and pestilent homes."[34] In San Diego, E. W. Scripps and his half-sister Ellen turned away from making money and began seeking to realize their more utopian ideal, while brother Fred and sister Annie were drawn to the region because of serious health issues. They also wanted their elderly mother to enjoy her final years in a more salubrious climate than that of Rushville, Illinois. They set about acquiring large plots of land; E. W. built a residence designed on utopian principles, Miramar Ranch, with forty-nine rooms and numerous comforts in which he hoped all the family members would live harmoniously. The social experiment in manipulating the physical environment failed to secure harmony within the family and reduce the individual anxiety and related "diseases of civilization" described by George M. Beard, a popular author of the time. But, as McClain points out, it profoundly changed E. W. from an aristocrat to a man who lived more simply and naturally. He also became a leading figure in local philanthropy and was an early and significant contributor to the fledgling Marine Biological Institute, which eventually became Scripps Institution of Oceanography. "Miss Ellen," as she was called, was also changed and established herself independently in a seaside cottage she had built in La Jolla, which as early as 1898 had become an enclave of intellectuals and artists, mostly from the East Coast.

The move to La Jolla significantly expanded Miss Ellen's social circle and, as La Jolla grew, she became pivotal to that growth through philanthropic gifts that established what today are major cultural, research, and health care organizations in the San Diego region: Scripps Institution of Oceanography, Torrey Pines State Park, the Bishop's School, the La Jolla Women's Club, the Scripps Memorial Hospital and Research Center (1924), and the Metabolic Clinic, which today is known as the Scripps Research Institute. Again quoting McClain: "San Diego was an experiment for the Scripps family—a place where the damaging effect of industrialism on both family and community could be lessened, if not relieved."[35] Thus the family vision shaped the development of San Diego up until World War II, and their interests in health, the environment, and research contributed significantly to the impressive growth the region experienced in these sectors during the postwar era.

A third major pillar of San Diego's modern economy, research and development of new technologies and scientific investigation, gained a toehold in the region with the world's first controlled heavier-than-air flight in 1883, and its presence expanded after 1900 as the military establishment grew within the city limits. The health industry was also expanding, thanks to progress through advancing technology enabled by scientific research. Influential citizens—some driven by personal intellectual curiosity, others motivated by their perception of civic needs—similarly invested in initiatives in 1902 that led to the founding of the Scripps Institution of Oceanography. On reflection, it is clear that, from the 1880s well into the 1950s, the military, scientific, and health communities pursued undertakings that from their earliest days depended on continuous innovation, focused constantly on adapting and upgrading their technologies and practices. All were animated by key human issues of their time, the military in terms of national security, science with regard to the quest for basic knowledge, and health in terms of longevity and prevention of disease. The fact that these activities that shaped San Diego's early years were characterized by a high interest and significant local investments in research and development suggests that citizens understood early on the importance of science and engineering to urban growth and economic advancement. The historical documents we encountered support this claim.

Endeavors in these directions only accelerated from the World War I years through the early 1960s, when the Chamber of Commerce published multipaged brochures to attract R&D to the region, describing the hundreds of research and development companies already resident in San Diego, with photos of white-coated laboratory workers. The documents detail the numbers of National of Academy of Science members and Nobel Laureates at work in local institutions. The Chamber's recognition and promotion of scientific research and R&D has signified since the early 1900 a clear and distinguishing characteristic of San Diego's DNA. The region's economy and culture appreciate science and technology, not as ends in themselves but in terms of the goods they can deliver, contributing not only to health, medicine, national security, or the betterment of the human condition, but also to the economic advancement on which the region has relied.

A second unique characteristic of San Diego's history relates to the first because, as we shall see, the military was not only the source of jobs and consumers but also a critical factor in solving the vexing problems related to early infrastructure development that included securing the city's supply of scarce water resources, elusive transportation links, and educational services. San Diego did not experience the accumulation of wealth and powerful multigenerational industries and families that occurred in cities that were more anchored in industrial and commercial activities. As a consequence, San Diego's civic culture has depended on different forms of organization to champion its economic growth and well-being. It is therefore not surprising that, for nearly a hundred years, the San Diego Chamber of Commerce was the city's most powerful organization, and in contemporary times entities such as CONNECT and BIOCOM, advocates of San Diego's high-tech clusters, represent significant centers of power and influence. This contrasts with many older industrial cities, where the names Danforth, Eastman, and Ford are more recognized and honored than are particular organizations.

A third characteristic that may be distinct to San Diego again relates to its long history of publicly funded military, scientific, and health enterprises. San Diego has *not* been tied to any singular industrial legacies such as automobiles or steel or to a commodity such as corn. San Diego, more than most cities across the United States, has depended on a single customer, the federal government, which has funded military forces and technology as well as much of the nation's R&D for the past hundred years. The government, however, although a single customer, has multiple interests, appetites, and constituencies. Especially noteworthy for San Diego is its ability to diversify its economy around the ever-evolving needs of the federal government, itself dependent on public funding. Long before the national government began to expand its investments in a wide array of endeavors during and since the era of the New Deal, San Diego had become quite adept at extracting major funding for its own needs from Washington, D.C.

The tremendous importance of extraregional linkages—especially to the federal government—as a pillar of regional economic prosperity stands as a fourth attribute that differentiates San Diego. With only a few exceptions, the city never fully developed its economy on the production or manufacturing of commodities or products that fed a large local market and eventually branched into regional and national consumer markets, the way the farmers in central California or companies like Levi Strauss in San Francisco were able to do. Until recently, San Diego's economic prosperity has not been tied to markets in Iowa, South Carolina, or Washington State, so much as to continued investment by the federal government in increasingly diversified products and, most especially, R&D needed within the military and health establishments. How that situation has changed since the 1980s will figure in our discussion of San Diego's latest "reinvention."

A fifth distinguishing characteristic is the extent to which San Diego society has readily integrated newcomers with talent and connections relevant to its economic growth into the city's life and leadership roles. In Chapters 4 and 5, we introduce some of the scientists, entrepreneurs, and business leaders who were attracted to the region with the promise of building major R&D establishments as well as new technology companies. The region possesses a long history of welcoming new people with talent and connections, and this likely contrasts with many other cities. In many communities there are multigenerational industrial enterprises and family influences that can create barriers to mobility and leadership roles among enterprising new residents. In many communities, established social hierarchies or institutions serve as gatekeepers, setting high standards for recent arrivals to meet before welcoming them into the fold.

Finally, collaborative activity represents a sixth theme significant to the invention and reinvention of the San Diego economy, a phenomenon that appears again and again not only in the diverse forms of collaborative activity within the business community but also among the business community, education, and government. This too may be a function of the absence of large industries and dominant families. Every key event that has helped San Diego from its earliest invention to the successive reinventions of the economic base can be linked back to loosely coupled collaborative efforts that emerged to achieve some economic value for the region. Outstanding examples of this include the Panama-California Exposition of 1915, which did more to put San Diego on the map than any previous efforts; the great gifts of land the city made to the Navy immediately following the end of World War I, which the city's voters endorsed all but unanimously; the deal that brought the Consolidated Aircraft Corporation to San Diego in 1935—the city's first large-scale heavy industry, which turned the city into a major player in the field of aviation; the inception of the University of California San Diego, culminating in the opening of the campus in 1960; the founding of CONNECT in 1985; and the formation of the San Diego Consortium for Regenerative Medicine (today called the Sanford Consortium) in 2006, which has placed under one roof an exceptionally high-powered team of scientists in the field of stem-cell research and application of their discoveries to medicine. It is a fascinating social dynamic, which contemporary analysis suggests is not always easy to establish in more hierarchical cities with more siloed industry associations, universities, and community groups.

It is tempting to dismiss the developmental trajectories of cities like San Diego as idiosyncratic. On the surface they can seem merely a function of the peculiarities of place, particular personalities, or propitious accidents of history; in other words, not instructive to other places seeking a path to revitalization or reinvention. We do not agree with such assessments; our investigations have led us to entirely different conclusions. We therefore endeavor to provide detailed accounts of the many small steps that have culminated in tipping-point events. Thus we strive to inform the reader how a civic culture whose stakeholders value collaboration among many capitalizes on its amenities of place to achieve its economic growth aspirations. To succeed, such a city must be opportunistic and flexible; by exploring the agency of small players, in the absence of any big players, we will tease out the relevance of the San Diego experience for others. The substantive middle four chapters of this volume of social and economic history, told through the lens of sociology, make the case, and our final chapter suggests the implications for others.

THE PLAN OF THE BOOK

In plotting the structure of this book, we determined that unfolding the region's social and economic history from 1870 through 2010 would be an optimally logical approach. We make the case that the current taken-for-granted interpretation of San Diego's emergence as a twenty-first-century global technology center, resulting primarily as a function of the creation of a new University of California campus there in the 1960s, grossly oversimplifies the reality.

Lacking the historical data and sociological insights provided in this book makes it easy even for knowledgeable people to identify as lackluster the character of San Diego's economy and civic culture prior to the 1960s. This can minimize the important role a technologically sophisticated absorptive and adaptive business community represented for the manifold commercialization and technology cluster developments the region has experienced since the 1980s. The State University of New York at Stony Brook and the University of California at Irvine are just two examples of AAU-member research universities founded at the same time as UC San Diego that have *not* resulted in the regional clustering of thousands of new tech companies and tens of thousands of new high-wage tech jobs. We will argue that San Diegan's early commitment to the military and health as economic growth opportunities was propitious. Both of these industries had an early dependence on science and technology, and both triggered a consistent pattern of land-use decisions, federal relations strategies, and collaborative business investments and initiatives, which by the 1980s proved extremely favorable to the growth of the critical mass of R&D enterprises and global technology businesses on the Torrey Pines Mesa.

In Chapter 2, "The Invention of a Twentieth-Century City: The Rise of a Martial Metropolis," we document the many unsuccessful efforts by San Diego's early founders to extract economic value from its temperate climate and visually magnificent shoreline, hills, and canyons, none of which favored traditional agriculture or industrial development. The health-enhancing character of San Diego's natural environment, coupled with the promise of its harbor once deepened through dredging, converged in the first decade of the twentieth century into a civic culture that harnessed the new American empire on the Pacific for economic ends. The persistent cultivation of the Navy, the communitywide social integration of the military, and the launching of the Panama-California Exposition against great odds in 1915 firmly established San Diego's path to becoming one of America's most important military cities. The chapter further documents how, subsequent to the Naval Act of 1919 and well into the 1930s, San Diego expanded and consolidated its military reach, becoming one of the nation's few Federal Cities with the War Emergency Act of 1939, experiencing what was referred to as a "blitz-boom" until 1945.

In Chapter 3, "The Postwar Invention of the Martial Metropolis: Building the Foundation of R&D to Serve the Cold War Economy," we turn our attention to the first of a number of reinventions of San Diego's economy in response to the growing military and federal appetite for research and technology in the postwar era, fueled largely by the Cold War. Recognizing the significant contributions made to the war effort by SIO on behalf of the University of California's Division of War Research and by Convair/General Dynamics to both naval and aviation technology development and manufacturing, San Diegans rallied behind R&D as a way to help retain the military as well as to continue to attract federal investment in the region. This was reflected in numerous public referendums to cede land to promising R&D institutions. A series of signal events highlight San Diego's sudden agglomeration of scientific talent within the span of just a few short years: the expansion of SIO's research agenda; the establishment of a privately funded think tank by Convair, General Atomic; the rapid expansion of medical research through Scripps Hospital and Metabolic Institute; and the establishment of the Salk Institute. On the heels of these came the founding of a University of California campus on the Torrey Pines Mesa in the early 1960s—an institution focused on science and technology contiguous to all these other R&D enterprises. Chapter 3 presents the individuals, the public incentives, and the private investments and strategic choices that enabled this unparalleled consolidation on a geographically distinct site known as the Torrey Pines Mesa.

In Chapter 4, "San Diego's Economy Comes of Age: 1869–1984," we interpret the consolidation of R&D on the Torrey Pines Mesa throughout the resource-rich Cold War, during the war on cancer, and with the national expansion of medical schools and research funding well into the 1980s. The Torrey Pines Mesa enjoyed twenty years of institution building: laboratories, offices, classrooms, and high-tech industrial parks representing billions of dollars in construction contracts, funded in large part by the federal government.

In addition to building facilities, the multiplying not-for-profit R&D institutions on the Torrey Pines Mesa aggressively recruited senior-level talent in their quest for "instant greatness," understood in the scientific community as high levels of research funding, prolific publications in peer-reviewed journals, as well as election to honorific academies and awards such as the Nobel Prize or Fields Medal, and they succeeded spectacularly. And so the Torrey Pines Mesa flourished, aided by the mushrooming federal research budgets, California's growing investment in faculty and infrastructure across the UC System, as well as the fact that American industries were increasingly outsourcing important components of their R&D functions. In a number of cases they also began to align with some of the early start-ups or spin off their own, as in the cases of SAIC and Titan Industries in defense, Linkabit in communications, ISSCO in software, IMED and IVAC in medical devices, and Hybritech in biotechnology in the later clustering of tech companies on and around the Mesa.

Chapter 4 discusses the parallel strategies utilized by each of these institutions in pursuit of instant greatness and documents the enormous gains in funding and reputation the region made by the mid-1980s. Coincidentally, San Diego as a whole struggled. The savings and loan crises of the 1980s pulled the rug out from under the construction and financial industries; demand for military manufacturing declined, especially for the expensive planes and missiles being developed by General Dynamics; and, in spite of its being dubbed "America's Finest City" by Mayor Pete Wilson, the city experienced a string of failures to attract major companies or research consortia to locate in the region. Even before the collapse of the Berlin Wall in 1989, civic leaders recognized something must be done to assure not merely economic stability but growth moving forward. The greatest opportunity they could see in the mid-1980s was to create some initiative that would stimulate high-tech start-ups and growth companies coming out of the R&D institutions on the Mesa, as had happened twenty-five years earlier in Palo Alto around Stanford University. A new chancellor at UC San Diego with Stanford and National Science Foundation credentials empowered a small group of campus leaders to work with the community to devise a plan. Chapter 4 illuminates that process and the characteristics of the CONNECT program, which, according to both the Monitor Group and the Milken Institute, represented the catalytic agent for San Diego's next reinvention as a center of innovation and entrepreneurship.[36] This represented a move to build globally traded high-tech and life science clusters drawing on the inventions, talent, and capital concentrated in and around the not-for-profit research institutions such as UCSD, Salk, The Scripps Research Institute (TSRI), Sanford Burnham, and dozens of others, most of them located on the Torrey Pines Mesa.

Chapter 5, "Connecting Science and Business: San Diego's Next Reinvention," presents San Diego's second reinvention. In a word, the founding of CONNECT triggered the region's growth and transformation from 1985 through today. It occurred as Eli Lilly acquired San Diego's first biotech company, Hybritech. Qualcomm, today a Fortune 500 company, was just getting started, and defense contractors such as SAIC, Titan, and General Atomic (GA) were seeking commercial contracts, anticipating reductions in defense contracting. This chapter underscores the reengineering of San Diego's civic culture and political economy that during these decades accompanied significant growth in science and technology clusters, venture capital investments, and high-wage jobs in those companies, which themselves indicated a complete restructuring of professional business services such as accounting, marketing, and legal services. Additionally, a variety of new civic organizations focused on technology, innovation, and small business were created, and during this period San Diego experienced exponential growth in philanthropy, much of it dedicated to progress in science and technology. Finally, in the wake of the terrorist attacks of September 11, 2001, the defense sector, both the military installations and defense contracting companies, became more robust than ever. In fact, the Navy's Space and Naval Warfare Systems Command (SPAWAR), which invests approximately $3 billion annually in procurement of R&D relevant to the services, is now located in San Diego in buildings originally occupied by Consolidated Aircraft Corporation during World War II. The result of all this, as we noted in the beginning of this introductory chapter, is that San Diego fared much better than other parts of the country in the terrible economic downturn of 2008 through 2010. The chapter concludes with a suggestion that San Diego is in the midst of its third reinvention, realigning its R&D, economic development, and civic initiatives to capture the opportunities created by the reengineering of global corporations and the convergences of multiple technologies to address megaproblems such as renewable energy, personalized health, and new Web applications.

The book concludes in Chapter 6, "Innovative, Evolutionary San Diego," with a reflection on the possible implications the San Diego experience might have for other places. Our analysis clearly suggests that even very similar natural assets (such as sunshine) and core industrial capabilities (that is, traditional manufacturing) can vary dramatically in how they are leveraged over time for new economic purposes, depending on the civic culture of a region. The San Diego story suggests the importance of nimbleness, opportunism, collaboration, and most certainly external connections to the essential talent and resources that enable economic transformation and reinvention. Thus, our recommendations for action emphasize ways to reinvigorate civic culture and even reengineer regional social dynamics to enhance the absorptive and adaptive capacities of communities seeking to navigate an economic transformation in the face of new global economic forces. We in no way intend to present San Diego as a model but rather as an example of principles and practices that may prove useful in other communities.

2 THE INVENTION OF A
TWENTIETH-CENTURY CITY:
THE RISE OF THE MARTIAL METROPOLIS

San Diego's evolution from a sleepy town on a spectacular bay into a major "martial metropolis" began at the turn of the twentieth century and was complete within a generation. The city's residents combined persistence, imagination, and opportunism to accomplish this, characteristics that proved essential to the building of a solid economic base that tied the region's growth strategies to the nation's evolving political role in the world.

California itself took on growing importance, in particular its harbor cities, as the United States became increasingly engaged in the dawning "Pacific Century"; these events were pivotal to the invention of San Diego's unique civic culture and political economy. Los Angeles and San Francisco were already booming metropolises by 1900. They had major commercial harbors and continental transportation links, significant industries, growing populations, and increasing personal wealth and cultural and civic amenities. San Diego, in contrast, was little more than a village on a bay yet to be fully exploited.

The invention of San Diego's core economic activity, however, was about to occur. Many of those who had come to San Diego after 1850 were at least to a degree educated, successful, and affluent; they came from many parts of the United States. All wanted to enjoy the health-giving qualities of San Diego's unique environment, while replicating the amenities of the big cities from which they had migrated. But they also wanted a true metropolis and a booming economy without any of the costs the Industrial Revolution had extracted from other great cities.

After 1900, San Diego's visionaries and entrepreneurs seized the U.S. Navy's need to expand its activities in the Pacific as an economic growth opportunity. The Navy represented federally employed people, demand for the development of local

facilities and housing—a boon to the construction industry—and an array of sec-
ondary services to support the military employees and their families, all of which
translated into jobs and growth for the region. San Diego's invention of itself as a
"martial metropolis" marked its takeoff as a city, but it also created a dependence
on the federal government that persists today.[1]

Understanding the early history of San Diego's partnership with the military
and the city's links to Washington, D.C. as a primary economic strategy that first
began to materialize more than a hundred years ago is critical to any understanding of its current achievements. With its emergence as a major military center
after 1900, a distinctive and enduring civic culture took shape. Since then, San
Diego's business community has been characterized by abundant boosterism, opportunism, dogged persistence, and tolerance of setbacks and failures. The city's
leaders have focused on cultivating the federal government as the main investor
in the region and as a customer for its industries. San Diegans have also embraced
entrepreneurial outsiders capable of enhancing federally related activities. Finally,
San Diego's civic culture has been driven unceasingly by a belief that its climate
and natural environment need to be protected against the ravages of traditional
industrialization and urban growth.

THE DAWN OF THE "PACIFIC CENTURY" AND THE PARADOX OF SAN DIEGO BAY: THE INVENTION OF SAN DIEGO'S CORE ECONOMY

American settlers who trickled into San Diego after the Mexican War saw before
them a wide-open space that must have awed them on the one hand with the possibilities it suggested and cowed them on the other with the limitations that the
semiarid, desert landscape naturally imposed. Approaching San Diego from the
sea, newcomers first saw hills and bluffs, backed by an arc of granite-gray mountains in the near distance. In the spring of the year, those hills would be covered in
verdant splendor, if only for a few weeks. The rest of the year, though, the grasses
and shrubs reverted to various shades of gold and brown—clear evidence of a dry
climate. Entering the sparkling Bay of San Diego, they saw what appeared to be
a marvelous landlocked harbor; their imaginations might have told them at this
point that, despite its near emptiness, someday the bay would teem with ships and
commerce and industry. But for the moment, only a few sparse settlements dotted
its shores.

For the next fifty years the vision of a thriving city on the Pacific frontier largely
eluded San Diegans. U.S. Boundary Surveyor John Bartlett, who arrived early in

1852, expressed what was probably a popular opinion at the time; there was, he said, "no business to bring vessels here, except an occasional one with Government stores . . . [and] without wood, water, or arable land, this place can never rise to importance."[2] The scarcity of basic resources to which Bartlett referred mentioned only some of the obstacles to growth that San Diegans faced during the early years. Most notable on the longer list were geographic isolation from the rest of the United States, rugged mesa-and-canyon topography that promised to inhibit large-scale agriculture, a scarce and unreliable indigenous water supply, and a harbor that in its undeveloped state was difficult and dangerous to navigate.

Despite the best efforts of an energetic and enterprising business community to generate sustained development, San Diego experienced several spasms of growth followed by dramatic contractions before 1900 that kept it struggling, deep in the shadow of San Francisco and Los Angeles. The tide began to turn in San Diego's favor only in 1898 as a result of events far to the west, principally the U.S. acquisition of Hawai'i through annexation and victory in the Spanish–American War, which eventually brought the former Spanish colonies of Guam and the Philippine Islands under American control. Now a true "empire on the Pacific" extended a great distance beyond the California coast. To San Diegans, these events carried special significance. They believed their geographic assets—their bay and southernmost position on the coast—provided them as never before with the opportunity to participate in the nation's expansive future. The U.S. Navy would surely need to increase its presence on the West Coast to deal with the evolving situation. Its mission had suddenly grown to include defense of the nation's new overseas territories and of the merchant shipping that would expand to serve them. Concern with Japan's imperial intentions—its interest in Hawai'i, Guam, and the Philippines—contributed to San Diegans' sense of their own role in the emergent "Pacific Century."

After 1901, Theodore Roosevelt's administration began to provide the Navy with the infrastructural elements necessary to carry out the new Pacific strategy—an expanded, modernized battle fleet, coaling and repair stations at various points around the Pacific basin, and the Panama Canal. Roosevelt is also credited with initiating War Plan Orange, the Navy's code name for its reformulated mission in the Pacific.[3] Given Japan's rising prowess, the president and Navy Department certainly had sufficient reason to begin to map out possible scenarios of a future conflict in that part of the world. In this, the city's leaders saw a possibility that they might finally start to attract federal investment in the improvement of their harbor, which would inevitably lead to the other kinds of urban growth they so earnestly desired. Now, at long last, their city might begin to transcend its isolation and its reputation for having missed the train.

News of the Navy's potential interest in establishing a small industrial plant—a coaling station—on the south coast gave San Diegans some hope that they might make the Navy at home on their vaunted bay. Thus, the mayor, city council, and directors of the Chamber of Commerce launched what became San Diego's hallmark for the next century: an intensive lobbying campaign directed simultaneously at several different committees in Congress, the Department of the Navy, and even the president himself, all intended to generate a decision in Washington to invest in San Diego. They didn't understand quite yet the significance of the course they were about to pursue, but within a decade a coherent strategy began to emerge: Use the Navy to "upbuild" the city and "put San Diego on the map." Even before World War I broke out in Europe, and long before the United States became directly involved, the business community started to create a viable urban political economy based on *their* perceptions of what the armed forces needed and what the federal government might be willing to spend on them. Imagine the audacity of these small-town business leaders as they attempted to shape national policy—indeed a major theme of their efforts over the next several decades. They framed their wish list for the city around much larger issues of national security and geopolitics and were never afraid to go right to the top of the nation's power structure to stake their claims.

At this moment, federal funding to upgrade the harbor topped their desires. The bay required extensive improvements before it could be of any real use to the big ships of the Navy, and Congress was not inclined to pay for these without solid confirmation that it needed to do so. In 1900 the Chamber obtained an estimate of $219,500 for all the work to bring the harbor up to a more useful standard. The government was spending a great deal elsewhere for similar purposes. San Diegans wanted only their fair share, but they had to compete with obscure and remote harbors such as Eureka in California's far north, which had recently received $1.7 million. Congress had awarded nearly $4 million to create an artificial harbor near Los Angeles that soon achieved enormous commercial success.[4]

If federal and naval officials could be persuaded of the Navy's need for even a small installation at San Diego, with some improvements to its harbor using the monies provided, perhaps ensuing events (ultimately, the Panama Canal, further expansion of U.S. trade across the Pacific, or war with Japan) would drive federally funded harbor development on a much larger scale. Building up the Navy's enthusiasm for San Diego was the essential challenge. With only a little action on the Navy's part in return for a great deal of agitation, the Chamber's directors obtained the endorsement of the mayor and more than a hundred citizens to address a "memorial" to the Secretary of the Navy that pounded home the theme of

San Diego's strategic importance. In this document, titled "The Pacific Ocean and Its Shores Are Destined to Be the Theater of The World's Greatest Commercial Activity," they noted that of the three natural harbors on the Pacific coast, theirs was "in some respects . . . the most important," while it remained "the most neglected and the least developed." This moment marked "but the beginning of the glorious future in store for the Pacific Coast states of our great Republic," a future that would bloom once "the waters of the old Atlantic . . . eventually meet the virile Pacific," an event that would only "accentuate the strategic value of the bay of San Diego." Thus, they argued, the federal government must finish dredging the channel, expand the capacity of the coal depot, establish a naval training station, build a naval hospital and wireless telegraph station, and do some additional dredging in order to make available "the best site for a dry dock and repair station on the Pacific Coast."[5]

Unfortunately, the Navy had no such plans for San Diego. In fact, Admiral of the Navy George Dewey, the hero of the Battle of Manila Bay, had classed San Diego "among the ports of the second order of strategic importance," and nothing had yet occurred to change his mind. Much correspondence passed back and forth for the next ten years among the several parties before anything substantial occurred; the Navy simply was not yet ready to rise to San Diego's bait.

Aided by the strenuous efforts of San Diego's business community, global events shaped what happened next. In 1906 President Roosevelt oversaw reorganization of the Navy's sixteen battleships, many of its cruisers and smaller craft, into a single concentrated "battle fleet" that operated mainly in the Atlantic Ocean. In the far western Pacific, however, Japan had defeated Russia in 1904–1905, proving that its naval power could easily threaten the precarious stability of American possessions and policy in that part of the world. Roosevelt thus sent the Atlantic Fleet on an around-the-world cruise to impress the Japanese and European admiralties with the modernity and prowess of the new American Navy and at the same time test the fleet's speed, endurance, and mechanical reliability.

More than a month before the great armada's departure, the San Diego Chamber of Commerce requested that the California congressional delegation and the Secretary of the Navy order the fleet to stop first in San Diego as it headed up the coast before crossing the Pacific. The San Diegans especially desired the consent of its commander to bring his big ships into the harbor. When ominous evidence appeared that Los Angeles was plotting to usurp the honor, a citizens' committee spearheaded by the Chamber raised $20,000 by a citywide subscription campaign to send a delegation of leaders aboard a chartered fishing boat to Magdalena Bay, 650 miles south of the border, to intercept the fleet there.

When the committee of San Diegans (which included the mayor, the president of the Chamber, and several other Chamber directors, as well as "one of the ablest [harbor] pilots of San Diego") met up with the fleet, they managed to convene a meeting with the fleet's commanders on the deck of the flagship; here they learned that the ships would indeed make San Diego their first port of call but also that the Navy men judged the condition of the harbor too shallow, narrow, and dangerous: The warships would not enter the bay.[6] Again, imagine the boldness of these boosters, who risked their reputations both at home and in the eyes of the Navy as they pursued their still-nascent strategy.

Once the fleet arrived and anchored off Coronado, parades, ceremonies, balls, guided tours, dinners, luncheons, teas, theatrical presentations, and "private drawing-room functions at the homes of prominent San Diego people" were all the order of the day—April 15, 1908. The *Union* newspaper reported that 75,000 people turned up for the procession that ran nearly two miles from the bayfront landing to the terrace in City Park. At Coronado, distinguished guests from across the nation gathered to honor the seamen, and patriotism "ran riot" all over town. The governor of California extended the state's welcome—a real coup for San Diego.[7] The visit was by all accounts a success, and now San Diegans redoubled their efforts to win the coveted appropriations for harbor improvements and more naval bases while the Chamber directors strove to capitalize on the gains they had made during these dramatic events. A civic culture animated by the promise of the military for the region's growth and identity was starting to take root.

The fleet having departed, a surplus of $8,000 remained in the coffers of the Fleet Welcoming Committee. Chamber directors contacted donors to the fund, asking if they might keep the money "for advertising purposes. . . . [to promote] the City and County of San Diego and its various advantages and benefits."[8] Their approach in this matter to newspaper magnate E. W. Scripps generated a blistering reply, in which he informed them that he had not been aware of this purpose or intention, and that "nothing would have been more repugnant to [him] than this idea of the community seeking to make a profitable speculation out of an ostensibly patriotic demonstration." Imagine the effect, then,

> on the national administration, on Congress, and on the American people as a whole, if they should learn to believe that this whole, mighty demonstration attending the visit of the fleet to the Pacific Coast was nothing more than a huge real estate advertisement.[9]

Scripps's response called into question all that the Chamber had been doing for the past several years. By this time, San Diegans must have understood that a natural harbor and an equable climate did not by themselves a city make, that industrial and commercial capital was not going to roll into town on a Santa Fe or Southern Pacific train, and that what other people had done to build up other places might not have any particular relevance to San Diego's peculiar circumstances. Under the leadership of the Chamber of Commerce, the people of San Diego remained determined to obtain the interest, recognition, and hard cash that they still needed to build their city, but they knew by now that they would have to find their own way. They sought urban growth on their own terms. They asked no one's permission, and they never wavered in the face of failure.

In the fall of 1909, the Chamber's board of directors appointed a committee, all drawn from its own ranks, to honor the opening of the Panama Canal, scheduled to occur in 1915. The committee chartered a corporation capitalized at $1 million (raised by public subscription) to start the processes of creating a world's fair in motion. As banker and Chamber stalwart Fred Jewell put it, "Now is the time for San Diego to become a city, or lay down and be out of the running for good and all. . . . By all means, boost for the fair."[10] They placed a proposition for a $1 million dollar bond on the ballot of the 1910 election that ended victoriously by a margin of seven-to-one. In advance of this, the *Union's* editors dubbed an affirmative vote "the most important civic function . . . ever . . . imposed upon [San Diegans] in their capacity as citizens of this community."[11] The resultant Panama-California Exposition earned a place for itself in local lore. It provided a powerful stimulus to both the business leaders and the community at large to rally around a common cause, pool their resources, and finally develop the 1,400 acre City Park—a diamond in the rough that had long languished as a "barren waste" until then. It also drew precisely the type of attention to the city the leadership so earnestly desired.

As San Diegans began to prepare for the exposition's opening, other elements of the Chamber's emerging strategy blossomed as well, none more important than what resulted from the election of 1912. Early in that year, the Chamber had made a tremendous effort to urge the federal government once again to complete the dredging for which it had been begging since 1902, improvements that "should be made not in the interest of the people of San Diego or of California alone, but in the interest of the government as well."[12] Before this could occur, Congress would have to allocate the funds—a mere $219,000. Nothing happened, though, until the last days of 1912, when relations between San Diego and the federal government suddenly changed in some remarkable ways.[13]

In mid-December 1912, just a few weeks after the election, the Navy at last endorsed the dredging project that would make the coaling station accessible to the current and coming generations of capital ships.[14] Just one month before, San

Diegans had finally sent one of their own—a director of the Chamber of Commerce, no less—to Congress. And even before he was sworn into office, San Diego's new congressional representative William Kettner had hastened to the nation's capital to do his constituents' bidding. No individual better personifies both the promise locked up inside San Diego's challenging early twentieth-century environment and the "invention" of the modern city than Kettner, who articulated and effectuated the city's coming partnership with the federal government.

An insurance broker and resident of San Diego only since 1907, Kettner was quite popular in town. He had risen to prominence in 1908 when he had been selected by the Chamber of Commerce to replace the ailing Fleet Welcoming Committee's chairman; he remained popular despite the fact that he was a Democrat in a strongly Republican town (in 1912, 20,000 registered Democrats resided in the congressional district to which San Diego belonged and 70,000 Republicans).[15] When an out-of-towner won the Republican nomination by a wide margin, Kettner jumped into the race. Despite the huge disparity in party registrations, he won the support of a majority of San Diegans. As he noted in his memoir, "After my nomination, the directors of the Chamber of Commerce of San Diego, almost as a body, left the ordinary business of building up the city and entered into politics."[16] In the final vote, Kettner eclipsed his opponent 10,545 to 6,793 in San Diego County, approximately the same margin that obtained throughout the district. Democrat Woodrow Wilson's plurality in San Diego was also significant. The residents of San Diego now had their own representative in Congress.

Within days of the election, Kettner swung into action. The City Council dispatched the congressman-elect (as yet unsworn) to Washington to see if he could generate action on the stalled dredging project that might lead to an early appropriation from Congress. His enterprising persistence, first in front of the Army's Board of Engineers, then with Admiral Dewey himself, and finally with his soon-to-be congressional colleagues, involving two cross-country trips and much self-effacement over a period of two months, had the desired effect. Kettner had done all of this legwork months before he was sworn into office, and with success in hand he returned home a hero.

Admiral Dewey never revealed his strategic reservations about San Diego's naval future, instead couching his lack of enthusiasm in economic terms. In March 1913, he informed the secretary of the Navy that "appropriations [could] be spent more advantageously at other places." He stated quite flatly, however, that "San Diego would probably be the last place of attack by an enemy coming across the Pacific," which meant that it is not needed as a base for anticipated operations against any strong maritime power south of us, and is not nearly so well situated geographically and has not as good communications with the rest of the country as San Francisco and Puget Sound for operations west of us.[17]

The imminent completion of the Panama Canal and the nation's increasing engagement in trade and politics in the Pacific basin boded well for yet more local growth. Having their own man in the House of Representatives, pledged to obtain whatever help he could from the federal government to push the city-building project along, now contributed to the business community's sense that a golden age was about to dawn over San Diego.

While Kettner's initial success at Washington appeared as a portent of good things to come, it was a rather modest first step. The Chamber's directors vigorously increased their efforts to "agitate the national government" for items further down their list of needs and desires.[18] Through such activity the Chamber defined its most useful civic role for many years into the future, in this way forging San Diego's civic culture as a leading martial metropolis. Kettner soon earned himself the reputation as the city's "million-dollar congressman" because of the money the federal government now started to trickle and then pour into the pipeline straight to San Diego.

Close on his success with Dewey and the dredging project, Kettner negotiated the Navy's first purchase of land in San Diego—a small but exceedingly difficult transaction that almost disintegrated at several junctures. In this case, the service desired to acquire a property on which to place a powerful radio transmitter, part of a global network of such stations then under development. While several of the congressman's Chamber colleagues attempted to sell the Navy properties they either owned themselves or represented, the naval board in charge of selection preferred one that belonged to an outsider who asked a price higher than the Navy wished to pay. When the seller testily expressed his unwillingness to accept the Chamber's demands to lower his price to accommodate the Navy, naval representatives threatened to pull up stakes and seek their second choice, a property in Orange County.

At this point, Kettner stepped in and arranged a compromise, saving the deal for San Diego. This meant a number of things for the city. First was a further federal expenditure of $278,700 to construct and equip the station.[19] Second was the quartering of "fifty families, officers, operators and recruits . . . at the new station." Third was the prestige of having the entire volume of the Navy's trans-Pacific radio traffic pass through San Diego (as the Chamber put it, "The words 'Via San Diego' will be found each day on the telegrams received by the Departments in Washington.").[20] Fourth, San Diego had established a toehold as a center for development of some of the highest technology of the time. Fifth was the greatly enhanced sense of friendship among Navy officials, the federal government, and San Diegans. Sixth, and most important of all, was the special position that Kettner's expert midwifery had established for the Chamber of Commerce—from now on, the organization would act as the Navy's exclusive broker in San Diego, while doing a much better job of promoting the interests of its members (especially its directors).

The persistence and ultimate success in Washington demonstrated by Kettner have been repeated again and again over the history of San Diego. Subsequent civic boosters, defense advocates and contractors and, eventually, champions of federally funded basic research and big science have been critical to San Diego's growth.

THE CANAL, THE EXPOSITION, AND THE EMERGENCE OF TWENTIETH-CENTURY SAN DIEGO

The opening of the Panama Canal provided San Diegans with a tremendous opportunity to turn a corner in their quest for growth, an idea that had incubated in the minds of the city's leaders for years before the event occurred. Having decided to celebrate the "joining of the old Atlantic with the virile Pacific" in the grandest possible fashion, the business community, taxpayers, voters, and most ordinary citizens prepared to show off their city to the world.[21] They petitioned Congress for the right (and the funding) to stage a real world's fair in honor of the canal but lost a bruising competition with San Francisco. Undaunted, San Diego went ahead with its plans and put on a much more modest "Panama-California Exposition," acting as if this were the only such extravaganza. While the Exposition itself barely generated the operating profit its boosters had promised, it spun off myriad long-lasting benefits to the struggling city. Of greatest significance was the way San Diegans used the fair to showcase the city and its harbor to influential outsiders, top military decision makers in particular, and thus seduce them with the potential of the place. The events that followed remain one of the great tipping points in the course of the city's development.

In carrying out their plans, San Diegans undertook incalculable hard labor and huge expense to make it work, and their efforts paid off in ways and to an extent that they had not dreamed possible at the outset. Slated to operate for a year, the Exposition opened on New Year's Day, 1915. While attendance was lighter than expected at first, by the summer its popularity seemed sufficiently assured that the directors extended its run for a second year. More than 2,000,000 people paid to attend during 1915, and 1.7 million more did so before the Exposition closed for good on January 1, 1917; remarkable, given that the population of San Diego itself had not yet reached 70,000. During the first year, the fair hosted the vice president of the United States; the secretaries of the Treasury, Interior, and Labor Departments; the speaker of the house; and former presidents Theodore Roosevelt and William H. Taft, as well as William Jennings Bryan, Assistant Secretary of the Navy Franklin D. Roosevelt, Commandant of the Marine Corps George Barnett, and numerous governors, U.S. congressmen, and senators.[22] Representative Kettner came several times, once with the largest congressional delegation ever to visit San Diego.

Military exhibits, including model encampments, parades, concerts, mock attacks, and more, comprised a feature especially well liked by visitors. Particularly significant was the presence of Colonel Joseph Pendleton, whom Exposition organizers had invited to reside on the grounds for the duration along with his 4th Marine Regiment. Although the Marines had to leave the fair on two occasions to pursue military interventions in Mexico and Santo Domingo, Pendleton had proclaimed himself a confirmed "San Diego booster" and seized his own opportunity to agitate in favor of a permanent base for Marines somewhere on San Diego Bay, a project Kettner had been working on behind the scenes for more than a year.

At various times during the first half of 1915, Kettner and Pendleton met with their superiors (General Barnett and FDR key among them) to further the idea, which soon took on a life of its own. By the summer of 1915, the Navy Department had entered into negotiations with the San Diego Securities Company (whose principals were Kettner's Chamber of Congress comrades George Burnham, Rufus Choate, and retired admiral Henry Manney) for the purchase of 232 acres of former pueblo lands located on a semisubmerged tideland called Dutch Flats near the company's largely undeveloped Loma Portal tract. The city council voted unanimously to sweeten the deal with a gift of 500 acres of adjacent submerged tideland that the city supposedly owned. Between these two tracts, the Navy Department would possess sufficient land for a Marine base and perhaps a submarine base for the Navy as well and area for a deepwater channel approaching the bases. The timing of this move was critical: The members of the House Committee on Rivers and Harbors—Kettner's own—happened to be in town just then.[23]

Events now all but collided. The Navy had recently decided to pursue a major increase in strength, and the Wilson administration moved decisively to prepare the nation and its military services for possible engagement in the war in Europe; San Diegans made the federal government an offer they hoped it could not afford to refuse. Having learned a valuable lesson during the 1913 radio station transaction,

Chamber directors now moved as one to ensure that both the publicly and privately held portions of the Dutch Flats property changed hands as intended. There was much discussion in the Navy's upper ranks about what was to be done with the property once it was acquired—the Navy Department remained reluctant to turn San Diego into a major naval complex for some time to come, but with so much land at their disposal, begging to be obtained so inexpensively, they decided to act.

CONSUMMATION AND FULFILLMENT: THE BIRTH
OF SAN DIEGO'S MARTIAL METROPOLIS

Almost as soon as the Exposition closed for good—January 1, 1917—the Chamber of Commerce, at Kettner's urging, convinced the city council to lease the Balboa Park grounds to the Navy to use as a wartime training complex and hospital, at a rent of $1 per year. In the meantime, the Army and Navy both ramped up their aviation activities on John D. Spreckels's North Island. The Navy had tried on several occasions to purchase the property from Spreckels, but to no avail; Spreckels had always said he intended to build a first-class resort and subdivision on the property, and besides, intensive military aviation activities would devalue what he had already created at Coronado. Congressman Kettner said he would accede to the Navy's condemnation action only if the service promised to "play fair" with his friend Spreckels; when the court case was finally settled in 1921, the magnate accepted the astonishing amount of $6,098,333.33 ($4,783 per acre) for the Island.

The situation heated up considerably, however, once the war ended in November 1918. Several branches of the Navy Department now pressed for new peacetime installations on the Pacific coast, all of which had been under discussion for the past several years. Of particular interest to San Diegans was a repair base for destroyers, and where surplus ships could be held in ready reserve; a major naval hospital; a supply depot and pier along the downtown waterfront; and a permanent naval training station to replace the one still operating on Goat Island in San Francisco Bay. With one bold stroke on New Year's Day of 1919, Secretary of the Navy Josephus Daniels divided the monolithic Atlantic Fleet into two equal fleets, one of which was to reside in the Pacific.[24] Whatever other actions the nation might make with regard to demobilization, disarmament, and world peace, the Navy remained the first line of defense. To the editors of the *Union*, Daniels's landmark resolution meant, above all, that San Diegans should "seize the opportunity," because the city was soon to be "lifted into the prestige of a great seaport metropolis."[25]

The idea that decisions made in Washington could suddenly turn San Diego into a great urban center underscored a sense of civic inferiority characteristic of the city's history. San Diegans still believed that certain vague malevolent forces—principally the disdain of the railroad companies and "the antagonism of other cities"—had hindered their course of urban development. Now, however, San Diego was finally going to receive its due.[26] As if anticipating the momentous changes that Daniels was about to effect, the Chamber of Commerce offered up three properties free of charge to the Navy for its new West Coast training station in December.[27] Chamber leaders knew exactly what they hoped to gain in return for their ostensible generosity: a more fully developed harbor, millions of dollars in construction contracts for bases and related infrastructure, thousands of naval trainees and sailors permanently stationed at San Diego, and, not least, satisfaction in the knowledge once and for all that San Diego was on the map. Kettner told his committee that if the Navy accepted one site in particular, at Loma Portal, next to the Marine base, the service would thereby acquire a mile-and-a-quarter-long bay frontage in addition to what it already held. The net result "would practically give the navy department all of San Diego Bay."[28]

A great sense of urgency now gripped San Diego's leaders, so strong was their desire to secure favorable decisions from the secretary, the Navy Department, and Congress in the shortest possible time. William Kettner explained to his constituents the need to do their part. He pointed out that the city of Chicago had recently donated a site worth $2 million for the Great Lakes Naval Training Station, "which was one of the best investments [that] city ever made." Thus it made economic sense to trade the Navy undeveloped real estate in return for guaranteed income of perhaps $400,000 per month in local merchants' coffers as a result. Moreover, the salaries of the trainees would amount to another $250,000 a month, plus the $1 per day it cost to feed a sailor, plus the many thousands of dollars spent on supplies each time a ship entered the harbor.[29] With the Navy thus in place, there would be no postwar economic recession in San Diego.

The forces within the city—all "the usual suspects," including the mayor and city council, directors of the Chamber of Commerce, other businesspeople and landowners, and the voters themselves—over the next months rallied to turn what had been a somewhat scattershot but clearly evolving strategy into a coherent program for urban growth. All of their past efforts seemed pale in comparison to what was about to transpire. All the small-scale agricultural development, the efforts to establish a railroad connection, the attempts to lure industries to San Diego or to turn the city into a haven for health seekers and retirees, faded into the background as San Diego mobilized to recreate itself as a true "martial metropolis," to invoke the expression coined by historian Roger Lotchin. According to Lotchin, a number of cities across the country sought to overcome economic and especially industrial "backwardness" by offering the military services various inducements to locate there, thus contributing in some significant way to the local economy.[30] Elements of this type existed elsewhere, but San Diego now built a model "metropolitan-military complex" in a pure and concentrated form.

First, the city's leadership engineered a complicated yet effective assemblage of privately and publicly owned property at Loma Portal to give to the Navy for its new training station. To collect the money needed for the purchase of the privately owned acreage, the mayor, city council, and directors of the Chamber went door-to-door through the city (as they had done in 1908 at the behest of the Fleet Welcoming Committee), accepting "subscriptions" from citizens in amounts as small as $1. Next, the city offered nineteen acres in Balboa Park at Inspiration Point as the site for the naval hospital, a parcel that the executive secretary of the Board of Park Commissioners described as "unquestionably one of the most attractive in the entire park system." Proceedings also got under way to transfer a much larger (98.2 acres) waterfront site south of the downtown area for the destroyer and repair base and a whole city block located at the foot of Broadway, on the waterfront, where a supply depot and pier might be built. The city government had authorized the mayor to deed these to the Navy, along with the land and bay frontage for the supply base. In the Naval Act of July 1919, Congress authorized the Navy Department to accept the former two properties; in the meantime, Congressman Kettner placed the deeds to the latter into escrow, pending naval approval.[31]

Consummation of these transactions required approval by the city's voters. Kettner, the *Union*, the Chamber, and the Navy men involved all looked forward to a unanimous vote in favor of the gifts. And that is almost what they got. For the hospital site in Balboa Park, the tally was 9,341 to 134; for the supply depot and pier, 9,321 to 68; for the destroyer repair base, 9,339 to 65; and for the training station, 9,115 to 70. San Diego's voters had spoken, and their sleepy little city was soon to become, in the words of a top admiral, "the Hampton Roads of the Pacific."[32] By 1923, all these bases had been built and staffed, and what's more, before the end of 1919, Secretary Daniels had designated San Diego headquarters of the Eleventh Naval District, which included Los Angeles within its boundaries—a tremendous coup for the formerly beleaguered Harbor of the Sun, whether measured in psychological or economic terms. So influential in the affairs of the city was the position of the District's commandant (always a two-star rear admiral) that this officer has been called "the naval mayor of San Diego" ever since.

By the time of the special elections, only twelve years had passed since E. W. Scripps had excoriated the Chamber for turning the celebration in honor of the Grand Fleet into a "real estate promotion." As real estate developer and die-hard booster Oscar Cotton now told his compatriots at the San Diego–California Club, the Chamber's advertising arm, "San Diego [had] arrived. Prosperity [was] here, for every bank, hotel, laundry, and restaurant report[ed] business [was] good." Cotton attributed this grand success to three factors: the completion of the San Diego–Arizona railway (in fact, never a factor in the city's bottom line), "the federal government's building program here, and the activities of the San Diego–California Club."[33] Of the three, it was obvious that only one had really brought home the goods.

Thus, San Diego, like all great American cities, having struggled in its early years to find a workable path to growth, finally found its modus vivendi. Unique to San Diego, though, was the combination of local and far-flung circumstances that included the Spanish American War, the digging of the Panama Canal, World War I, an opportunistic civic culture, and a highly resourceful leader—William Kettner—so well suited to the main chance; these enabled the city to mobilize and exploit its natural assets and thereby pave a durable path to a prosperous future. A set of social dynamics and cultural values became deeply embedded after 1920, serving San Diego for decades to come as its leaders continued successfully in their opportunistic pursuit of federal dollars in the service of economic growth.

THE PARADOX OF THE MARTIAL METROPOLIS

Even before the vast changes in the Navy's postwar program took hold in San Diego, an editorial in the *Union* expressed what many felt to be the meaning of recent events: San Diego had finally arrived at a position

> fully within the concern of the national authority. . . . The action of the government in sending this splendid fleet into our waters, establishing this port as an important naval and military base, is an indication of our permanent inclusion in the broadening scope of a policy consonant with the demands of a new era now developing in the history of the world.[34]

In a letter to the editor, an anonymous "taxpayer" spelled out the city's new political economy in terms of a crude cost-benefit analysis, claiming that the Navy provided a much better deal than indigenous investment in industry and infrastructure. According to his simple explanation, all the millions of dollars needed for development would come from outside, population growth would be greater, and a naval training station would be much more benign toward the environment than any factory. San Diego could thus avoid the gross mistakes made by Los Angeles. He noted:

This small city [the training station] will consume less than 500,000 gallons of water each day. The new Goodrich plant at Los Angeles with an annual payroll of $7,500,000 will use daily 8,000,000 gallons of water, or 16 times as much water as the training station. This new suburb will require no expenditure for schools, sewers, paved roads or upkeep of streets. Fellow taxpayers, this is our opportunity to increase our assets on a far better basis than any previous proposition. Let's go while the going is good.[35]

"Taxpayer's" theory made sense to San Diegans. Whatever benefits smokestack industries might provide, there were always costs to pay, whether for infrastructure, environmental degradation, or overconsumption of scarce resources. Had "Taxpayer" studied the wartime record of Camp Kearny, a huge wartime Army cantonment a few miles north of Mission Valley, in particular the considerable expense to which the city and utility companies had gone to accommodate the post, he might have modified his calculations. Nevertheless, the logic of relying on the federal government to cover some of those costs while increasing the city's commercial and demographic assets proved irresistible. If San Diego could not have Los Angeles's factories, it would be delighted to have the Navy.

Now the Navy's transformation of the city's physical environment began in earnest: The top brass wanted nothing less than an "unbroken water front owned and controlled by the Government, of about four miles in extent, including the Marine Depot, the training station . . . , and the fuel depot," which would require acquisition from the city, "free of charge," of course, of just one more strip of land along Point Loma. The bay, however, would still not be sufficiently useful to the Navy without extensive further dredging to provide space for navigation as well as anchorage for the hundreds of ships that would soon call San Diego home. To this end, federal agencies drew up a grand plan that included dredging, filling, and a very great deal of construction.[36] In his report for the fiscal year ending June 30, 1920, the Navy's public works officer noted that, in San Diego, "$3,500,000 worth of work has been under construction and $4,000,000 worth of work [has been] proposed."

The city was on the map to an extent it had never been before. But there was a paradox inherent in a military-based economy. San Diego lacked the breadth that industrial companies and personal wealth brought to other cities. It could, however, through its thickening web of connections with Washington, D.C., generate the financing needed for essential infrastructure associated with the military expansion. Additionally, San Diegans were naïve compared to their peers in Los Angeles and San Francisco in how they addressed major infrastructure problems.

San Diego's civic culture has been characterized by a reluctance to make major investments in the fundamental, physical urban necessities, a quality that continues to haunt the city today as it struggles with an inadequate water supply, a faltering sewer system and an undersized regional airport. Clearly, not all of San Diego's underlying problems had been solved once the Navy established itself in such force. In fact, the perennial issues of water supply, transportation, industry, harbor development, and housing weighed even more heavily on the minds of San Diego's leaders because of the sudden pressure that the expanded naval activities now exerted on all of them. Throughout the 1920s and 1930s the city's problems grew larger in magnitude and more difficult to address, while the Chamber—with the municipal government in tow—continued to attack them only with old and rather ineffectual weapons. Thus the post–World War I victories seemed harder won, and the spoils considerably more scant. Perhaps the most difficult problems facing the boosters existed within their own minds. While they all seemed to know what they wanted and needed to make their city grow, they often acted in ways that obstructed the realization of their good intentions.

The matter of a city hall and civic center present a case in point. San Diegans had never built one; instead, most municipal offices occupied rented space in a commercial office building. Planner and city-beautiful advocate John Nolen had pointed out the need for such a complex in his 1908 design for the city, and he did so again when the Chamber invited him back to formulate a revised plan in 1926. To Nolen, a well-conceived civic center was not only necessary for a city's "municipal life" but would "transform the civic spirit of the community, raise the civic pride of the citizens, and attract favorably the attention of visitors." Nolen now chided San Diego's leaders, telling them that they should have taken his advice the first time and moreover that they "had no reason to rest content" with the beauty of the city's natural setting. Worse, the leadership's apathy meshed only too well with the city's characteristic "haphazard, inconsistent, and wasteful" development, to the extent that the increased cost of land made the proposition far more difficult to accomplish than ever before.[37]

Nolen's pointed criticisms highlighted a curious shortcoming in the boosterism that the city's leaders had practiced for so many years: Although they had a good and valuable product to sell, that is, the city's beauty, climate, and potential for commercial growth, the business community had always found it difficult to transform these natural attributes into worldly economic assets. No matter how well they advertised San Diego to the rest of the world as a present and future metropolis, the city remained tightly wrapped in its small-town skin. They might argue that their vast efforts to bring the Navy to town had paid and would continue to pay tremendous dividends, but they had never managed to do the ordinary things they needed to foster the metropolitanism needed for San Diego to mature, and thus compete with Los Angeles or San Francisco on a more equal basis.

On what should San Diego build the rest of its economy? Chamber of Commerce directors had long debated the type of growth to stress, whether the marketing of fruits (for the particular benefit of agriculturists), tourism to stimulate further colonization of the city's hinterland, the commercial tuna fishery and packing industry, or efforts to attract more manufacturing.[38] San Diegans worked hard over the years on the first three while manifesting a great deal of confusion in their handling of the fourth. They achieved a significant degree of success in creating a wider market for local produce; tourism had become a mainstay of the city's economy and culture during the first quarter of the century; and the tuna business became well established during World War I. Even in the realm of heavier industry the city's leaders could boast of at least one major attainment—the Navy, which according to its secretary, Edwin Denby, was the largest industrial concern in the United States by the 1920s.[39]

As rewarding as San Diego's growth in the naval arena had been, commercial and industrial development of the harbor and the city itself by the 1930s never rivaled what had occurred in Los Angeles during the same era. Although San Diegans had touted the commercial splendors of San Diego Bay for more than sixty years, they still had little to show for the effort. The city's leaders had always taken inordinate comfort in their assertion that the bay was one of the world's great natural harbors, which they felt provided them with a significant moral advantage over Los Angeles in particular, whose harbor was human created. Clarence Matson, a leading figure in the development of the Los Angeles waterfront, correctly noted that

> San Diegans had poked a great amount of fun at the harbor aspirations of Los Angeles. The San Diego newspapers referred to Los Angeles Harbor as a "harborette," and if the truth must be told, this practice rather irritated those of us in Los Angeles whose duty it was to make the world understand that Los Angeles was a real seaport.[40]

Unfortunately for the San Diegans, imaginary moral superiority served them not at all. The three major events the boosters had counted upon to improve their fortunes—the opening of the Panama Canal, the completion of the San Diego & Arizona Railroad in 1919, and the federal dredging operations—had done practically nothing over the years to fulfill the bay's supposed commercial promise: San Diego remained a minor player with regard to California's ocean-borne trade. Most cargo passing through the port of San Diego was inbound rather than outbound; clearly, the city was a consumer rather than a producer, indicative of lagging industrial and commercial development. Moreover, southwestern cotton growers and other agricultural enterprises, from Texas to the Imperial Valley (immediately to the east of San Diego), preferred to ship their goods through Los Angeles, San Francisco, or Seattle rather than deal with the bottlenecks and higher freight rates they encountered at San Diego.

THE MARTIAL METROPOLIS: A BUFFER AGAINST THE GREAT DEPRESSION

San Diego was not immune to the dislocations that the Great Depression caused across the country, but the peculiar nature of the city's growth during the 1920s attenuated some of the economic distress. As the dire effects of the slump became increasingly visible around the country, the city's leaders largely stayed their course. Real estate values fell, as did bank deposits, and the general level of commerce in the city also deteriorated. But because so little of San Diego's income derived from manufacturing and because so much of the regional product depended on ongoing federal appropriations, naval activities in particular, the Great Depression in San Diego proved considerably less severe than elsewhere.[41] The Navy had channeled nearly $126.4 million into San Diego since the turn of the century, which provided the city with a substantial shield against the massive nationwide economic downturn.[42]

The city's basic agenda hardly changed during this troubled period. The water problems and their tentative solutions that had always generated such pressing concern remained on the table. Even as the cities of the Los Angeles region created the powerful Metropolitan Water District, engineered a great aqueduct to bring Colorado River water into Southern California, and invited San Diego to participate, San Diegans voted in 1933 to remain aloof in the hope of someday developing their own aqueduct further to the south. The Chamber's industrial and transportation committees continued to struggle with the same old issues, mainly in the same old ways. The perpetual nationwide advertising campaigns seemed to occupy an even higher priority than they had earlier, perhaps getting in the way of more substantive action. A striking example of this was the decision to reprise the 1915–1916 Panama-California Exposition in 1935—good public relations, but no cure for the city's many ills. Meanwhile, the naval connection and harbor development continued to be the real staples of the local economy and the city's raison d'être.

San Diego's civic leaders seemed to have locked the city into a comfortable condition of stasis, although to leave it at that ignores the remarkable long-term cultural evolution that now indelibly identified San Diego as a navy town. The Navy, and the federal dollars that accompanied the service in such a number of diverse ways, represented by the early 1930s the very essence of the city and the image it projected to the world. San Diego's leadership continued as it had throughout the 1920s to fuss over the matter of an independent source of water for the naval bases without really attacking the problem, and harbor dredging remained another urgent concern. But other thorny troubles that had arisen from the recent expansion of the naval establishment began to share the spotlight early in the depression period. Notable among these was a shortage of housing, accompanied by the perception of inflationary rental rates, serious issues from the Navy's point of view. The business community's and the military's efforts to build and sustain San Diego as the self-proclaimed "aviation capital of the West" provided another source of anxiety, mainly because the much-publicized slogan was less than accurate.[43]

By 1935, the Navy had leased eleven sites around San Diego County as auxiliary airfields for specialized training and emergency landing purposes, but no permanent acquisitions were undertaken at the time.[44] San Diego proved a perfect venue for naval flyers to show off their derring-do. On a regular basis, the Chamber directorate petitioned the bureau to hold air shows for the benefit of the public, and the Navy almost always complied with the requests. Thus, Chamber-requested "massed flights" of military aircraft often filled San Diego skies with machinery, noise, and gasoline exhaust, which was only one of several environmental problems that the Navy had created in the area since the World War I period. Citizens in fact lodged numerous complaints in this regard, often stating that the airplanes were responsible for degrading their domestic peace and equanimity.[45]

The loss of the Navy's main dirigible base to the San Francisco Bay Area after a protracted competition disturbed San Diego's leaders, who hoped never to allow such a defeat to blemish their record. To ensure success in the years to come, they courted their naval benefactors with an intensity that sharply distinguished the 1930s from earlier periods, signifying the single most noteworthy aspect of San Diego's unique civic culture, as well as the business community's most important pursuit. San Diegans had always taken great care to lavish gifts, entertainments, travel expenses, and perpetual red-carpet treatment for naval officers whenever the opportunity arose, but now they eclipsed all their previous efforts by a wide margin, always framed in terms of friendship, honor, patriotism, national defense, or San Diego's "natural rights." Far surpassing these, however, was the starkly mercantilist, if not mercenary, point of view that by now appeared innate among civic leaders. All other considerations aside, more naval activity in San Diego meant more business activity, more real estate development, and more money flowing through the pipeline from Washington, D.C.

Three more landmark events occurred in San Diego during the mid-to-late 1930s that served not only to bolster the local economy against the ravages of the Great Depression but to further refine and fuse the civic culture. First, the business community secured the location of a major industrial concern other than the Navy. The forces with the power to do so—the Chamber's industrial development committee and the municipal government—had been reluctant over the years to offer manufacturers the kinds of inducements that other cities made available, that is, free or cheap real estate, tax incentives, and cash (with regard at least to the real estate, not unlike what they had been doing for the Navy); they now did precisely this for the Consolidated Aircraft Corporation of Buffalo, New York, in 1935. The second was winning in 1936 a multimillion-dollar harbor dredging appropriation (by far the largest to date) through the New Deal's Public Works Administration (PWA) and Works Progress Administration (WPA), all for the benefit of the Navy. And third was President Franklin Roosevelt's declaration of a "war emergency" in September 1939 that signaled a wholesale takeoff in San Diego's aviation factories as well as a manifold increase in the Navy's presence in and around the city. The term that appeared in popular media to describe the combined effects of these events, *blitz-boom*, which sounded so positive, in fact covered a host of urban and environmental woes that changed the city's landscape forever.

Because San Diego was supposed to be the "air capital of the West," aircraft manufacturing might fit the city as well as the Navy did. It was also, in principle, at least, a clean industry. In the pre-World War II era, it was still small in scale and did not include mass-production assembly lines. Moreover, it mainly employed skilled (that is, white) workers of a better sort—which San Diegans classified as a desirable situation overall. An ex-Army pilot and former barnstormer, Claude Ryan, set up an airplane manufactory/flight school/airline in San Diego in 1924 and attracted international attention three years later when he built Charles Lindbergh's *Spirit of St. Louis*. This certainly added some cachet to the boosters' claim, although Los Angeles was by this time home to three budding plane manufacturers—Lockheed, Douglas, and Northrup—which gave that city a better claim to the title.[46]

The situation changed dramatically in the mid-1930s, with the arrival of Reuben H. Fleet and his Consolidated Aircraft Corporation. Fleet had first come to San Diego in 1911 as a member of a National Guard unit that patrolled the Mexican border during that country's revolution. He returned six years later with the Army Air Service and learned to fly at North Island. When Fleet left the Army in

1922, he received employment offers from some of the leading airplane builders of the time. He organized his own company in 1923, naming it Consolidated Aircraft, moving from Dayton, Ohio, to Rhode Island and ultimately to Buffalo, New York. The firm had always specialized in military aircraft, although Fleet and his designers often modified these to suit civilian needs.[47]

According to a history of the company, the rigors of the Buffalo climate were "a real detriment to Consolidated's flying-boat business," and Fleet yearned to move his plant to a place where he could test his planes out of doors and on the water all year long. Because transporting his finished product by rail to Navy bases on either coast was costly, dangerous, and in some cases impossible, Fleet searched the country for ten years to find just the right location. Florida, Seattle, and Southern California all ranked high in his mind, and he found himself so attracted to San Diego's new bayside airport at Lindbergh Field in 1929 that he tried to buy it outright for $1 million.[48]

Naturally, Fleet's interest pleased the San Diego Chamber of Commerce, and the organization's aviation expert, Tom Bomar, kept after him for the next several years. In search of the best deal he could get, Fleet dragged the Los Angeles Chamber into a bidding war with its southern neighbor. The city of Long Beach offered Consolidated more than twenty-two acres of land free next to its municipal airport, which delighted Bomar, who claimed that *that* property was always under water during winter and was five miles from the ocean, meaning that the company would still have to haul its planes overland to the sea before they could be flight- or water-tested. Fleet made no decision on the matter until May 1933, when he received one last impassioned plea from San Diego Harbor Commissioner Emil Klicka, who convinced the manufacturer on the spot to choose San Diego. The company entered into a lease with the city for seventy acres of choice property adjacent to Lindbergh Field and the bay at a price that Fleet could not afford to refuse: $1,000 per year for fifty years.[49]

Fleet commenced operations in his $300,000 custom-designed plant on the waterfront in September 1935, at which time the Chamber announced a renaissance in community interest in its affairs thanks to the arrival of Consolidated—"the first major industrial plant ever to be located in this city"—but noted that it was not about to rest on "its well-earned laurels." Because Consolidated had placed the city so spectacularly on the industrial map of the nation, many "other industrial plants [were] now giving serious consideration to the advantages that we unquestionably possess." When Fleet wanted a $500,000 loan to defray the cost of moving, Congressman and Chamber Director George Burnham helped to arrange it with the Federal Housing Administration, although the Chamber directors had made it clear at almost the exact same time—in reference to several other companies then interested in San Diego—that "it was not the duty of the Chamber of Commerce to secure finances for such concerns."[50]

Like the Navy, Fleet's operation promised to bring thousands of people to San Diego who would want to live in houses they could rent for $25 per month or less. Consolidated hoped to have 1,500 people on its payroll by the beginning of 1935, but because the Navy was pressing him to complete a $6.5 million contract on time, it added 2,500 more workers to its force by March of that year. The company planned to employ as many San Diegans as it could, but it needed "only experienced aircraft workers," most of whom would have to migrate from elsewhere. This put heavy pressure on the already oversold housing supply, but Fleet was quick to engage in such civic matters, attending public meetings in search of solutions to practically all of San Diego's long-standing urban woes, in very similar fashion to the naval commandants who had over the years played such prominent roles as civic leaders. The city and the Chamber, however, came under increasingly harsh criticism from all sides due to the lack of affordable housing, and before long Consolidated employees began to seek a more modest cost-of-living by moving to Los Angeles and finding aircraft work there.[51]

Like the Navy, Consolidated needed to modify San Diego's cityscape to meet its own special requirements. To provide sufficient space for the company's workshops, aprons, and taxiways, the several tuna canneries then in the immediate area had to move south of downtown, near the destroyer base. The small boats anchored in the bay offshore of the airport had to move as well, and the dredging apparatus then in use had to get out of the way too. The Chamber's aviation and industrial development committees recognized the importance of keeping the company's executives happy, realizing that Consolidated had the power to attract yet more aviation industries to the city; thus the organization coordinated such activities enthusiastically.[52]

The company soon more than fulfilled the boosters' mercantilistic expectations. Before the end of 1936, the aviation committee reported that Consolidated employed 3,600 people, "with an annual payroll of approximately five million dollars." The committee therefore outlined a vigorous agenda for the immediate future:

> To continue efforts to secure additional aircraft factories; contact a selected group of manufacturers in regard to plants at San Diego; develop an industrial airport at Chula Vista and complete Lindbergh Field; continue study of the industrial housing problem; study utility and water rates, study State and Federal legislation

affecting industry . . . and [publicize] our fine climate and its benefits to manufacturing, by carrying weather data on the letterheads of local firms.[53]

In other words, given the emphasis on study and public relations over concrete, concerted action, there was nothing new under the San Diego sun.

Reuben Fleet immediately found himself at the top of the city's leadership pyramid. He became a large contributor to the Chamber and commanded great respect wherever he went, including the highest offices in the federal government. He had something to say on practically every subject of concern to the Chamber, the city council, and even the Navy, and when he spoke, people listened. Sensitive to the citizens' concerns about "labor troubles," for example, he told the Chamber's executive committee that he opposed the organization's recent proposal to create "a municipally owned and operated coastal steamship line" because it would "undoubtedly" bring the wrong kind of working person to town.[54]

Having instantly established himself as the single largest employer in San Diego other than the Navy, and a substantial power broker who had the ear of cabinet secretaries, congressional leaders and President Roosevelt as well, Fleet began to reshape the city as he saw fit. Claiming the ground by the airport and the waters of the bay for the sake of his company's welfare was a modest beginning that he soon eclipsed. He served as the de facto "industrial mayor" of San Diego, who sat right at the head of the table with the commandant of the naval district and the real mayor, and his impact on the city only grew over time—just one more unintended consequence of the acts of the boosters. San Diego's economy had become one that was directly dependent on federal dollars not only through military bases with large payrolls, but also through a growing cluster of private industries that served the military by providing the R&D, equipment, and services needed by the expanding U.S. forces.

THE WAR EMERGENCY

By all accounts, World War II profoundly changed California and the American West, with spectacular growth in industry, population, and wealth. According to Gerald Nash, "It transformed a colonial economy based on the exploitation of raw materials into a diversified economy that included industrial and technological components. . . . A major influence was the dynamism of the federal government, which invested at least $40 billion in the West during wartime."[55] San Diego had been preparing for war in the Pacific since the turn of the century. Thus it was ironic how unprepared San Diegans found themselves to cope with the great naval buildup of the late 1930s and the war that followed. Between the naval bases and Consolidated Aircraft, the city's leaders had proudly fashioned San Diego into a sprawling armed-camp-by-the-sea; as well, they had studied and mastered the tortuous art of generating federal appropriations to pay for many of the city's basic urban amenities, including the park, the waterfront, the harbor channels and anchorages, water and sewer systems, and streets. They had also configured the city's general economy to depend on ever-increasing federal spending. And finally, they had created a unique civic culture—an all-encompassing societal outlook—the heart and soul of which was the U.S. Navy.

By the time of World War II Los Angeles had enjoyed the lead as California's preeminent city for a generation, the culmination of a trend that had begun to manifest itself statistically in the early 1920s. San Diego's leaders now had to concede that their city would *never* occupy first place and would *never* outpace its rivals commercially, industrially, and perhaps even in the case of the Navy as well. Under these circumstances, planning for the postwar era became a pressing priority for the Chamber and municipal government. To their credit, they began a formal process of review and sought recommendations relatively early in the war and were thus armed with a comprehensive plan fully two months prior to VE Day and nearly seven months before the end of the war with Japan. The national government had taken extraordinary measures to underwrite the community's ability to deal with problems generated by the war, but nobody knew what the future held in store once the war ended. Business leaders feared the worst, anticipating a reprise of the Great Depression they thought would arrive with the historical certainty of rapid postwar demobilization. The leaders' dream of a perfect city nevertheless remained alive. Unfortunately, many elements of their peculiar utopian vision had become quite obsolete during the war, leaving San Diego to appear hopelessly stuck in the past. Fifty years later, a prominent local journalist characterized San Diego as a "cul-de-sac city" that might suffer forever from a long history of questionable decisions.[56]

The American "war emergency" began officially eight days after Germany invaded Poland on September 1, 1939. The ostensible purpose of the president's declaration was to observe, safeguard, and enforce American neutrality, as the nation remained officially at peace; it did not yet put "the nation on a war basis."[57] San Diego's military population began steadily to rise, and Consolidated Aircraft continued to generate boom conditions as it received order after order for its warplanes. City leaders viewed these effects as an unmitigated, if temporary, good. The jobs that the company offered were themselves responsible for attracting many new residents to San Diego. All signs pointed to an unprecedented takeoff: San

Diego was indeed about to attain its long-sought metropolitan status, although at a considerable price.

As the city's response to the War Emergency gained momentum, economic output soared. The number of industrial wage earners, their wages, and the value of their output tell an important part of the story but give little indication of the larger transformation that was then occurring across San Diego. The statistics suggest enormous growth, so much of which had resulted from the Chamber's leadership and community building; beyond the statistics, the benefits that accrued to the city from the growing federal partnership were undeniable. Since World War I, the Navy alone had spent $50 million building its installations in and around San Diego and was presently spending $40 million dollars per year on operations and maintenance there.[58] By the time of the War Emergency, San Diego was home to 38,000 sailors, plus quite a few members of the Marine Corps and Army. The multilayered harbor dredging-and-filling program had made it possible for the bay to accommodate nearly 200 warships. The city's support for military aviation, and more recently its aviation industries, had indeed turned San Diego into something of an "air capital," as the business leaders liked to boast, and the urban infrastructure that had recently appeared (much of it thanks either to New Deal programs or the Navy Department's commitment to the city) really had transformed the landscape in positive and useful ways.

Within a year of President Roosevelt's declaration, however, evidence emerged to counter the ebullience expressed by so many of the city's leaders. Reuben Fleet became so alarmed by the rapidly deteriorating conditions that he urgently called on the secretary of the Navy and the secretary of the Treasury to come to San Diego to confer with him early in the fall of 1940. Such was his influence that both cabinet secretaries immediately sent their top assistants—Undersecretary James Forrestal for the Navy and General Counsel Edward H. Foley for the Treasury. They arrived at North Island Naval Air Station in the morning of October 4, 1940, without any of the fanfare that usually greeted such important federal officials, and were spirited across the bay to Fleet's office. There, they also met the assistant to the commandant of the Eleventh Naval District and other ranking sailors, several representatives of the War Department, and a delegation from the "British Purchasing Mission," no doubt concerned about Consolidated Aircraft's ability to fulfill its contracts under the trying circumstances. Before the day was over, Forrestal and Foley returned to North Island, boarded their plane, and departed for Washington.[59]

Foley's report of the meeting to his boss, Henry Morganthau, stated the astonishing conclusion that Fleet had delivered to the assembled dignitaries: The federal

government would "ultimately have to provide for the comprehensive development of San Diego as a new Federal city."[60] It was now up to the national government to finish building San Diego. Fleet had told them that the city needed $1
million to complete the sewer system, $10 million for a federal aqueduct to bring
water into San Diego from the Colorado River, and $1.5 million more to finish
some of the roads that connected his aircraft plant to the various naval and military
installations around town, among other pressing and costly concerns that included
housing, schools, and more. All that was necessary to convince Forrestal and Foley
of the city's dire condition was the brief transbay excursion aboard Fleet's yacht.
Here they were treated to a whiff of the raw sewage that was still being pumped into
the harbor because San Diego could not afford to build a proper disposal plant.[61]

Which among the city's current problems best demonstrated how completely its
leaders had lost sight of their City Beautiful ideals as they built their martial metropolis? The sewage disposal situation certainly rates highly, considering the vast
degradation of the bay that had become so nauseatingly evident. Failure to prepare
the city's housing stock and related infrastructure adequately for the influx of aviation workers and Navy families also deserves mention, at least when juxtaposed
to the great victory that attracting Consolidated Aircraft represented. And while
everyone found the city's dearth of efficient streets, roads, and railroads troubling,
in the end, the water supply must take the prize. It is a fundamental rule of urban
development that a city cannot grow demographically, commercially, or industrially beyond the limits of its supply of fresh water. Since the turn of the century,
private entrepreneurs such as John D. Spreckels and Ed Fletcher, the Chamber of
Commerce, and the city government had worked on the water problem, generating studies; building dams, reservoirs, and a distribution system; and otherwise
fretting about the future of the supply as the city grew. Although the Chamber had
always promised all comers—including the Navy—an inexhaustible volume of the
"purest mountain water," the Navy's presence constantly threatened to overtax the
precious resource, a source of considerable friction between the service and the
city at various times. The War Emergency, which caused the explosive growth of
the Navy's operations and the industrial population, plus the demand generated
by the aircraft plants, combined with a prolonged drought to cause a near collapse
of the entire system. Unable to solve its own problems, the Navy itself intervened
in 1945 by undertaking construction of the long-awaited aqueduct (in fact, connecting San Diego to the Metropolitan Water District's pipeline at San Jacinto,
eighty miles or so northeast of the city) from the Colorado River. To this day, San
Diegans continue to deal with many of these same infrastructural issues, and even
now civic boosters believe they can do so without significant public financing or

tax increases. As Steven Erie has demonstrated in his recent work, the city borrows from its pension accounts to fund vital public works and services rather than facing reality in a more responsible, more sustainable way.[62]

Once the United States was completely embroiled in the war, all of San Diego's affairs became more complicated. Total mobilization and total war in the Pacific strained the city's resources to their utmost limits. While various government projects attempted to deal with some of the worst aspects of the numerous crises, many of the city's problems remained unsolved until late in the war, if they were solved at all. Basic public services gradually caught up with the new government-built housing tracts, but a high level of discomfort in the new suburbs persisted for years. Moving the expanded population to and from work, shopping, and leisure pursuits proved extremely difficult, as the existing transportation system was not up to the task. The streetcar system alone experienced a staggering increase in ridership between 1939 and 1943 of 430 percent. San Diego's central business district had become so congested that the Chamber of Commerce persuaded the aircraft companies to structure their daily shift changes so that their employees would avoid commuting during peak shopping hours to keep space on buses and trolleys available for defense workers, no matter how much this might have displeased the city's retailers.[63]

One of the major phenomena of the World War I period, the "great migration" of people—primarily African Americans from the rural South—to northern and western cities in search of employment, occurred again during World War II, although in somewhat different form. This time, the scale and scope of the war were much larger, and thus the demands for military personnel and civilian workers swelled beyond anyone's expectations; the migration included Americans of all ethnicities and quite a few Mexican nationals as well. Given the vast technological advancement in weaponry, especially aircraft, many thousands of the new migrants sought and found work in Southern California's aviation factories. In response to intense pressure from African American leaders, President Roosevelt issued an executive order in June 1941 that required factories doing war work to desegregate and otherwise ban racial discrimination in all defense industries. San Diego's small African American population (4,143 people in 1940, out of a total population of 182,500) benefited from this turn of events, as did the nearly 10,000 black wartime migrants. Out of a total black workforce of 5,000, by war's end approximately 1,500 African Americans in San Diego worked for the federal government, 1,200 worked in the aircraft plants (mostly at Consolidated), and 500 or so worked in construction—relatively high-paying jobs. Most of the rest worked in domestic service.[64] Black workers in San Diego, however, still faced the city's history of discrimination (the president of Vultee Aircraft—the company that merged with Consolidated—for example, told a group of black employment-seekers to their faces that "it [was] not the policy of this company to employ people other than the Caucasian race"), as well as the fact that so much defense work in San Diego required skilled or semiskilled experience, which surely limited the range of opportunities for many African Americans.[65]

Mexican workers entered the United States in great numbers during the war under the bracero or guest worker program, although census statistics, which did not then include a separate category for Latino ethnicity, make it impossible to determine accurately how many people of Mexican descent lived in the area. Other sources have noted that numerous braceros took employment on farms and railroads elsewhere in the country; in June 1942 the *San Diego Union* reported that local farmers found it "impossible to get Mexicans." The farm labor situation became so acute in San Diego County that farmers considered asking the government to allow prisoners to work their fields or even to release interned Japanese and Japanese Americans from their captivity.[66] The Chamber of Commerce objected vigorously to this idea, and Phil Swing, simultaneously a director of the Chamber and the city's representative in Congress, proposed a new constitutional amendment to abrogate the clause in the Fourteenth Amendment that "automatically conferred citizenship upon anyone born in the U.S., regardless of his descent."

San Diegans of Japanese ancestry, despite the obstacles presented by state anti-Asian laws and policies on the one hand, and residual racial discrimination on the other, had nevertheless over the years earned a strong reputation as hard workers and good neighbors on their farms and in their businesses. They suffered a sudden shock when the War Relocation Authority ordered them to report for internment a few weeks following the attack on Pearl Harbor and were probably equally shocked by the crude animosity expressed by the Chamber of Commerce and county agricultural department. These agencies now saw in this productive and highly patriotic segment of the community the immediate potential for such treachery as the poisoning of the fruit, vegetable, and water supplies by pesticides or bacterial agents capable of causing massive epidemics. The county agricultural commissioner went so far as to suggest that white farmers would "now have a chance to get the vegetable industry back into their [own] hands" and that *their* produce "would probably be of better quality." Clearly, the internment and its attendant racism destroyed what had once been a vibrant, successful community in San Diego. Most of the internees eventually returned to San Diego, and among them were some of the most highly decorated combat soldiers who themselves had been drafted (some had indeed volunteered for military service) while in the internment camps. They rebuilt their lives but never their community. The San Diego to which they came back, and which they now shared with a larger and more ethnically diverse population, had changed in many ways thanks to the war. The city had become, perforce, more inclusive, and yet even as a great national movement for civil rights took shape and came to dominate American society, some of San Diego's small-town attitudes persisted, making it difficult for minority segments of the community to advance.[67]

In the midst of the war emergency, the city's leaders came to realize the impact that national and international events might have on the future of San Diego in the postwar world. Having witnessed the rapid rate of change that the "federalization" of the city had already produced, they quite reasonably feared that they were losing the initiative in dealing with local issues. The city's phenomenal growth, which had begun with the arrival of Consolidated Aircraft in 1935, had surpassed all predictions by 1943, causing severe congestion in residential neighborhoods and housing projects, the manufacturing and business districts, and the areas surrounding the airport and naval bases. Alarmed at the clearly visible consequences of the war on the standard of living in the city as well as the impairment of its military and industrial functions, Congress sent major investigative committees to San Diego twice between June 1941 and April 1943 to study the situation there. At both sets of hearings, city officials, businesspeople, naval officers, and interested citizens told their stories of the blitz-boom in generally less than glowing terms.[68]

No one at the hearings had much good or hopeful to say about the situation, and that made an interesting contrast to the city's actual growth statistics of which the boosters were so inordinately proud. For example, 4,000 people worked in manufacturing in San Diego in 1935, and this figure increased to 70,000 in 1943. In the same period, industrial payrolls exploded nearly 4,000 percent, from $5 million to $192 million dollars. Such figures make a clear statement with regard to the relationship between war and the city's economic growth, although they offer no reference at all to the various social or environmental costs incurred along the way.[69]

To San Diegans alone fell the task of planning for the postwar era. The business community must have sensed that the war boom could not last forever; early in the war, they sought to regain their customary control of urban development processes in preparation for war's end. The Chamber of Commerce's board of directors engaged the services of the Day & Zimmermann Company of Philadelphia to perform a survey and create a plan for the future. Day & Zimmermann (D-Z) ultimately provided an up-to-date assessment of the city's productive resources as well as numerous suggestions with regard to maintaining commercial and indus-trial expansion long into the future.

Day & Zimmermann delivered its eleven-volume opus in May 1945. From its first page to its last, the report strove to answer all of the questions that the Cham-ber had been asking for many years about how to turn San Diego's unique combi-nation of assets and liabilities into a reliable, profitable, durable, yet well-tempered growth machine. To its credit, the company criticized the city's economic history, although in subtle ways. For example, with regard to commercial use of the harbor, the report stated that the city was "a consuming rather than a producing commu-nity," where waterborne business lagged far behind the city's "industrial and trade activities." For these reasons,

> railroad and . . . truck traffic from inland points does not funnel through the port but is directed to Los Angeles. The latter can be accounted for, in part, by more frequent and better rail service from inland points to Los Angeles and by easier grades over highways used by motor trucks in reaching Los Angeles.[70]

The statistics that the company marshaled to support this assertion illuminated the status of San Diego Harbor as perhaps no previous study ever had: Despite all the massive harbor development projects in the name of commerce, the port of San Diego ranked twenty-third out of twenty-four Pacific ports in 1940 with respect to volume of trade, even though the city itself ranked sixth in population and eleventh in value of manufactured products. The harbor had been closed to commercial shipping during much of the war, but its reopening provided only a small benefit to the local economy. To improve this situation, the consultants recommended the creation of a unified port authority, a "free-port" foreign trade zone, and expanded wharf and airport facilities to allow San Diego to assume a "place of importance in the economic distribution of consumer goods for a large Southern California and Arizona market."[71]

In the realm of water development, D-Z discussed the fact that growth of con-sumption during the war outpaced population growth by a factor of 100 percent and that San Diego was now using an amount of water equal to what earlier studies had predicted for 1965. Thus the company looked forward to the day that Colo-rado River water would begin to flow into the city. Only then would San Diego and "other parties to the San Diego County Water Authority . . . be assured adequate public water supplies for many years to come."[72]

Day & Zimmermann's analysis of labor-force participation showed clearly the special quality of San Diego's martial metropolis. First (in 1940), a higher proportion of the local population held paying jobs than was the case elsewhere; and second, "Government employment predominated in importance." In San Diego over 26 percent of workers were employed by one or another government agency, while the national average was a little less than 3 percent. On the other hand, less than 14 percent of the city's working population engaged in manufacturing, as compared to a national average nearly double San Diego's. The report noted that such job dependence on the government indicated the vulnerability of San Diego's economy. In the manufacturing category, the city's workforce was a little less industrialized than the rest of the state but only 57 percent as much as the rest of the United States. Because most of that employment became available between 1935 and 1940, and had begun to dry up after 1944, its future hardly seemed assured.

The preponderance of government employment naturally attested to the success of the boosters' long-term campaign to militarize the city. On San Diego's future as a Navy town, however, D-Z offered two contradictory forecasts. On the one hand, the report predicted that curtailment of aircraft production and military demobilization would cause many men "to return to their former homes . . . accompanied by the exodus of wives and other members of their families now temporarily working and residing in San Diego." On the other hand, the report estimated postwar government employment would be sustained "at approximately present levels to allow for the planned expansion of the naval destroyer base and operation of other establishments on a peacetime basis."[73] Could the city have it both ways?

Between 1939 and 1943, San Diego's rank as an industrial center rose from seventy-ninth in the nation to twenty-eighth, most of which was attributable to specific "war production."[74] Thus defense cutbacks might have a negative impact on the local economy, which indeed came to pass. Within months of the war's end, aircraft industry employment had dropped from its 1943 peak of 60,000 to 6,000, and the resident population of soldiers and sailors also declined sharply.[75] The tourist industry, however, bounced back and soon exceeded its pre-war income level, as did the tuna fishery and agriculture. Payrolls in the manufacturing sector also remained well above the pre-1940 mark.[76]

As Figure 2.1 below suggests in geographic terms, the Navy remained the outstanding pillar of the economy and of the community as well, even after demobilization, in place on vast tracts of some of the city's choicest property. In 1947, the Navy's 45,000 active-duty personnel stationed in San Diego, plus its 15,000 civilian workers, comprised fully 41 percent of the city's labor force "and poured $105 millions in wages into San Diego's merchants' tills."[77] This trend would continue long

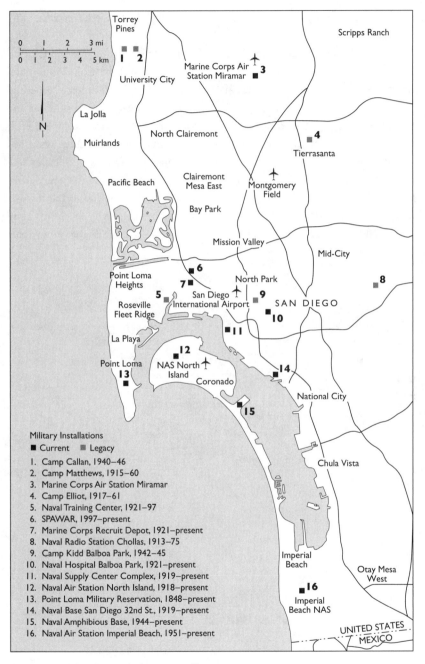

Figure 2.1 San Diego military installations.

Source: Robert Summers, PhD.

into the future; as always, the Chamber of Commerce led a perpetual campaign to keep it that way.

What San Diegans did not—and, very likely, could not—anticipate was the impact the atomic bomb, the dawning of the nuclear age, and the Cold War would have on the city's economy. The national security and national defense appetites for R&D and advanced weaponry in the late 1940s and early 1950s postwar era presented San Diego with new opportunities to leverage the civic culture and economic capabilities imbedded in its long love affair with the military. Once again, local boosters, entrepreneurial outsiders, and new opportunities to secure expanded forms of federal largesse converged into a concerted strategy to aggressively grow and attract new federal R&D investments and defense contracting to the region. This resulted in a series of land use decisions and lobbying activity in Washington that enabled the martial metropolis to reinvent itself as a Cold War economy, the subject of Chapter 3.

3 THE POSTWAR REINVENTION OF THE MARTIAL METROPOLIS: BUILDING THE FOUNDATION OF R&D TO SERVE THE COLD WAR ECONOMY

With only a slight stretch of the imagination, San Diegans may trace the origin of research and development of high technology in the region all the way back to 1883, when the Montgomery brothers experimented successfully with their home-made manned glider, ultimately attracting aviation pioneers Octave Chanute and Glenn Curtiss to the city a few years later (1895 and 1910, respectively). Curtiss trained the first naval aviators at his school on North Island starting in 1911. By the 1920s, a small but significant aircraft industry had taken root; Claude Ryan's company built Charles Lindbergh's *Spirit of St. Louis* very near the site of today's Lindbergh Field—San Diego's international airport. Shortly after the turn of the twentieth century, civic leaders recruited University of California zoologist William Ritter to establish a marine biological research station, first on the bay and then a few years later on the coast at La Jolla. They saw scientific research as a way to help put their isolated and long-suffering town on the map; this venture ultimately became the world-renowned Scripps Institution of Oceanography (SIO), progenitor of a new general campus of the University of California by 1960. The U.S. Navy installed radio apparatus on Point Loma in 1906, a key link in what soon became the first global wireless communications network.

The World War II era witnessed tremendous growth and inventiveness in research and development in San Diego in fields related to the war effort, primarily in aviation, electronics, and oceanography; with regard to the latter two, this was largely thanks to a distinctive collaboration between SIO scientists and the Navy. All of these events represent elements of evolutionary trends in the city's own development: In the early decades of the century, leaders imagined San Diego as the "air capital of the West"; the Chamber of Commerce and the Scripps family thought that their support for scientific research and higher education would attract business, industry, and culture; and of course the Navy itself became the city's chief source of income and growth—its principal "industry"—for nearly three generations.

As World War II drew to a close, however, San Diegans with good reason worried about their future. They correctly anticipated massive military demobilization along with an end to the prosperity the city had enjoyed by virtue of its booming defense—mainly aviation—factories. Business leaders sought to diversify the city's economy, but they had only limited resources they could invest to that end. While the city had accumulated some remarkable intellectual capital over the years, it was still saddled with the same limitations with which it had grappled for a long time: relative isolation and a narrow commercial/industrial base. It still possessed the same old assets that had helped it grow earlier, including its fine climate and natural beauty. And the city still owned great tracts of well-located pueblo lands that it could distribute or use as its leaders and citizens saw fit. Strategic combinations of these elements soon led San Diego into its first major postwar reinvention, as the stories that follow will illustrate.

At the end of the war, San Diego's economy remained highly dependent on the federal government with more than 60 percent of its GRP generated by military installations and defense contractors, a much larger proportion than in other California cities in the 1940s. The city's third-largest industry, tuna fishing and packing, remained strong at least for the time being, employing 40,000 workers at its peak during the immediate postwar years, even earning San Diego the nickname "tuna capital of the world."[1] Tens of thousands of defense manufacturing jobs, however, disappeared as the military's demands declined, shifts in commands occurred across the country, and military bases consolidated or closed down altogether. By 1945, San Diego entered a severe recession that did not fully abate until the outbreak of the Korean War in 1950. After a number of efforts aimed at diversification met with only limited success, civic leaders in San Diego began to see a new path to economic growth that entailed leveraging historical assets while conserving the natural amenities of the region. The demands of the Cold War significantly enabled this transformation, given the importance of basic research in projects related to national security.

Throughout World War II the federal government had been increasing its investments in basic research to support technology development for the war effort under the leadership of Vannevar Bush. During World War I, Bush as a young scientist had invented a magnetic submarine detection device and belonged to the

National Research Council, the organization that pioneered wartime collaboration between scientific research and the armed forces.[2] During the 1930s, he had become a leading figure in American science and technology; as war clouds gathered again he sought from his position—first as president of the Carnegie Institution and then as chair of the National Advisory Committee for Aeronautics—to push President Roosevelt to establish a new federal agency to coordinate scientific research in behalf of national defense.

When France fell to invading German forces in June 1940, Roosevelt accepted Bush's proposal during the course of a ten-minute meeting (and over a single sheet of paper), creating the National Defense Research Committee with Bush as the chair. Many of the committee's members also belonged to the National Academy of Sciences. Their task was to coordinate collaborative scientific efforts; later most agreed this enabled the Allies to win the war. Bush further convinced FDR to create a fund to award large sums annually for collaborative research among military, industry, and academic researchers without congressional or any other oversight. The Manhattan Project, nuclear weapons, sonar, radar, and amphibious vehicles, as well as penicillin and sulfa drugs, were developed with these resources. In his treatise *As We May Think*, Bush spoke of the war as "a scientific war."

As the war ended, Bush continued to advocate "technical superiority as a deterrent to future enemy aggression," and, in his 1945 report to President Truman, *Science, The Endless Frontier*, he argued that basic research is "the pacemaker of technological progress" and that the new principles and concepts developed in basic science laboratories become the new products and processes that enable technological advancement. Bush worked closely with generals and admirals through the war and was equally adept with Congress later. By late 1949 it became clear the Russians had developed an atomic weapon, and so the race in basic science began in earnest. Under Bush's guidance, Congress created the National Science Foundation in 1950 to support basic research, much of it geared to answering the emerging exigencies of the Cold War.

These facts illuminate the San Diego story with regard to the growing importance of advanced technology development to naval warfare and aviation and because of the significant involvement of the Scripps Institution of Oceanography's research programs in setting the war and postwar priorities of the U.S. Navy. In 1938, Robert Gordon Sproul, president of the University of California system, created a UC Division of War Research that strongly supported the sorts of military, industry, and scientific collaborations Bush championed. Roger Revelle, Scripps's director, was intimately involved with these efforts at the federal level, as was John Jay Hopkins, soon to emerge as a key figure in San Diego's first post–World War II reinvention as CEO of General Dynamics/Convair. Both men saw the postwar opportunities for San Diego to become a major center of advanced R&D; by the early 1950s, civic leadership, the Chamber of Commerce, and other local boosters came on board. In the 1950s, while San Diego's local economy still rode a postwar roller coaster, the city had two strategic assets it leveraged effectively, thus enabling the phenomenal growth of a critical mass of well-funded research institutions by the late 1960s on the undeveloped Torrey Pines Mesa: thousands of acres of city-owned pueblo land at its disposal for economic development and superb connections to influential people in Washington, D.C., thanks to the city's long military history and R&D activities during World War II.

THE EVOLUTION OF NAVAL RESEARCH IN SAN DIEGO
AND ITS ROLE IN THE REINVENTION

As reported in the previous chapter, the extreme demands of the War Emergency in 1939 and the war that followed provided the impetus for the significant augmentation of San Diego as a "new Federal city," which meant injecting millions of federal dollars into San Diego's woefully inadequate infrastructure, a package worth $44.5 million, all told.[3] The impact of this program lasted long after, for it provided many of the elements the city required to attain the status of a "metropolis" to which its boosters had aspired for generations.

By war's end, metropolitan status carried other less obvious meanings as well, primary among them potential for the city to pursue a gradual, partial divergence from its all-encompassing dependence on the Navy. With better housing, sanitation, roads, and a secure water supply, San Diego became more attractive to other kinds of businesses, industries, and residents. The Chamber of Commerce and city government, which had so relentlessly pursued the Navy for the past forty-five years, now began to seek a more diversified economic base, focusing in particular on some old ideas that now seemed more likely to succeed. The report generated by the Day & Zimmermann firm called on the city to expand tourism, build new and enlarge existing institutions of higher education, improve the city's external transportation links, and cultivate new industrial activity. This, however, did not mean San Diego would abandon its old habits. Reasonably fearing that cancellation of defense manufacturing projects as well as postwar military demobilization would erase the gains the city had so recently realized, the Chamber of Commerce in particular maintained pressure on the Navy Department to keep much of the fleet and other commands happily at home on the bay, despite the wholesale downsizing then occurring.

Even as they did this, they sought to capitalize on some of the other effects that the war had produced within the city, and here they began to generate a transformation of wartime activities into what soon became mainstays of the evolving economy: high-tech research and development and manufacturing geared to the emerging peacetime/Cold War environment. In this regard, one of the most important wartime developments was the partnership between the Scripps Institution of Oceanography (SIO) and the National Defense Research Committee (NDRC) and its successor, the Office of Scientific Research and Development (OSRD), which resulted in the establishment of UCDWR—the University of California's Division of War Research at Point Loma, to administer a new laboratory on the grounds of and in coordination with the existing Naval Radio and Sound Laboratory on Point Loma. Much credit for this goes to Scripps scientist Roger Revelle, who, serving as principal liaison officer between the Navy and certain divisions of NDRC, engineered transinstitutional collaborations that not only made huge contributions to the Allied victory but also firmly established the foundations for San Diego's high-tech future.[4]

The history of SIO deserves mention here, for it is as characteristic of San Diego as the emergence of the martial metropolis. Beginning in 1902, a small group of local citizens began to attempt to induce the University of California to establish a marine biology laboratory somewhere on the shores of the bay or seacoast. The kernel of the group formed around Dr. Fred Baker, a physician and serious amateur malacologist. Baker and his wife Charlotte, who was San Diego's first female doctor, had lived in San Diego since 1888, and both were "very active in civic affairs."[5] Baker enlisted his shell-collecting companion, H. P. Wood, secretary of the Chamber of Commerce, as well as another prominent civic-minded physician, Fred R. Burnham. The three formed the core of the Chamber's "biological committee" and began earnest pursuit of their mission in 1902.

The Chamber of Commerce took up this project as just one more way to help put San Diego on the map by harnessing the region's natural capital. The founders of the association along with University of California zoologist William Ritter, having subsequently gained the interest and financial support of newspaper magnate E. W. Scripps and his half-sister Ellen Browning Scripps, mixed their intellectual curiosity with their "local patriotism," initially to create a summer laboratory for Ritter and his students and then to transform it in a few years' time into the University of California's first permanent function at San Diego. As Patricia Schaelchlin has pointed out, the Marine Biological Station, which officially became SIO in 1921, had established itself as "the cornerstone of La Jolla's educational community, and its second economic base" after it first set up shop on Alligator Head in

Scripps Park in 1905.[6] From modest beginnings, a multivalent relationship began to grow among scientists, the business community, the Scripps family, the city, and the state of California, all of which suggested a civic culture capable of nurturing great creativity, especially as the institution itself developed its reputation as a leading center for marine biological and, later, oceanographic research. During the early 1930s, SIO scientists began to focus on the kinds of oceanographic issues that, when applied to naval war fighting, became critical to the success of the Allied war effort. And these events had a direct impact on the course taken by the city in the years following World War II, as this chapter will reveal.

Within two months or so after Roger Revelle completed his doctorate at SIO in 1936, the institution placed him on board a submarine tender during a Navy training cruise to take hydrographic measurements—including temperature, salinity, and chemical composition of the water at various depths—across a large swath of the Pacific. According to his biographers Judith and Neil Morgan, the scientific results of the expedition were uncertain, but that type of data was essential to the research then underway to improve SONAR, the antisubmarine warfare (ASW) tool then still in a rather crude state of development. Revelle immediately grasped the potential connection between the budding science of oceanography and naval warfare and more particularly the opportunity to partner the scientists at SIO with the needs of the Navy. From that point forward Revelle's actions and interests shaped SIO's thrust for years to come, affecting "the directions of oceanographic research worldwide, and even the outcome of World War II."[7]

Revelle applied for and received an officer's commission in the Navy Reserve, noting that on future research missions aboard Navy ships he preferred to "give and take orders rather than being in the anomalous position of a paying guest."[8] By the time he was called to active duty in July 1941, he had helped to forge a strong research partnership between the two entities, remarkable considering how little stature the field of oceanography had attained by that time and especially remarkable given the near invisibility of SIO, which then possessed only "five full-time graduate students and ten or eleven maverick scientists pursuing wildly independent studies."[9] Revelle spent a few frustrating months at the Navy's sound school on Point Loma training radar operators before finally obtaining a transfer to the Hydrographic Office itself, in Washington D.C., where he hoped to do more productive work.

Establishment of the sound school on Point Loma in 1939—the Navy's first—provided a glimpse of the great collaboration that soon emerged between SIO and the Navy. The sailors and scientists together studied the underwater thermal gradients affecting subsea sound propagation and reception, while a flotilla of destroyers and submarines applied what they had learned and trained new sound operators in the adjacent waters.[10] Between 1936 and the first months of the war, Revelle participated in research related to radar and sonar, essential to SIO's growing relationship with the Navy's research establishment, which now began to rival the longer-term affiliation between the military and the better-known Woods Hole Oceanographic Institution (WHOI) on the East Coast. The genesis of these efforts traces all the way back to the World War I era, when, sponsored by the Naval Consulting Board and National Academy of Science's National Research Council, scientists from private companies as well as prestigious eastern schools began their work on sonar. In fact, it was the potent threat of the German U-boat during that conflict that, according to Gary Weir, provided the "the catalyst that accelerated American naval oceanographic studies, dramatically altered scientific practice, and profoundly affected the selection of new subjects for investigation," a process that the emerging exigencies of renewed global warfare only reaffirmed during the early 1930s.[11]

When Roosevelt's new secretary of the Navy authorized the creation of the Navy's first laboratory on the West Coast, the Navy Radio and Sound Laboratory (NRSL), to be located on Point Loma, the idea had been under discussion among naval leadership for the past year. This event occurred in response to recognition that the Navy needed much more in the way of coordinated research and development than other recently established organizations, such as the Navy's sound school (founded to train sonar operators), could provide.[12] The naval establishment in San Diego, along with the conditions that had enabled it to thrive since early in the century, contributed greatly to the R&D revolution that followed. Of special value were the proximity of deep ocean waters, the extensive local oceanographic knowledge SIO had generated since its founding, the Navy's existing sound and sonar school, and the fact that almost all of the Point Loma peninsula belonged to the federal government.[13] Essential to this future was the contract between the University of California and the national government, which created the university's Division of War Research (UCDWR) in April 1941, for which Revelle was also project officer.

Assigned to the Navy's hydrographic office in 1942, Revelle soon transferred to the Bureau of Ships; his influence there on the Navy's electronics program was enormous. An admiral who oversaw Revelle's work commented after the war that "the large role which oceanography now occupies in the Navy research program is in part due to Dr. Revelle's effectiveness and foresight in planning and promoting the Bureau of Ships research during the war."[14] Revelle continued his naval career until 1947–1948, during which time "the Office of Naval Research signed contracts with Scripps assuring the institution of its interest and pledging funds to support basic research." Back in civilian life, he became associate director of SIO and director in 1950.

Within a few months of the end of the war, the Navy combined its two San Diego labs into the single Navy Electronics Laboratory (NEL), a sure sign of the Navy's "emphatic commitment for peacetime R&D, even as it demobilized its big wartime fleet."[15] UC scientists continued their collaborations with naval research on Point Loma at the new Marine Physical Laboratory, commissioned in 1946 to continue the pure scientific research endeavors begun during the war. In fact, the research programs and the infrastructure they required grew apace, as new labs, test beds, docks, and forests of experimental antennae took over some of the Navy's earliest San Diego installations, including part of what had once been the old coaling station. The Allied victory had proven the value of scientific research applied to military ends, convincing the Congress, the military services, the general public, and university administrations. According to Nancy Scott Anderson, scientists now appeared "not as irrelevant intellectuals, but as saviors of western civilization whose genius could mobilize strategy, arm and feed troops, and inform policy. By 1946, with the Cold War freezing Eastern Europe into a hostile nuclear camp, the entire country seemed to believe it needed science and technology to survive."[16] Oceanographic research in particular, as pursued by Revelle and his SIO colleagues, had made vast contributions to the effectiveness of American pro- and antisubmarine warfare as well as to the success of amphibious landings from North Africa to Normandy and across the vast Pacific. SIO's parent institution, the University of California, had provided the lion's share of scientists, lab space, and administration for the Manhattan Project, whose atomic bombs had contributed to the war's conclusion in August 1945.

Having been kept out of the Army's Manhattan Project during the war, the Navy hastened to take a leading role in the atomic weapons tests that occurred at Bikini Atoll (Operation Crossroads) in 1946. Revelle was there, "as commander in charge of the Navy's Bureau of Ships [and] in overall command of the oceanographic survey" work that occurred before and after the tests. Numerous SIO scientists were involved, including biologists Marston Sargent and Martin Johnson, and Walter Munk, who provided "assistance in mathematical and theoretical problems of ocean diffusion."[17] The Navy made it clear that it wanted and needed such collaborations with academic scientists to continue. Referring to the fundamental studies of the physics and acoustics of underwater sound and related work in electronics started by UCDWR, Vice Admiral E. L. Cochran, Chief of the Bureau of Ships, suggested that to University of California President Robert G. Sproul early in 1946: "The wider intellectual interests involved in academic positions would attract more capable personnel to this work and would also militate against the possible stagnation of the program," he said. "It appears, moreover, that such a program should be of intrinsic interest to the university."[18] To the university, this meant secure long-term federal funding, which at the time SIO truly needed. This Navy money came to the institution, at least for the time being, with practically no strings attached.[19]

Among NEL's most important projects during the late 1940s were precision radar navigation systems and electronic recognition systems whose utility soon migrated from the military to the civilian sector, with important applications in commercial shipping and civil aviation. By the early 1950s, with the endorsement of the Eisenhower administration, this growing partnership among the university, military research institutions, defense contractors and civilian industry became the central feature of San Diego's postwar reinvention, a pattern that persisted until 1966, at which time the Navy reorganized its entire research establishment.[20] For SIO, defense work post-1950 included more involvement in atomic and thermo-nuclear weapons, but a major project to investigate the sudden disappearance of the sardine fishery from California's waters brought in $300,000 from the state at first, followed by nearly $1 million per year in grants over the next several years. The so-called Marine Life Research program was carried out on Point Loma, near the Naval Electronics Lab. Between 1950, when Revelle was appointed director of SIO, and his departure in 1964, the institution's budget had grown from $1.5 million per year to $12 million.

SIO's relationship with the Navy's research establishment grew in such a way as to give the Institution the scope and leverage to press for the creation of a new general campus of the University of California, an idea that San Diego boosters had advocated since the 1920s. The impact of World War II on SIO proved decisive, thanks in particular to the agreement that led to NDRC's charter to undertake basic research and development but not the manufacture of military hardware. The naval establishment in San Diego, along with the conditions that had enabled it to thrive since early in the century, contributed greatly to the R&D revolution that followed.[21] SIO had become a powerhouse of basic scientific research, and its local, national and international reputation carried with it enormous influence, which Roger Revelle and his colleagues wielded as a rationale for establishing a much larger presence for the University of California in San Diego. Other forces, large and small, near as well as distant, also contributed significantly to San Diego's emergent reinvention.

THE BIRTH OF GENERAL ATOMIC

Although in mid-1944 the war was still far from over, by then the tide of battle had turned decisively in favor of the United States and its allies. Business leaders, politicians, workers of all descriptions and their families—to say nothing of the uniformed service members themselves—looked forward to the coming peace with a mixture of relief and trepidation. Victory would settle some of the questions of what the future would look like, but no one at this point could know if the promises offered earlier in the war period of an "American century" or a "century of the common man" might actually take shape and endure.[22] The great defense plants in San Diego had already passed their peak employment levels and productivity, and their contracts soon dried up, ultimately reducing their workforces by tens of thousands of employees. Civic leaders had worried as far back as 1939 about the potential impact of demobilization on the city's economy. And no one knew then that the parlous alliance between the United States and the Soviet Union would turn into the tense half-century "Cold War" rivalry with its constant threat of mutually assured nuclear annihilation.

Thus San Diegans scrambled to maintain if not augment the gains their city had made during the run-up to and prosecution of the war. Managing the Navy's downsizing and the conversion of defense industries to civilian production were both part of the city's program for the immediate future, as was a series of moves intended to diversify the local economy. These changes did not come easily; Consolidated Vultee Aircraft Corporation's struggle for survival represented a large fraction of what the rest of the city was going through. The company's response to rapidly changing circumstances—indeed, its unforeseen adaptations over the next decade or so—similarly came to represent San Diego's own evolution.

On the one hand, Consolidated's wartime record signified enormous success. Its designers had in short order created and built airplanes essential to Allied success—in excess of 33,000 aircraft, or 13 percent of the nation's total, including the Catalina and Coronado flying boats and no fewer than 18,000 B-24 Liberator heavy bombers.[23] The company and its subcontractors were San Diego's largest non-Navy employer and key contributors to the city's growth from 1935 on. Consolidated and Vultee, the company with which it merged in 1943, pioneered use of the mechanized assembly line for large-aircraft production, among other engineering and social advances (for example, providing day care for the children of its employees). On the other hand, management problems plagued Consolidated, leading to the company's merger with Vultee and founder Reuben H. Fleet's retirement. According to a history of General Dynamics Corporation

(GD), Consolidated's ultimate successor, the federal government's "unlimited state of national emergency" meant these were issues of national importance; "Consolidated was too important to be allowed to flounder."[24]

The merger with Vultee turned Consolidated-Vultee (also known as Convair) into a member of the postwar defense conglomerate giant General Dynamics (a veritable "General Motors of defense," as its principal organizer and first president himself said) between 1953 and 1954.[25] The General Dynamics chain of descent extended all the way back to the Holland Torpedo Boat Company and its immediate successor, the Electric Boat Company, founded in 1899. Electric Boat's checkered history included selling submarines simultaneously to Japan and Russia while the two were at war in 1904–1905; building eighty-seven submarines for the U.S. Navy during World War II (the largest single supplier); the Atlas Corporation, maker of ballistic and NASA missiles of the same name; and acquisition of the Aviation Corporation (later, AVCO), of which Vultee was a founding subsidiary. These several entities were reorganized in 1952 as General Dynamics, under the leadership of John Jay Hopkins, who had become Electric Boat's president in 1947. All of these companies became divisions of General Dynamics through a series of highly risky mergers and acquisitions, and they all struggled with the slowdown and then virtual halt in defense contracts. Hopkins's leadership, however, brought them through the early postwar transition, greatly aided by outbreak of war in Korea in July 1950. Two related factors undergirded General Dynamics' meteoric rise: first, "the technological revolution of the postwar era, together with the rising tempo of Communist aggression, which convinced the Congress and the civilian public that defense was a permanent business"; and, second, the "growing recognition of the importance of science, both to industry and defense, and an imperative need for new management concepts to cope with the increasing complexities of a rapidly changing and dynamic world."[26] General Atomic thus represented the realization of Hopkins's dream—that well-applied research and development might save the world for democracy.

By 1954, Hopkins's "empire" included two San Diego companies destined to become major players in the emerging Cold War defense establishment—Convair and Atlas. Typical of what his biographers have called his daring and innovative entrepreneurship, he had obtained for Electric Boat the contract to build the Navy's first nuclear submarine, the *Nautilus*, "without having in hand the scientists, engineers or the facilities to do an unprecedented job."[27] This meshed with his own passionate interests in nuclear energy, a central motivation in his decision to establish an entirely new company he called General Atomic (GA), to pursue basic research and development.

Hopkins' ideal research agenda—what he wanted General Atomic to accomplish—resembled at least to a degree that which the oceanographers and their colleagues at SIO sought: an "exploration of basic forces," although GA's scientists would focus their investigations on the workings of the most minute possible elements in existence. Similar to what the UCDWR and the Navy had tried to accomplish during the war and thereafter, in other words a practical application of that knowledge, GA would seek the "generation of bold ideas" and try to turn them into "salable hardware," primarily for the nation's defense. Where they differed, though, was in GA's intention to develop its discoveries further for the sake of medical and physical research, transportation, space flight, and even for the potential benefit of consumers.[28]

The man Hopkins chose to run the new undertaking, the thirty-two-year-old Dr. Frederic de Hoffmann, a strong advocate of the "atoms-for-peace" movement, seemed especially well suited to the task. Already a world-renowned nuclear physicist, De Hoffmann set the John Jay Hopkins Laboratory on a course that, again, resembled in some ways the collaboration that had occurred during the war on Point Loma among the scientists, the warriors, and the politicians. De Hoffmann assembled a team of top scientists, engineers, and businesspeople who composed a heady mix of talent that quickly began to fulfill Hopkins's vision. Early members of GA's scientific leadership included Edward Teller, Hans Bethe, Freeman Dyson, Ed Creutz, and others.

Locating the enterprise was a crucial decision GD/GA managers needed to make. Representatives of sites from all around the United States courted the company with offers of free real estate; prominent among them were the state of Florida and the bucolic Northern California city of Monterey. Late in the previous year, according to the *Union*, Hopkins had told the UC Regents that "location of a scientific and technical campus at La Jolla would probably mean location in San Diego of the company's 10 million dollar scientific research project." But, said Hopkins, "I do not want it understood that location of our research project in the San Diego area would be entirely dependent on the decision of the Regents on locating a scientific and technical school in the La Jolla area. We may locate it there anyhow."[29] To De Hoffmann the scientist, however, San Diego's charms proved undeniable. Questions of quality of life seemed paramount. As noted in a report in *San Diego Magazine*, De Hoffmann stated that the 300 or so people he anticipated would staff GA would "not be satisfied to look back in ten years and say they have made a lot of money. They will want to say they have lived wisely and well."[30]

What precisely did De Hoffmann mean by "wisely and well"? For the better part of eighty years, the Chamber of Commerce had been touting the weather, the bay, the natural beauty of the place, the possibility for unlimited growth of agriculture, industry, and trade. According to newspaper publisher James Copley, arguably one of the most powerful people in San Diego at the time, La Jolla specifically provided "the finest of recreational resources in beaches, together with two picturesque golf courses on Torrey Pines Mesa. Municipal and state-owned adjacent properties to the north are planned and developed as park reserves."[31] These qualities certainly represented real attractions to potential settlers, but what indeed did De Hoffmann and others see as special about San Diego and superior to the other places eager to land GA? The city's growth and economic development since the mid-1930s—its emergence as a metropolis still in possession of vast untapped land resources—was one likely issue. Better yet was the synergistic relationship that had emerged during the war years among the military, SIO's research capacity, and defense contractors. The fact that, under Roger Revelle's leadership, the Navy and SIO had continued to collaborate since 1945 on high-profile, big-budget nuclear research was of even greater significance. This confluence enabled other forces within the city now to press harder and with better chances than ever for success for establishment of a greatly increased presence of the University of California: GA's interest in San Diego in this regard proved decisive. Director of SIO since 1950, Revelle himself led this effort, calling for a "new campus that would be 'something like' a publicly supported Caltech" that would provide "education for the new profession of scientific research rather than the older professions of law, medicine and engineering."[32] An outfit like GA might fit right in.

THE RAPID RISE OF UCSD

The chair of the Chamber's education committee happened to be vice president of General Dynamics/Convair; he passed the word to his colleagues on the Chamber's board of directors that John Jay Hopkins sought to build a research center that in connection with an "appropriate academic atmosphere" would locate in San Diego. Hopkins himself said he felt "very strongly that a university devoted to the sciences [would] be a great aid to the industrial growth of San Diego." More to the point, according to Nancy Scott Anderson's history of UCSD, Hopkins had long hoped that the university would "provide a branch for Convair's would-be scholars."[33] Such a school appealed to some, but clearly not all, influential citizens with a stake in the city's future. When the question of providing land for a new UC campus came before the city council in December 1955, majority sentiment countered the Chamber of Commerce's proscience agenda and supported the idea of an undergraduate school primarily geared to turning out engineers, not scientists.

That idea was anathema to Malcolm Love, president of San Diego State College, whose school had a strong undergraduate program in engineering; a UC school of engineering would certainly devalue his institution. While San Diego State and Love himself were highly respected pillars of the community, the city council reprised its vote of thirty years earlier anyway, offering to donate a large parcel of undeveloped land adjacent to SIO for the purpose.

Three days later, according to Anderson, Hopkins accompanied a Chamber-led group that included NEL director Henry Bernstein, Convair's director of science Ed Creutz, Frederick de Hoffmann, and others to a meeting of UC's Board of Regents in Los Angeles to plead their case. Over the next few months, this group stumped, lobbied, and otherwise exerted considerable overt pressure on university officials to create their ideal "Institute for Pure and Applied Physics" along with an "Institute of Mechanics" at La Jolla, all intended to "powerfully accelerate scientific progress." Hopkins wrote to UC President Robert Gordon Sproul in March 1956 that General Dynamics would invest $1 million in the university if that might help generate a favorable disposition to implement the La Jolla campus. Putting the new UC side-by-side with SIO and his General Atomic lab, and only a few miles away from Atlas Missiles' new $40 million plant in Kearny Mesa, became the combined vision of San Diego's business and scientific elites.[34] A few months later, on June 5, 1956, voters ratified the City of San Diego's offer to General Atomic of a spectacular 300-acre site on the Torrey Pines Mesa, a stone's throw from SIO. Such support from the community was absolutely essential to securing the regents' approval for the new campus. As Roger Revelle said in a 1985 interview,

> Companies here had engineers who needed more basic science. Companies such as GA, Convair, Solar, Rohr, Cubic, Ryan. Freddie De Hoffman and J. J. Hopkins were great supporters. The City Manager, the Chamber of Commerce guys, Pat Hyndman, Jim Archer, all went to The Regents. Rossi, the director of the Naval Electronics Lab and later the US Office of Naval Research (with whom I coauthored a paper on sonar), made speeches in San Diego supporting the Graduate Institute.[35]

Within days of the election, President Sproul reported the recommendation made by the Regents' Committee on Educational Policy as follows:

1. There is a definite need for the expansion of the University's facilities for instruction, research, and public service in the San Diego area.
2. Our industrial civilization and the very survival of the nation depend critically on increasing the number of young scientists and engineers. The type of

expansion proposed for the San Diego area would aid greatly in carrying out this responsibility of the state and nation for the training of young people of this kind.

3. Development of the University's activities in the La Jolla–San Diego area could be carried out most effectively and economically by expanding the La Jolla campus [SIO], which already contains a center of specialized scientific research and graduate instruction that is internationally recognized . . .

4. The expansion of the La Jolla campus activities should be along the lines of natural growth in mathematics, physics, chemistry, and the earth and biological sciences, with both undergraduate and graduate instruction. In addition to the core of sciences there should be sufficient undergraduate teaching in the humanities and social sciences to afford a well-rounded education.[36]

In a recent speech to the San Diego Executives Association, presented on the eve of his ninety-eighth birthday, Pat Hyndman recounted the role of the team to which Revelle had referred in convincing the UC Regents once and for all to accept the idea of creating UCSD. Convened by the Chamber of Commerce, the group included the Chamber's Director of Development Arnold Klaus, prominent real estate broker Philip Anewalt, attorney Jim Archer, and Hyndman. Revelle had provided the team with his detailed proposal for an institute of applied mechanics, which they all felt could hardly fail to sway the skeptical regents.

According to Hyndman, when they presented the idea, all they received in return was "a cold shower." Chairman of the Regents Edwin Pauley, who feared that a new campus at San Diego would dim the luster of his much-loved UCLA, informed the San Diegans that, for any such new campus, the city would have to provide a vast tract of land, much larger than the parcel then under consideration. The group worked furiously to consolidate the much larger gift of property that UCSD now occupies (1,000 acres of city-owned pueblo land, plus 545 acres from the Marine Corps's Camp Matthews), and thus armed returned to face the regents, where Pauley gave them "another cold shower." It seems that the flight path of the planes departing Naval Air Station Miramar would unduly disturb the students and faculty. The group promptly obtained the Navy's agreement to shift the flight path to the north, and with that they appeared before the regents again, only to receive a third cold shower—the state could not possibly afford to begin to develop such a campus at that time. John Jay Hopkins was in attendance; at this meeting, says Hyndman, Hopkins reached into his jacket pocket, pulled out the famous $1 million check, and presented it to Pauley. No cold shower this time; Pauley didn't say a word, and the regents agreed to go ahead with UCSD.[37]

At that meeting of the regents, the board appointed Clark Kerr as president of the University of California system; at this same meeting they also decided to build two other new campuses—Irvine and Santa Cruz. Kerr commented in 1983 on how important he felt it was for each campus to have "a distinctive personality." He further observed that, because of the population growth in San Diego and SIO's long-established research record, there was an opportunity for the campus to become "another Berkeley, whereas our expectations of Irvine and Santa Cruz were quite different." Then-Governor Edmund G. "Pat" Brown expressed similar sentiments rather more poignantly in an interview conducted in 1985, noting that he had never gone to college but was nonetheless "very attracted to the idea that the citizens of the State of California could have access to an elite university experience through the University of California."[38] This alignment between the vision of men such as Revelle, Brown, and Kerr and the advocacy of regional civic leadership proved essential to both the establishment and character of the UC San Diego campus.

Over the next months, a number of constituencies fiercely debated the nature of as well as the location for the new UC campus. Some argued that a graduate school focused on the scientific disciplines should nestle between SIO and GA, while an undergraduate campus should be located more centrally, perhaps even as far south as Chula Vista. James Copley, publisher of the *Union* and the *Tribune*, argued persuasively in favor of locating the new UC campus between SIO and GA, citing the "extraordinary beauty and attractiveness" of the location, the proximity of the two existing institutions, and the fact that the public had spoken so clearly on the gifts of real estate. Of particular interest, Copley noted that other "'idea' industries of the kind that should be close to a university are also being established in the vicinity."[39]

The Navy weighed in as well before the deal could be sealed: The Marine Corps would vacate its extensive rifle range (Camp Matthews), and naval aviators using the base at Miramar just a few miles to the east had already agreed to alter their flight path in answer to concerns related to noise and safety. San Diego State College dropped its opposition, too, secure in the knowledge that UCSD would not overly encroach on its programs. In the end, all the pieces fell into place. General Atomic broke ground late in 1956 and occupied the first of its new buildings by mid-1957. UC president Clark Kerr told the *Tribune* in June 1959 that he wished "to proceed as rapidly as funds will permit with the full development of a general campus . . . at La Jolla to take its place alongside Berkeley and Los Angeles. The generosity of the people of San Diego in making the gift of 450 acres of property for the purpose is an act of great vision."[40] The battle over the decision to build UCSD at La Jolla finally ended in October 1959.

Despite the tremendous advance the foregoing events suggest, San Diegans still had cause to worry over their economic future. In the summer of 1960, the County Planning Department revived the old "Smokestacks versus Geraniums" conundrum as it predicted a continuing slide in military aircraft production that "put the region in a most precarious position as far as sustained manufacturing employment is concerned." If the county were to "continue to support the million people who now live here" and otherwise avoid at least two virulent strains of economic decline, the planners urged a course "to capitalize on [the region's] advantages to attract many types of highly desirable industry."

To attract "selected industry" of the desirable type, planners needed to:

1. Create an appropriate industrial climate that would pay workers higher than average wages;

2. Retain and enhance "those features of the San Diego Region which make it an attractive, pleasant area in which capitalists, managers, and scientists and their families want to live, as well as a magnet for tourists"; and

3. Diversify existing industry and add new ones "compatible with our existing environment, suited to our location, resources and facilities."

These might include "research institutions like the Navy Electronics Laboratory, the John Jay Hopkins Laboratories," and the Salk Foundation; electronics plants, shipyards, boat and sporting goods makers; "space age programs like General Dynamics Astronautics Division"; and clothing manufacturers. The agency went on to suggest various programs intended to make these ideas feasible.[41] As prescient as this document appears given the shape the future actually took in San Diego, a large element of the coming economy was just beginning to emerge—health and biomedical research were about to take off due to the expansion of the Scripps Clinic and Research Foundation and the city's commitment to Jonas Salk and his research foundation, both located on the Torrey Pines Mesa. In a number of critical ways, the new campus of the University of California that began to materialize after the mid-1950s tied these elements together, making the value of the whole of the Torrey Pines Mesa much greater than the mere sum of its parts.

As booster-in-chief and prime operative of the UCSD project, SIO director Roger Revelle framed his vision for the startup in grand terms. The new university should be "like a cathedral: 'the center to which all men turn to find the meaning of their lives and from which emanates a wondrous light, the light of understanding.'"

Moreover, any delay in its establishment "would be tragic, and might affect to a significant degree the very survival of the United States."[42] Revelle harbored no thought whatsoever of creating a conventional university campus. The city's business leaders pressed for a university that would turn out physicists and engineers to work in nuclear-oriented defense industries; Revelle accepted this view as part of his grander vision. Thus the vision that coalesced among Revelle/SIO, John Jay Hopkins/GA, and the Chamber of Commerce became the first full iteration of the plan for UCSD: a graduate school composed of an "Institute of Pure and Applied Physics" and an "Institute of Mechanics."

Throughout this quest Revelle maintained his ties to his network of war and postwartime contacts within the national defense community—federal funders and local defense industries alike. At least in part due to his urging, all among these diverse constituencies rallied in favor of the advanced science campus. In his 1985 interview, Revelle reflected on the relationship between SIO's mission and UC's ambitions for growth:

> In the early '50s, we specialized in areas that were primarily related to ocean research and we were primarily a research institution working on very applied problems. Our guys were good sea-going scientists. A graduate school of science and technology would improve this. We needed a publicly supported Caltech [the California Institute of Technology].[43]

Although today's UCSD differs from Caltech in numerous significant ways, Revelle's vision, to a large extent, was realized over the next fifty years.

Once the regents gave their go-ahead for the new campus, Revelle began his faculty recruitment program from the top down, beginning with Nobel Laureate chemist Harold Urey, whose august presence provided the new school with "instant legitimacy" and "a guarantee of seriousness" that soon attracted other leading academicians—a "dream faculty for a dream campus," as Revelle's biographers put it. Revelle's early recruits comprised a prestigious roster of highly qualified, restless, ambitious leaders in their fields who aspired to be the "best research faculty in the world," even before the bulldozers started to prepare the ground for the new campus. As early as 1961, UCSD's graduate program in physics "was second to none in the country"; biology, chemistry and experimental psychology were not far behind.[44]

Other early arrivals included Jim Arnold, Keith Brueckner, and geneticist David Bonner. Bonner in particular hoped "to establish at UCSD a series laboratories and interrelated institute-like departments that would mix work and faculty from physics, chemistry, the Scripps Institution, and a barely mentioned medical school." Recruitment, institution building, and academic success took off. Those hired brought with them "funded grants, labs, and graduate students." Jim Arnold, who was also interviewed for the UCSD archives in October 1985, was a distinguished professor of physical chemistry recruited from Princeton. He described the early faculty at UCSD as

> . . . captured by the vision. Coming from campuses such as Chicago, Princeton, and Yale, they had a chance to break away from the past. Therefore, UCSD was attractive to certain kinds of renegade academics. Our attitude was that somebody good was full of "piss and vinegar." We wanted people that were challenging the status quo intellectually and defining many of the new fields of science that were developing at that time.[45]

Arnold also illuminated the "intellectual framework" behind forming the departments on the new campus, noting, "We hired people who were in the news, such as the Meyers and of course Harold Urey. We identified areas of emphasis that were emerging and important, such as particle theory, plasma physics, low temperature physics, and later, astronomy when we brought the Burbidges here. Physical chemistry fit with SIO's earth sciences department."

Arnold's comments were echoed in an interview from 1999 with a distinguished physicist, Sol Penner, who began visiting GA and the campus in the 1950s and eventually moved to UCSD to start the applied physics and information sciences departments. "Our focus was an exceptional person rather than a particular subject. . . . [Harold] Booker for example, was a physicist in systems and control and we brought him to the campus to build an applied physics and information sciences program. He built the nucleus of the department." Moreover, "in the early '60s, the Cold War was the driver of basic research and engineering companies. Engineering was becoming indistinguishable from physics, like at Caltech, where seventy engineers and scientists might be working all in one group."

The strong science orientation of the campus was echoed in numerous interviews with founding faculty of the UCSD campus. Herb York, a physicist who was selected to be the first chancellor of the UCSD campus, having served as undersecretary of Defense in Washington, D.C., during the 1940s, returning in the 1950s to be director of the Lawrence Livermore Lab, commented on the campus as he found it:

> I had done a good job in Washington, DC and that was the reason I was attractive to Kerr and many of the early scientists here. I had no background in education, had been working in the Pentagon. When I came, the Los Angeles division of the

UC Senate was still very present. People were eager to get out from under them. They had already hired physics, chemistry, and biology faculty at the senior level and were beginning to create departments.

In fact, Penner referred in his interview to a number of the early faculty as "McNamara's Whiz Kids" because of their involvement with the space race stimulated by Sputnik and inspired and financed by President John F. Kennedy.

Everything, according to Judith and Neil Morgan, "soon fell into place: Scripps Clinic moved to Torrey Pines Mesa near General Atomic, and vastly enlarged its research institute. Scripps and [the] Salk Institute could offer dual appointments or adjunct research roles to enhance the synergy of the new campus." Thus Revelle's vision for an ideal Cold War university took shape, marred only by his being passed over for the position of its first chancellor, partly due to his poor relations with President Kerr, the domineering Edwin Pauley, and other regents, as well as opposition from the community that likely emerged in response to his perceived arrogance and imperiousness.[46]

Atomic physicist Herbert York received the appointment that Roger Revelle—on the scene and deeply involved since 1936—felt should have been his own from the start. Highly placed within the national security and national defense establishments as well as within the UC system, to York fell the task of consolidating the complicated real estate transfers, conversion of military buildings to academic uses, initiating the enormous development, construction, and administration of the new campus. York also had to breathe life into the "semblance of a full-service undergraduate school," and this "meant physicist York had to hire in mathematics, the fine arts, humanities and social sciences." He was furthermore under orders to start up the medical school, all the while "working with a collection of faculty members described . . . as a gifted group of academic outlaws who saw in San Diego the chance to shed the constraints of ordinary university life."[47]

UCSD admitted its first class of undergraduates in 1964. Replacing Roger Revelle's "highly unorthodox" dream of a complex of "institutes," a more conventional educational structure emerged. The remnant of Revelle's vision, the School of Science and Engineering, initiated in 1960, had enrolled 269 graduate students as of fall 1963, but with the arrival of the first class of undergraduates a year later it was "collapsed" into UCSD's emerging system of colleges. At first there was one college—Revelle envisioned twelve—but the scheme evolved into the central organizing principle of the school's undergraduate program one college at a time until in 2001 there were six. The college system earned a reputation as "an exciting innovation in an era of educational novelty," but graduate instruction and research remained much more the focus of "local budget-makers," to whom it appeared that "the university's future was steaming toward San Diego on a money-laden research train." Thus the graduate and research programs grew apace. As of 1963, the faculty numbered eighty, mostly scientists, including two Nobel Laureates and thirteen members of the National Academy of Sciences.[48]

Throughout UCSD's first decade, scientific faculty on the one hand generated spectacular successes in the growth of the campus and in receiving outside funding by virtue of inter- and cross-disciplinary collaborations. On the other hand, they engaged in irritating, debilitating factional academic feuds. In the early years, physics dominated, then biology, then physics again—a challenge that emerged from the "explosive experimental activity" occurring at the crossroads of chemistry, physics, and biology.[49] Part of such turmoil could be attributed to the scientists' superstar status and sensibilities; the "generalized fever for establishing centers, programs or research units," funded from outside the university by government agencies, industrial concerns, and philanthropic foundations, surely contributed as well. The movement to establish organized research units (ORUs) or institutes outside the purview of academic departments increasingly became, according to the Academic Senate's Committee on Educational Policy, "the only way to get money [for the campus] to thrive," and without which the university could not hope to fulfill its "dual commitment of research and of instruction." In 1966, however, the vice chancellor for graduate studies and research explained that ORUs were intended primarily to "facilitate the development of advanced research programs . . . essential to excellence in graduate education," and secondarily to cultivate outside funding.[50]

While benefiting greatly from the ORU program, departmental research and instruction in engineering followed a somewhat bumpy path. David Bonner expressed amazement in 1962 "that relatively little thought [had] been given" to its long-range development. Roger Revelle's promise, made in 1955, to avoid orthodoxy in the school's engineering curriculum, led planners in the direction of physics as the "foster parent" of various academic engineering disciplines. The physicists involved, however, preferred to keep to their own specializations, even though the coming regime of "engineering sciences" would include applied electronics, astronautics, and chemical engineering. Within a few years of the formation of the Division of Engineering in 1981, these programs garnered more than 20 percent of all UCSD's undergraduate majors and graduate enrollments, and 17 percent of the university's departmental expenditures. David Bonner's "innovative but unrealistic ideas for the applied sciences," as well as the original idea that engineering at

UCSD would pursue the commercial application of atomic energy, had long fallen by the wayside.[51]

Early recruits to the program, such as Sol Penner from Caltech and Henry Booker, late of Cambridge and Cornell, came to UCSD with first-rate connections, whether within the defense establishment or the National Academy of Sciences. Their rarified studies in applied sciences attracted other luminaries and soon led to research in "combustion and propulsion, applied plasma physics, sonic flow and turbulence theory," as well as solid-state and quantum electronics, the physics of the solar system, radio astronomy, computer science, and information and communication theory. They championed crossover research that defied the old boundaries between physics and engineering, calling them arbitrary and punitive. Their programs and departments changed focus and names on several occasions within a few short years. For example, Penner's department of aerospace engineering became aerospace and mechanical engineering sciences, which later became applied mechanics and engineering sciences. Applied electrophysics became electrical engineering and computer sciences, which was later divided into departments of computer science and engineering and of electrical and computer engineering. The number of undergraduate majors in these several fields rose exponentially, as did the graduate student population, faculty and staff.[52]

By the late 1960s, UCSD had become a renowned center for classified research, "founded on the fortunes [provided by] outside funding and already . . . one of the principal recipients of federal research grants in the nation."[53] Quite a bit of the $40 million worth of outside funding (spread across 135 contracts) was indeed classified "mission-oriented" work and thus a subject of concern to university administrators, students, and the general public during the politically turbulent period. In January 1971 the Academic Senate expressed strong opposition to research related to defense—a far cry from the institution's critically important research and development activities during and after World War II. It was clear, as Nancy Anderson has pointed out, that UCSD had by now "outgrown its beginnings as a creature of the national and local military-industrial complex. It would continue to progress as a stellar scientific research institution supported by vast sums of outside funding, but UCSD had become independent."[54]

Over the next decade, federal funding for university research projects only grew in importance as state financing diminished. The Academic Senate's earlier resolution against classified research made the task of landing federal contracts much more difficult while at the same time generating a dangerous rift—what former UC President Clark Kerr had called a "new hierarchical point of tension . . . between humanists and scientists."[55] The university's decision to pursue a more humanistic avenue of scientific research finally came together in the late 1960s with the open-ing of UCSD's School of Medicine—an event that had been under discussion and considered a foregone conclusion since the mid-1950s despite more than a decade of "complicated, shifting war," a source of "great pulling and hauling," and, perhaps needless to say, vacillation.[56] Participants and affected parties included the regents, the governor of California, the state legislature, UCSD science faculty (led by David Bonner), the local medical community, medical faculty members at UCSD and UCLA, campus deans and chancellors, the Chamber of Commerce, the Veterans Administration, the County of San Diego, and, of course, the citizens of the region, who comprised the prospective population of patients to be served by the school and its affiliated hospitals and clinics.

At the heart of the often acrimonious debate was the nature of the school itself: Was it to be the school's mission to train clinicians, or should its main function be in the realm of primary medical research? The rapidly growing San Diego commu-nity wanted and needed the services that a clinically oriented school could provide: the hospital beds, medical specialties, and perhaps most of all, a growing popula-tion of medical practitioners. According to the Chamber of Commerce, strongly in favor of the idea for years, the region already possessed all the main criteria necessary for the successful establishment of the school—a thriving metropolitan area, an existing university, "enough patients with illustrative medical problems," and a sufficiently large and diverse clinical pool of physicians on whom the school could draw "as needed."[57] Committees within the university, however, hewed to David Bonner's plan for a research-based school—"an appendage of his School of Human Biology," although critics of this idea felt that such a focus might "produce graduates who would never practice medicine."[58]

When the regents approved a plan in the fall of 1962 intended to educate "phy-sicians for service," the stage was set for nearly two decades' worth of fractious-ness. After several pushbacks of the entry date for the first enrollment of students (from 1964, and finally to 1968) and considerable difficulty in recruiting a dean, the university hired Joseph Stokes III in January 1964 to set the school in motion. Stokes attempted to implement the Bonner Plan through "interdigitation"—a pro-cess whereby the medical school would integrate its faculty positions with partici-pating campus departments, thus eliminating the need for separate basic science departments within the medical school itself. According to Nancy Scott Anderson, "Clinical departments would serve the campus and county hospitals and would have access to a new, 1,000-bed Veterans Administration hospital planned for the campus." A major flaw in these arrangements arose with disagreements in regard to the mix of county "charity patients" and private patients that the hospitals would have to serve and how fees from private patients and state welfare funds would be intermingled and "used to support the general medical school operation." Relations between UCSD and the local population of medical practitioners became highly strained over questions of compensation, poor usage of the UCSD/county hospital, and the academic ideology of the school; the bad feelings so generated persisted for many years to come. As plans for the size and estimates of the costs of the various facilities went up and down between 1962 and 1966, and amid all the political turmoil these events caused, heads rolled—first that of Dean Stokes, and later Chancellor John Galbraith.[59]

In the midst of this tumult, the university managed to hire Robert Livingston, formerly of Yale, UCLA, and the National Institutes of Health, as chair of the medical school's neurosciences department and eminent surgeon Marshall Orloff. Orloff enjoyed something akin to the superstar status of Roger Revelle's early hires—Markle Scholar in Academic Medicine and professor and chief of surgery at UCLA. "The esteemed Eugene Braunwald" came as chief of medicine in 1968 (he soon obtained a $5 million heart–lung grant from the National Heart Institute); several other internationally respected leaders in their fields also joined the faculty around that time, "acting as magnets for the medical school in ways that early faculty had for the science departments." The leadership of the dean who replaced Joseph Stokes, biologist Clifford Grobstein, who had initially been hired to chair UCSD's biology department after David Bonner's untimely death, seemed to help greatly to calm the situation after his appointment in May 1967; in 1968, the School of Medicine finally opened its doors.[60]

THE ROOTS OF SAN DIEGO'S HEALTH
AND BIOSCIENCE CLUSTERS

San Diego leaders aggressively leveraged the region's R&D assets relevant to the advanced technology needs of the military and the national security priorities of the Cold War in their efforts to diversify the city's economy. Equally, they sought to benefit from San Diego's long identification with health and well-being to support an expanding investment in science and clinical applications relevant to health and medicine. Here again, as with the formation of the marine biology lab that became the Scripps Institution of Oceanography, the largesse of Ellen Scripps was pivotal. She enabled the founding in 1924 of the Scripps Metabolic Clinic, which in the 1950s became the Scripps Clinic and Research Foundation. In the 1950s a group of basic scientists who had worked with Jonas Salk at the University of Pittsburgh undertook its leadership along with members of the founding faculty at the new University of California San Diego School of Medicine. The accelerated growth of the Scripps Clinic from the 1950s onward, the founding of the Salk Institute for Biological Research in 1960, and the establishment of an explicitly basic science–oriented School of Medicine immediately thereafter—all with the enthusiastic support of civic leaders and local philanthropists—was to pay significant economic dividends to the region within a few decades. The independent, yet parallel, growth of these three institutions subsequently has seeded more than thirty additional research institutes dedicated to the health and life sciences that now make their home in the region.

The Scripps Metabolic Clinic

In September 1924, Ellen Browning Scripps made a $250,000 contribution to establish the forty-four-bed Scripps Hospital in La Jolla. In December of that year she made an additional $50,000 contribution to create a specialized research facility, the Scripps Metabolic Clinic, as part of the hospital to diagnose, treat, and investigate diabetes (insulin had just been discovered) and other metabolic disorders. Dr. James Sherrill was the overall director from 1924 until his death in 1955, having hired a full-time director of research in 1928. When Ellen Scripps died in 1932 at the age of 95, she left an additional $300,000 in her will to the Metabolic Clinic, "preferably for research." By 1946, the clinic had separated from the Scripps Memorial Hospital and constructed a new research facility and began recruiting biomedical scientists. With Director Sherrill's death in 1955, Edmund Keeney— a self-confident and entrepreneurial physician-researcher originally from Johns Hopkins School of Medicine—became the director, just as the West Annex was being completed to house divisions of gastroenterology, allergy, and clinical immunology. Once hired, Keeney became a strong advocate for expanding the basic research program over the clinical practice, and a number of board members actually resigned in protest.

Keeney's vision prevailed, and in 1956 the institution was renamed the Scripps Clinic and Research Foundation. Keeney began aggressively recruiting new researchers, in particular a biochemist, A. Baird Hastings from Harvard University, in 1959 who, within a year, secured a seven-year grant from the NIH for basic science. Keeney scored a major coup recruiting Frank Dixon, the chair of the University of Pittsburgh School of Medicine Department of Pathology, whom Jonas Salk had tapped in the 1950s to start a research program in pathology at the University of Pittsburgh when Dixon was just thirty-one years old. As a teenager from Minnesota, Dixon had visited and fallen in love with La Jolla. He served in the military during World War II and attended Harvard, where he worked with Shields

Warren, who would become the Atomic Energy Commission's first chief of biology and medicine and an authority on radiation-induced disease. When contacted by Keeney in 1960 after more than a decade of outstanding research achievements, Scripps was still unknown, part of a small-town hospital and a risky career move. On the other hand, the position offered brand new space, resources to build a lab, and absolute freedom from teaching and faculty politics. "Our friends and colleagues in the East all told us we'd be back in a year," reported Professor Emeritus Charles Cochrane in a speech to the La Jolla Historical Society in 2010. "They were wrong," he went on to say, and at Scripps, under Keeney, "the scientists found exactly what they were looking for—a place they could do research full time, without excessive bureaucracy or requirement to teach, do rounds, or serve on committees; a place where science came first." When Dixon moved from Pittsburgh to La Jolla, he convinced six postdocs, a half-dozen support staff, and four faculty members, including Cochrane, to come with him. Lots of talent and time in the lab writing great proposals and good papers brought in the federal research dollars quickly, and many, including Dixon, spent their entire careers in La Jolla.

In rapid succession, Keeney recruited distinguished scientists from other leading medical schools to head the divisions of biochemistry and microbiology, so that by 1965 the Scripps Clinic and Research Foundation represented a powerhouse of world-class scientists similar to GA in physics and engineering by 1955, and UCSD in the basic sciences by 1960. Keeney was not only great at recruiting talent but also a phenomenal fund-raiser, engaging in particular the support of scientists, industrialists, and philanthropists, in particular Cecil H. Green (cofounder of Texas Instruments), who moved to La Jolla with his wife just as the region was developing as a center of science and medicine, thanks to the leadership of Keeney at Scripps, the founding of the Salk Institute, and the opening of the new basic-science-focused University of California campus in La Jolla. Fascinated by industrial applications to the field of medicine, particularly radiology and diagnostic imagery, Green made several gifts to expand the clinic's capabilities, including major gifts in the 1970s to construct the Ida and Cecil Green Hospital. On his wife's death in 1986, he made a major bequest to establish the Ida and Cecil Green Cancer Center at Scripps Clinic.

In the 1970s, Scripps Clinic moved all of its activities to the Torrey Pines Mesa, locating them within minutes to the rapidly expanding Salk Institute and the brand-new UCSD School of Medicine. Under the able leadership of the former director of NIH Charles Edwards (1977–1987) and then the internationally ranked biochemist Richard Lerner (1982–2011), The Scripps Research Institute, as it has been known since 1991, has grown into a major internationally recognized research institution with many Nobel Laureates and NAS members on its staff and in excess of $400 million in annual research funding—a fitting legacy for the visionary Ellen Browning Scripps.

The Salk Institute for Biological Studies

The strategic use of 48,000 acres of pueblo lands (San Diego's Spanish legacy)—the city's portion of the legal rights and land ownership California had acquired after the Mexican War in 1846—represented a valuable bargaining chip in luring research centers to the region in the 1950s and 1960s. City leaders had put them to strategic use to attract military installations to the region in the first decades of the century. So too, after World War II, free land was a tool for economic development, beginning with the 300 acres committed to General Atomic in 1955; a gift of twenty-seven acres on a bluff overlooking the Pacific Ocean to Jonas Salk, the developer of the polio vaccine, for his new Institute for Biological Studies, soon followed. Like Keeney and Dixon at the Scripps Clinic and Research Foundation, like Revelle and Bonner and other UCSD founding scientists, Salk had a vision of an interdisciplinary center where basic research scientists would be unfettered by academic silos and bureaucratic constraints in their pursuit of the rapidly expanding basic sciences. He also wanted the institute to be a place where scientists would explore questions about the "basic principles of life" and work together in a highly collaborative environment to achieve the kind of openness and exchange he felt was essential to the progress of science.

Salk sought to build a campus that was both aesthetically uplifting and functionally flexible. He collaborated with the architect Louis Kahn on the design of the facility he believed would enable this new paradigm for research and collaboration. In March 1960, with his vision, an architectural plan and a pledge of support from the March of Dimes, Salk and Kahn went to the San Diego City Council to request a gift of land on the Torrey Pines Mesa overlooking the Pacific Ocean. Salk had "a friend in court" in the person of the then-mayor of San Diego, Charles Dail, who had suffered from polio as a child. In June of 1960, in a special referendum, the citizens of San Diego overwhelmingly voted support for the gift of these pueblo lands to the Salk Institute, as they had done in 1919 for the Navy, in 1955 for the 300-acre gift of Torrey Pines land to General Atomic, and in 1959 for the UCSD campus.

Peter Salk described his father's reaction to La Jolla as "visceral." Unable to convince the chancellor of the University of Pittsburgh to support his vision of a new kind of interdisciplinary institute, Jonas Salk was exploring alternative sites when Ferd Fletcher, grandson of Colonel Ed Fletcher, introduced in Chapter 2, showed him a completely undeveloped site at La Jolla, overlooking the Pacific Ocean. Peter Salk said his father's response was unequivocal. "It was so beautiful; he saw infinity, space, unlimited opportunities to create something from scratch," and he knew this was where he wanted to spend the rest of his life.[61]

With his vision and the promise of complete intellectual freedom, by 1963 Salk began to attract full-time senior scientists and their research teams, including Jacob Bronowski, Melvin Cohn, Renato Dulbecco, Edwin Lenox, and Leslie Orgel. Salk also had a roster of nonresident fellows, who included scientists of the stature of Leo Szilard, Francis Crick, Salvador Luria, Jacques Monod, and Warren Weaver. The institute's research focused on genetics, molecular biology, neurosciences, and plant biology. Today, it employs sixty scientific investigators plus a staff of 850, who include visiting scientists, postdocs, and graduate students from all over the world. As of 2011, five scientists trained at Salk have won Nobel Prizes, and three resident scientists are Nobel Laureates. With an annual budget approaching $80 million, the basic research conducted at Salk commands worldwide respect.

The saga of the land deals of the 1950s and 1960s, the construction and expansion of research institutions, and the attraction of high-level talent underscore the fact that, by 1964, when the new UC San Diego campus admitted its first freshman class, the Torrey Pines Mesa was already a hub of innovative world-class science centers poised for further growth, given the booming economy of the United States at that time and the burgeoning commitment of the federal government to technology development and basic science throughout the Cold War. It would not suffice to say that San Diego had "come a long way" since its struggles at the turn of the twentieth century; over a period of sixty years or so, the city's leaders had invented and reinvented both an innovative political economy and civic culture, on which the next generation might build its own vibrant success.

CONCLUSION

In the 1950s and 1960s, San Diego, which since 1900 had become a martial metropolis, undertook the process of reinventing itself as a center of R&D, primarily in the service of the Cold War. As this chapter has revealed, a number of factors converged in the 1950s. Fueled by gifts of land, the federal government, the military services, and research establishments combined with visionary civic, science, and corporate leaders to transform the landscape. Together they converted the undeveloped pueblo lands on the Torrey Pines Mesa above La Jolla into a distinctive enclave encompassing a major nuclear energy enterprise, a well-funded Scripps

Institution of Oceanography, the Salk Institute for Biological Studies, and a major research university with great strengths in biology, applied physics, chemistry, and medicine, all in a period of ten years. During the 1970s, the already robust Scripps Clinic and Research Foundation moved from downtown La Jolla to the Torrey Pines Mesa, and a dozen new research institutes were founded—most notably, what today is the Sanford-Burnham Medical Research Institute.

Anxious to retain their nonindustrialized economy but eager for prosperity and metropolitan stature, civic leaders, decades before other communities across the United States (with the exception of Boston and San Francisco), were convinced by the well-connected distinguished scientists in their midst that an R&D-based economy might assure the growth and retention of the military and defense contracting in the region. History has proven them right. San Diego today continues to be one of the top centers of military and national security defense contracting in the United States, as well as a major home for naval ships, aviation, and the Marine Corps. What the civic leaders and science advocates of the 1950s and 1960s did not, and perhaps could not, anticipate were the effects that globalization and technological advances would have on the political economy of the world, particularly with the collapse of the former Soviet Union and the end of the Cold War, which provided the raison d'être for the growth of basic science support throughout the 1950s, 1960s, and 1970s—the subject of Chapter 4.

A number of common threads emerge from the story of San Diego's postwar reinvention, which may be relevant to understanding the transformation or stagnation of other places and other times. Clearly, different kinds of geographic assets matter more or less for different forms of economic activity. San Diego's long-barren mesas, hills, and canyons fronting the Pacific Ocean, for more than a century unsuited for agriculture or industrial manufacturing, today, in the knowledge age, represent valuable assets for the development of research campuses and science parks with the benefit of year-round sunshine and views of the Pacific. While the military was San Diego's primary "industry" from 1910 until 1950, leadership grasped the forces that were changing the character of that industry and, in particular, the growing importance of R&D. They mobilized their limited assets to adapt. In San Diego's case, that meant zoning the Torrey Pines Mesa for R&D and light industry, even though it had originally been projected for residential and recreational uses. Civic leaders also teamed with scientists to influence their complementary networks at the state and federal levels, as well as locally. It was also a period when key individuals took enormous personal risks, making commitments of personal time and resources to realize a dream, a vision. However, it is also important to point out that the opportunism and risk taking of the 1950s and 1960s was borne out of the absence of any legacy industries or families to buoy the local economy; the need to scramble for something new and different, because the choices available to many first-tier cities after the war—to go back to manufacturing cars, refrigerators, or glassware or to building furniture, or to large-scale agriculture or steel mills, or coal mines—had never been part of San Diego's history and had no promise for its future. So the new and the entrepreneurial, as well as military-related strategies, made sense.

4 SAN DIEGO'S ECONOMY COMES OF AGE, 1969–1984

San Diego's post–World War II reinvention incorporated a number of critical events, especially from the mid-1950s on. First, the city grew at a prodigious rate, and not only in terms of number of residents and gross regional product. Second, more and more of the virgin real estate within the sprawling city limits—much of the best of it owned by the municipality itself—was sold off for residential, commercial, and industrial development, and at least some of the property the city had given to the military services decades earlier came back into city hands to be recycled for other uses, including a portion of the vast tract that became UCSD. Third, a large part of San Diego's outward expansion—indeed its creation of model "edge cities" in the vicinity of UCSD and the research centers on the Torrey Pines Mesa—began to take physical shape nearly hand-in-hand with the makeover of the decrepit downtown, thanks in large part to the energetic leadership of Mayor Pete Wilson (1971–1982), a relative newcomer on the scene.[1] Neither of these large projects originated with Wilson; both had been under discussion and even active planning some years prior to his administration.

Called "Mr. Clean" by some to underscore the contrast between his youthful, progressive, aboveboard style and the murky self-serving underhandedness that his predecessors and their cohorts seemed to personify, Wilson remade San Diego's political landscape as he brokered the next generation of deals that came to define the city's place on the map of the nation's economy for years to come. These events occurred during a decade of national civil unrest, which stirred the conservative community's mistrust of the university. Unfortunately, this meant that the exponential R&D growth across all of the institutions on the Mesa was not treated as the kind of economic asset for the region it had been in the 1950s and 1960s in particular. The city's economy and the Mesa's growth during this decade and a half were parallel but not integrated. Few planning documents or public addresses from this period mention the economic promise of R&D as they had in prior decades.

San Diego's long tradition of boosterism and opportunism continued to characterize the city's transformation throughout the last third of the twentieth century. The early leaders who championed the use of undeveloped land on the Torrey Pines Mesa for the establishment of the innovative research institutes and a new kind of research university, with the possible exception of Roger Revelle, could not have imagined the extent to which the Mesa would grow into a major international center of research and development in fewer than twenty years. By the late 1960s, General Atomic had secured significant funding for a variety of projects, while Jonas Salk's Institute for Biological Studies had been built and populated with laboratories and internationally renowned researchers. UCSD's science departments had gathered some of the world's leading researchers as founding faculty, and the university had launched a new medical school with a focus on basic research. These developments by the late 1960s represented the platform from which a truly robust R&D community was able to grow over the ensuing decades.

The postwar expansion of federal research dollars across all agencies triggered by Vannevar Bush's call to increase basic research activities nationwide fueled this growth significantly. An intense spirit of global competition, frequently framed in the language of war, characterized the era. The expansion of the anti-Communist Cold War threats throughout 1960s and 1970s fueled burgeoning research activities in support of national security. The space race with the Soviet Union scarcely masked concomitant advances in ballistic-missile technology, starting in the late 1950s. And a growing national commitment to improving health and well-being through a major expansion of NIH funding, as well as a doubling of enrollments in medical schools across the nation, not to mention President Richard Nixon's war on cancer, accelerated the region's growth in medical research and education. The University of California founded three medical schools during the 1960s, at Davis, Irvine and San Diego.

This chapter illuminates the ways in which the regional economy negotiated the growth of R&D capacity on the Torrey Pines Mesa, as well as made the transition from an R&D infrastructure that was primarily federally driven and funded to a more market-oriented cluster strategy that allowed the region to build the market-driven infrastructure essential to creating distinct clusters of high-tech economic activity. Before examining the transition, however, it is important to understand the broader political and economic forces affecting the country and the region during this period that shaped the transformation.

CHALLENGES TO THE PROMISE OF R&D IN THE 1960S AND 1970S: THE GROWING SCHISM BETWEEN SCIENCE AND INDUSTRY

The consolidation and expansion of the research institutions on the Torrey Pines Mesa during the 1960s and 1970s took place in the context of a variety of national trends and regional events that had profound implications for the evolution of San Diego's innovation economy, in particular the long-championed establishment of a local campus of the University of California. The civic pride and hopes for its benefits to the military and defense contracting activities in the region were, however, soon dashed by social and political uprisings across America in the early 1960s. Civil rights marches in the South, the Watts riot in Los Angeles in the summer of 1964, Mario Savio and the Free Speech movement at Berkeley, the assassinations of Robert Kennedy and Martin Luther King Jr. in 1968, the rise of the Black Panthers, and, of course, the growing protests against the war in Southeast Asia all changed the American landscape profoundly. Through most of the 1960s, the UC San Diego campus, like GA before it and Salk and the Scripps Research Foundation, attempted to avoid the social turmoil of the period and focus on attracting world-class scientific faculty and researchers, building facilities and research infrastructure, and winning large federal grants, all with the support and admiration of the conservative business community.

During the 1960s, for example, the San Diego Chamber of Commerce published annual promotional reports on research and development in San Diego that summed up the tremendous gains the region had made in a mere decade. The 1966 report begins with a section titled "San Diego: Climate for Research and Development." It lists more than 200 enterprises in R&D under categories such as aeronautics, biology, computers and data handling, electromagnetics, electronic components, electronic instruments, electronic systems, energy conversion, medicine, nonmetallic materials, oceanics, optics, physics, processing, and chemistry. It also lists more than twenty research institutes and six educational institutions, including the young University of California. Twelve pages follow with photos and narratives on the research settings and companies in this sector. It even devotes a full page to the five Nobel Laureates working in the region, the twenty-two members of the National Academy of Science residing in the area, and the two members of the National Academy of Engineering. The report concludes with an invitation to "Please Join Us." Clearly, in the early 1960s civic boosters saw the promising economic returns of a vigorous R&D profile.

By the late 1960s, however, UCSD was turning into a more comprehensive university with humanities and social science faculties and a full complement of undergraduate and graduate students. This happened just at the time the national unrest caught fire, particularly among the young, with civil rights, the Vietnam War, and discontent with the "button-down" lifestyle of the 1950s and 1960s. The young UCSD campus became enveloped in this social tsunami, and an enormous schism developed between town and gown that would not be mended until the mid-1980s, a period of nearly twenty years.

In 1968, in what then-Chancellor William McGill referred to as "The Year of the Monkey" in a later book (1983), this terrible rupture occurred. In that year, not long after Ronald Reagan—much loved and widely supported by San Diegans—became governor, the regents of the university fired Clark Kerr from his post as president of UC, and several chancellors stepped down as well. Social unrest fulminated across American universities. At UC San Diego, McGill had to deal with a critical local press and a hostile community as he focused on the campus struggles around the reappointment of celebrated Marxist philosopher Professor Herbert Marcuse, whose graduate student Angela Davis began her rise to national notoriety. There was also a proposal for famous Black Panther leader Eldridge Cleaver to teach an "experimental" sociology course, a demand for a new undergraduate college organized by students focused on "Third World studies," to be named Lumumba-Zapata College, as well as major demonstrations on campus in support of the People's Park sit-ins at Berkeley and against the growing presence of U.S. military forces (many deployed from San Diego bases) in Southeast Asia.

Physicist Sol Penner remembered a deeper and more systemic chasm. As he pointed out in a 1999 interview, a vote of the Academic Senate mandated that the entire University of California abolish its program in classified defense-related research, which not only had been so important to SIO over the longer term but had also been a key element in UCSD's meteoric rise to prominence. The San Diego community could not help but interpret such events as a slap in its collective face. Penner rued the immediate consequences: closer supervision of academic activities and greatly reduced funding for research, which he said "after the turbulent '60s, hurt us for the next two decades." After all, until this moment, UCSD's basic research "was embedded in the Navy and military, and [those entities were] now unwelcome. There was uproar among academics about doing top-secret research."[2] On the same topic, Caltech-trained biologist Paul Saltman, appointed provost of Revelle College (the first of UCSD's six undergraduate colleges) in

1967, was horrified by what he encountered on his arrival on the campus—the "'all power to the people' faculty and curriculum that was fighting [against the] rigid scientific curriculum and values originally established at UCSD. The whole issue was freedom and anarchy."[3]

Such events did not endear the young campus or its activist faculty and students to the city's dominant conservative establishment. It would take years for these rifts to mend. In the interim, San Diegans, less enamored with the promise of science and academics to enrich the economy, were navigating more than their fair share of economic booms and busts.

CITY-BUILDING DURING THE COLD WAR

During the twenty years that passed between the end of World War II and the opening of the new general campus of the University of California on the Torrey Pines Mesa, the city of San Diego experienced a number of transformations large and small that indelibly shaped future events throughout the region. Despite the persistence of pervasive boosterism and dependence on the federal government, considerable changes in politics, leadership, economy, population—all important elements of its civic culture—emerged, whether for better or worse. Global, national, statewide, regional, and local trends all contributed to the changes that occurred. The intense desire for growth of all kinds continued to drive the actions of the city's leaders. They did remarkably well channeling outside forces and resources to their benefit, often in spite of tremendous resistance. But they also found themselves greatly limited, not only by virtue of their parochialism but by their strong tendencies toward "malfeasance, misfeasance, peculation and corruption," as a nineteenth-century critic of the early military-industrial complex so aptly expressed it.

The city's mostly positive economic performance during this period deserves illumination. Given its dependence on federal, mostly military, spending since the World War I era, the San Diego economy appeared precarious when examined against the cycles of war and peace. Strenuous efforts, however, by civic leaders, the Chamber of Commerce, and high-ranking officers friendly to the city generally managed to keep defense dollars flowing into San Diego at a high rate. Thus the city's economy manifested a certain long-term steadiness in most of its fundamental indices, although the waxing and waning of the Cold War generated some fluctuations. As noted in the previous chapter, San Diego's industrial base—primarily aircraft manufacturing—crumbled even before the end of World War II but recovered significantly with rising tensions between the United States and the Soviet

Union, the outbreak of war in Korea in 1950, and the revitalization of Convair after the takeover by General Dynamics in 1954. Convair, whose civilian and military aircraft programs then enjoyed a brilliant five-year run as a subsidiary of General Dynamics, soon suffered a series of crushing blows as its current models of bombers and fighter jets became obsolete. Its commercial jet airliners also lost the battle for viability to Boeing and Douglas thanks to a combination of technical issues and the failure of the company's dealings with Howard Hughes's TWA. Although Convair's travails by 1962 had caused the city's gross income from aerospace to fall from $1.1 billion to $215 million, the overall economy in San Diego was probably not quite as troubling as some critics have stated.

Convair's missile division, in fact, made a real contribution to the city's industrial well-being for years to come. It had undertaken a contract to develop what became the Atlas missile—the nation's first ICBM and primary satellite launcher—in 1946 (research only) and then full development leading to testing and deployment in 1955.[4] The project was subsumed a few years later by the new General Dynamics missile division, recently installed in a huge factory campus on Kearny Mesa, a few miles north of downtown. This successful venture employed thousands of workers from its inception and kept aerospace alive in San Diego even as Convair shut down its airliner and fighter jet assembly lines in 1962. According to the Economic Research Bureau's *San Diego Economic Bulletin*, a sharp decline in the aerospace industry had occurred between 1957, when 55,650 worked there, and 1962, which saw the number drop to 40,450. From this, *Time Magazine* inferred the city's quick transformation into a "bust-town," but clearly the economic situation was not as dire as that. Twelve thousand more aircraft manufacturing jobs disappeared over the next two years, but the city had other strengths on which it could rely. Even as strong a critic as Mike Davis noted forty years later that Korea and the Cold War combined to trigger a "new defense migration" that included federal subsidies for significant residential construction and an aggressive municipal campaign leading to the annexation of 100,000 acres of land between 1956 and 1962 for future suburbanization.[5]

Although the Korean War ended in July 1953, the escalating exigencies of the Cold War sustained a durable boom in defense spending in and around San Diego. The Navy's uniformed and civilian employees numbered 60,000 in 1947, received $105 million in wages that year, and comprised 41 percent of the city's workers. These figures increased fairly consistently over the next twenty-five years. For example, total military employment in San Diego (uniformed and civilian) rose to 120,000 in 1963, and their payroll for that year came in at $305.7 million. According to the *Economic Bulletin* in January 1967, the Navy had added "over $1 billion to the San Diego County economy in 1966, up from $872 million in 1965." The military payroll itself jumped to more than $1.2 billion in 1972.[6]

California was booming; not surprisingly, San Diego did well too. Population in the city and county increased, government employment in other sectors grew, the agriculture and tourist industries flourished, and the size of the workforce expanded year by year, while unemployment figures ranged between a high of 8.8 percent (1962) to a low of 3.3 percent (1969). While the local tuna industry had by this time entered its twilight period, the *Economic Bulletin* proudly announced in January 1968 that "education now rivals aircraft and missiles as a source of jobs." Many years would pass, however, before the city's investments in higher education and R&D paid off in a way more meaningful than the number of people so employed.

A wave of major real estate developments, an essential quality of the general boom, now occurred in San Diego as well, but it raised questions about the nature of the city's transformation, in particular the apparent rupture that occurred between shifting coalitions of "old guard" advocates of downtown revitalization and redevelopment and emergent "Young Turks" who saw great hope for San Diego's future (as well as their own fortunes) in the as-yet unturned earth north of the traditional boundary marked by Mission Valley. In the past, at least through the World War II era, San Diego's booster-developers seemed to speak with one voice, articulated by the Chamber of Commerce. Back then, when the city was so much smaller, the debates and decisions related to growth focused on an exceedingly narrow range of options, but by the 1960s a dissonant chorus of competing voices and interests argued fiercely about the best strategies to pursue. Many of the resultant decisions during the latter period led to the considerable enrichment of a small group of politically connected players who mired the government, business, politics, landscape, and culture of the city in a series of scandals that extended all the way to the White House, grotesque in the blatancy of their corruption.[7] And yet for the most part the city prospered. An outstanding irony remains: The chief institutional promoters for the old guard of downtowners, the Chamber of Commerce and then-Mayor (and unregenerate "smokestacker") Charles Dail, continued to seek opportunities in support of the quiet R&D revolution then gestating on the Torrey Pines Mesa, ten miles or so north of downtown, still a virtual wilderness in the early 1960s.

The principal battles for influence and turf between the factions approached a point of resolution in the late 1960s and early 1970s when, according to Mike Davis, the Young Turks "brazenly advertised their intention of building a new power structure and making San Diego 'more progressive.'" They were able to unseat long-entrenched conservatives, several recently having been exposed for grossly corrupt financial and political dealings, from high positions of leadership. Now, said Mike Davis, they allied themselves—at least nominally—with "elite critics of unrestrained and fiscally irresponsible growth, including influentials from Salk and Scripps" and posed as the "potential allies and financiers of all the city's disinherited elites: minority leaders, wealthy environmentalists, good-government types, [and] alienated UCSD liberals," all enemies of the bad old guard.[8] As John Davies, Mayor Pete Wilson's chief of staff, noted in a personal interview with the authors, the Young Turks really did represent a fresh and invigorating—indeed progressive—approach to long-entrenched ways of conducting the city's business.[9]

Critics contend that, prior to their protracted demise, the old guard had sold the city's soul in a two-pronged attack to defend their sunk capital, first "by using public policy and tax dollars to generate new headquarters, office and tourist development downtown"; and, second, to gut the retail activities not only in the city's own dilapidated center, but the downtowns of San Diego's satellite cities as well by building one giant new mall after another in strategic fringe locations. In so doing, they created uncounted square miles of sprawling asphalt and concrete and stucco blight all around the county. On a far more positive note, longtime city planner Glenn Rick had worked publicly, and after 1955 privately, to pursue the development of the area that included SIO, General Atomic, and UCSD and the Salk Institute and which would soon include the Veterans Administration Hospital, the Scripps Research Institute, the Sorrento Valley high-tech/light industrial area, and the huge University City retail-office-residential development, all of which would become a "second urban core: an eventual Golden Triangle defined by three intersecting freeways." As Mike Davis reminds us in a harsh but accurate assessment, "It was a classic formula already well rehearsed in Palo Alto and Boston: big public science promiscuously births private-sector spinoffs; engineers, medical researchers, and administrators, in turn need upscale housing, golf courses, and adjacent shopping."[10]

Pete Wilson came to office promising to pursue an agenda characterized by controlled growth, protection of San Diego's environmental riches, and minimal demands on the strained city treasury. He claimed special concern for the city's remaining open spaces. After hardly a month on the job, he expressed the need "to seek . . . the clear authority and tools needed to permit the city rather than the developer to determine the timing and location of new development" to prevent new residential construction from outpacing the city's ability to provide "adequate essential services," and to strictly limit development "in the far fringes of the city."[11] As Steven Erie, Vladimir Kogan, and Scott Mackenzie have pointed out, Wilson's

1975 growth-management plan gained acceptance despite the community's inherent free-market/antiplanning conservatism. The plan incorporated new public–private partnerships for the old downtown area that included the million-square-foot Horton Plaza shopping center, historic preservation of a "Gaslamp District" that had never been lit by gaslamps, a trolley system, and further residential, retail, and office redevelopment projects—all in all fulfilling San Diego's need "to create a downtown rather than bring one back to life." And, within a decade or so, all these projects had taken shape; today they serve successfully to identify San Diego's cityscape.

Two years later, Wilson articulated his ideal conception of the city's immediate future in terms that echoed San Diego's "city beautiful" advocates from early in the century, in particular planner John Nolen and merchant/booster/philanthropist George Marston, as discussed in Chapter 2. The latter's political opponents had derisively called Marston "Geranium George" when he ran unsuccessfully for mayor in 1913 and again in 1917 on a platform calling for environmental protection through carefully controlled industrialization and urban growth. In 1974 Pete Wilson told San Diegans that economic growth included attraction of new industry to San Diego, but it must "not degrade our environment and . . . it [has to] provide jobs for San Diegans." To this end, the mayor and city council were actively courting "several small manufacturing firms," a tuna cannery that might employ 1,400 "San Diegans who do not possess the industrial skills required for more sophisticated employment," an insurance company seeking to relocate its national headquarters . . . biomedical research firms, and a light manufacturing company."[12] Wilson was clearly less attentive to the city's heritage of development tied to the military, and he did include R&D within his scope, but he seemed primarily to focus his program on control of growth. In George Marston's day, such leadership came mainly from the Chamber of Commerce; now, however, City Hall was attempting firmly to set the course of development.

Concerned that new industry would necessarily entail population growth, the mayor pointedly asked:

> How many people can live in the San Diego air basin before air quality deteriorates to an unacceptable standard? . . . What population can our sewerage facilities accommodate before treatment produces an effluent that violates water quality standards? Or before we are compelled to build and pay for extremely costly facilities? What is the net effect of various increments of population growth upon the economic well-being of the present population of San Diego?

In answer, Wilson cited a recent report to the California State Commission for Economic Development by economist Irvine Reynolds that predicted a burden of

Figure 4.1   Smokestacks versus Geraniums. This cartoon appeared in the *San Diego Union* during the election campaign season in 1917.

Source: San Diego Union San Diego History Center; reprinted from Uldis Ports, "Geraniums vs. Smokestacks and San Diego's Mayoralty Campaign, 1917," *Journal of San Diego History,* Summer 1975 21(3); available at www.facebook.com/media/set/?set=a.337877966277998.74580.100001673925799&type=3&l=05f6e8a598.

great cost to the region as a result of continued high rates of economic and population growth, perhaps even to the point of "creating an explosive situation." Such expansion, said Reynolds, appeared "inevitable," and the mayor wanted to know how many newcomers the city could absorb "without injury to the basic quality of life that makes us all desire to live here."[13] How clearly this echoed the concerns raised by the War Emergency in 1939! Would the national government be prepared this time to recreate San Diego again as "a new federal city"?

SUBURBANIZATION ACCELERATES

Inevitable or not, the city's population increased by 25.7 percent between 1970 and 1980 and by almost exactly the same percentage in the decade that followed. Although revitalization of the city's core remained the heart of Pete Wilson's stated vision for the future, he endorsed and facilitated extensive development on the suburban fringe, most notably University City and North City West, which, according to Erie and his coauthors, seemed to contradict "the mayor's distaste for additional, large-scale development of San Diego's periphery."[14] Both of these edge cities were strategically located to serve previous as well as incipient commercial, industrial, R&D, and educational installations radiating outward from the Torrey Pines Mesa. In a 2009 interview with Mary Walshok, Wilson said that the R&D institutions on the Mesa had seemed to be developing at a splendid pace on their own, and thus his own main concerns lay with the balanced growth of the entire region.

University City had been on the drawing board since the late 1950s. According to its original master plan, a new community needed to grow up around the campus, to provide residences and services of all kinds to students, faculty, and staff (and their families) of the campus, a university-oriented population whose numbers were projected to reach a total nearly 56,000 within a few years. The plan further noted that:

> An attractive University Community can also be expected to draw a significant number of families who have no real connection with the University but desire the type of community atmosphere associated with a "college town." This group may be drawn from nearby Sorrento Valley, General Atomics, Daystrom, Miramar Naval Air Station, or other employment centers.[15]

In any event, University City was a well-established reality by Wilson's time, indeed necessary for the function of UCSD and the research establishments on the Torrey Pines Mesa. In what Erie and his coauthors described as a distinct change of course for Wilson, the mayor next allowed another major developer, Pardee, to build yet another huge edge city—North City West, just a few miles north of UCSD/University City. Did these moves represent a "broadening" of Wilson's thinking on controlled growth or a return to the kind of "growth machine politics" that had characterized the city's recent past?

As planned and executed, University City was contiguous to the Sorrento Valley area, which was zoned for light and medium industrial uses; Sorrento Valley quickly became a prime location for incubation of small-scale high-tech manufacturing and some R&D. Close by is the Torrey Pines Science Park, home to General Atomic since the late 1950s, as noted earlier, and many other scientific enterprises since then.

It is important to remind the reader that Sorrento Valley and the Torrey Pines Mesa had been a part of San Diego's pueblo lands—a legacy of the Spanish colonial era dating to 1791, at which time King Charles IV of Spain had placed in trust four square leagues (approximately seventy square miles) of land to encourage settlement and civil development of the San Diego area. At the request of the Mexican successors to San Diego, a retired American sea captain surveyed the pueblo in 1845 and greatly expanded the reserved lands to eleven square leagues, or approximately 192 square miles. When Mexico ceded California to the United States in 1848, the terms of the Treaty of Guadalupe Hidalgo promised to honor all previously established titles to real estate, and so control of the pueblo lands passed into the hands of the American municipality of San Diego. Over the ensuing years, evolving state as well as city laws prescribed the means by which the local government could dispose of this inheritance, although canny settlers often found ways to acquire title to pueblo lots at bargain prices, often in less than strict accordance with the rules. It seems too that the authorities kept their records of ownership and transfers rather sloppily.[16]

When Pete Wilson became mayor in 1971, only 49,000 acres (76.6 square miles) of the 192 square miles of the 1845 pueblo remained under the city's jurisdiction; several hundreds of those were on the Torrey Pines Mesa. Originally zoned for recreation, residences, and future urbanization, once UCSD, General Atomic, and the Salk Institute located there, the die seemed to have been cast for another type of use. Thus the city created a new zoning designation on a portion of the Mesa, SR, for scientific research, and created the Torrey Pines Science Park under that banner in 1973. The initial SR rules narrowly defined how such properties could be occupied and used; having gained authorization to sell pueblo lots in the park to suitable scientific enterprises, Wilson and his administration pushed for and obtained successive liberalizations of the zoning requirements when sales proved disappointing.

Wilson's commitment for downtown renewal led him to entice developer Ernest Hahn to build the million-square-foot Horton Plaza mall by allowing Hahn to build his own pet project, the massive University Towne Centre shopping mall, a controversial undertaking at the time that many in San Diego saw as a "sinister quid pro quo" for accepting the heavy challenges of downtown redevelopment. In the late 1970s the mayor also tried to arrange a deal that would have allowed Hahn to purchase a multiacre lot in the city's Torrey Pines Science Park at a price perhaps $1 million lower than its fair market value. Wilson's critics in San Diego's independent press called this a "scandal"; in fact, several other such deals were in the works at the time that greatly altered the original orientation of the Science Park while generating political controversy for the mayor. Prominent among them was sale of a prime parcel of land on the Mesa at a bargain price to the industrial conglomerate

Signal Companies, Inc., for its corporate headquarters (one of only a very few in all San Diego)—a rather different use for property intended for scientific research. Several members of the city council, the city government's in-house real estate consultants, the city auditor, other political opponents, the grand jury, and even the FBI found the way the mayor's office handled these transactions troublesome. No indictments were ever handed down, and the sense of scandal dissipated. Even so, the mayor's critics complained that the city should stick with the zoning stipulations and sell only to companies for purposes of scientific research. Moreover, the city on behalf of its citizens should realize the full fair market value of the land through properly constituted public auctions and *not* as "negotiated sales" that tended unduly to favor the mayor's political supporters, who were able to acquire these lots for between one-third and one-half of their real value.[17]

San Diego had long ago given away or sold very cheaply tremendous tracts of its choicest property for purposes related to its economic development. Sometimes the municipal government staged "public auctions" under rather obscure circumstances to sell its land to the "highest bidder" at suspiciously low prices, as had been the case in 1907 when E. W. Scripps purchased the acreage that became SIO. The Navy and Marine Corps enjoyed occupancy of pueblo lands deeded to them at various attractive locations in and around the city—indeed a number of such special real estate transactions characterized San Diego's first major reinvention during the World War I period. Voters and public opinion in general had supported this program all but unanimously. Now, however, lands adjacent to the nation's most expensive residential properties and ostensibly reserved for research were not only being sold to decidedly nonscientific users such as E. F. Hutton Life Insurance, Trade Service Publications, and Teleflorists, Inc., and occupied by travel agents and other such commercial concerns, but being sold to well-known speculator/developers such as Douglas Manchester, Ernest Hahn, and Robert Summers. Aside from the sweetheart quality of these deals, at least equally disturbing to Wilson's critics was the fact that the city agreed to install essential utilities to the sites at its own expense, often paying more than it had received from the sales. Also, contrary to Wilson's expectations, density of employment on the Torrey Pines Mesa proved far lighter than anticipated—Wilson's "jobs for San Diegans" seemed to have vanished into the sprawl.

Nevertheless, multiple interviews with San Diego business and community leaders suggest the overall positive impact of Pete Wilson's era. Although low-key, he was seen as a visionary leader, confident, intelligent, and capable of interceding when necessary on important issues. This was especially true with regard to the burgeoning technology industry on the Torrey Pines Mesa. On many occasions he reportedly used the power of the mayor's office to assure that science- and technology-based companies would locate on the Mesa and move through the city's bureaucratic processes effectively.[18]

In addition to the previously described growth management plan, establishing the Centre City Development Corporation for downtown redevelopment and strong advocacy for the region's enduring industries, Wilson also restructured the city's Economic Development Corporation to better market the remaining pueblo land. He amended the zoning of the Torrey Pines Mesa to include corporate headquarters and actively recruited new companies to locate there. When Irwin Jacobs couldn't get the help he needed in establishing headquarters for his new company, Linkabit, on the Torrey Mesa, Pete Wilson dispatched his staff to work out the details expeditiously to make land available. He recruited Aerojet General to the Mesa and was very helpful in assuring that a young startup company, Hybritech, would secure laboratory and corporate space in a project recently abandoned by Teleflorist International.

The development of the Hybritech campus on the Mesa, which housed San Diego's first biotechnology company, thanks in part to the give-and-take of the Wilson administration's flexible zoning policy, is a good example of how Pete Wilson used pueblo land and buildings as a magnet to draw good "clean" companies to locate in the region. He had a number of willing partners who helped him in this effort. Initially, the land on which Hybritech built its structures was offered to Teleflorist so that it could move its national headquarters to San Diego. The land was made available at virtually no cost to the tenants. University Mechanical, a major engineering and construction company that had previously built General Atomic's headquarters and the San Onofre nuclear power plant, began designing a complex for Teleflorist and securing the permits and approvals needed for a multistory corporate headquarters. In the midst of this design and development process, Teleflorist was bought out and informed the city and the construction company that they would not be moving to the region. The investors and developers immediately began thinking about how to repurpose the project for some yet-to-be-identified tenant.

The city's Building Department, according to Pete Garcia, the manager of this overall effort for University Mechanical, was totally uninterested in any kind of special concession. He and his team described to the mayor their desire to find a new tenant. Dick Redmond was an independent real estate developer who had partnered with University Mechanical to develop this among other projects. He had originally been the person who found Teleflorist, recruited them, and worked with the city and the construction company to bring the company to the region.

By the time the deal fell through, the developers and the construction company already had sunk considerable funds into the project. The mayor's office again interceded to enable a conversation among the Redmond Development Company, Neilsen Construction, University Mechanical, and principles from Hybritech, who at the time were seeking a new headquarters. A decision was made at no cost to Hybritech to repurpose the building in a way that would serve their needs, as well as increase the likelihood that the early investors would eventually do well on the project.[19]

While scientists were still working in crowded temporary buildings, development of the permanent space accelerated, and the labs were shoehorned into the building. Garcia described it as "a pick-up game" where the attitude was "we are going to make this work." The construction loan had been secured and permanent financing put in place in 1980. As a consequence, everybody wanted to move quickly. The developers finalized all of the loans and fronted all of the cash, and, once the building was occupied, quoting Pete Garcia again, all parties "prayed every month the Hybritech folks would pay their rent because they now had a building that was useless for anything other than the kind of applied research that Hybritech was doing." Hybritech did stunningly well in a matter of a few years, and University Mechanical and Redmond Development built a second building on the footprint and eventually sold both buildings to Bank of America for a significant profit in a matter of only five years.

Everyone associated with the Hybritech deal remembers the important role the mayor's office played in interceding on their behalf, as did the principals in Linkabit with regard to their securing space on the Torrey Pines Mesa. Pete Wilson repeatedly voiced his support to assure that companies would be based and prosper there. The companies that were established in the 1970s on the Mesa, largely because of the commitment of Pete Wilson's administration, created the platform out of which future clusters of science-based companies would form.

Locating both Hybritech and Linkabit on the Torrey Pines Mesa within close proximity to the research institutions is a dramatic example of decisions made in the 1970s that enabled the reinvention that would take place in the late 1980s. These companies formed the essential foundation for San Diego's life sciences and telecommunications clusters. In the meantime, additional companies located nearby. They included Data Sciences, Calbiochem, RAMCO Energy Consultants, National Cash Register, Spin Physics, and IRT Corporation—some more closely identified with scientific research than others. The fact remained, however, that scientific research as well as research and development had taken root on the Mesa—a decisive factor in the next phase of San Diego's reinvention.

Mike Davis and Steven Erie both deliver some sharp, well-considered criticism of the city's leadership throughout the post–World War II era, with Pete Wilson coming in for his fair share of it. Certain crucial elements of San Diego's metropolitan life—fiscal governance, or race and labor relations, for example, to say nothing of the kind of sprawl and its discontents that came to be called "Los Angelization"—improved little or not at all during these years. During Wilson's time as mayor, however, San Diego began to realize more fully than ever before the old vision of a great city built on environmentally "clean industries" that produced more knowledge than effluent. The reinvention of the city, in particular the blossoming of city's reputation as an apt and attractive location for high-tech R&D and manufacturing, now only accelerated.

THE EMERGENCE OF THE LIFE SCIENCES IN SAN DIEGO, AN ADDITIONAL ENGINE OF ECONOMIC GROWTH

It was also during this period, the 1970s and 1980s, that life sciences funding from federal and foundation sources began to grow significantly while the engineering and physical services remained essentially flat. The numerous life science research programs on the Mesa and most especially the UCSD School of Medicine were well poised competitively to tap into these new resources. The amount, number, and variety of health-related R&D activities on the Torrey Pines Mesa now increased substantially; Figure 4.2 documents federal funding increases.

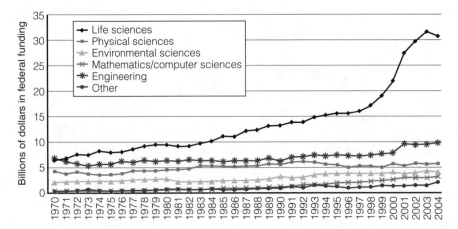

Figure 4.2   Trends in federal research funding by discipline, fiscal years 1970–2004.
Source: National Science Foundation.

Nothing symbolized the groundswell of national interest in health more dramatically than President Richard Nixon's 1971 declaration of a "war on cancer." As signed by Nixon, the National Cancer Act of 1971 included three far-reaching recommendations. The first called for the establishment of a new government agency, the National Cancer Authority, whose mission would be defined by statute as the "conquest of cancer at the earliest possible time." The authority was to be independent of NIH and would absorb all research activities related to cancer.

The second recommendation envisioned a comprehensive national plan to systematically attack the complex of cancer and a greatly expanded federal budget for cancer research, including significant annual increases. Third was establishment of an appropriate, permanent home—a center for research funding and a strategy for research management; in other words, an appropriate "organizational home for cancer."[20] This development on behalf of cancer research was the result of a variety of political forces throughout the 1950s and 1960s, committed to achieving some of the most important goals of the National Institutes for Health, which funded research across the health sciences. The National Cancer Research Act galvanized enterprising institutions and individual researchers to build major labs and centers focused on finding a cure for cancer. By the late 1970s, the Torrey Pines Mesa was home to three world-class cancer centers: UCSD, Sanford Burnham, and TSRI. The growth of TSRI and Sanford Burnham during this period deserves special notice.

The Evolution of the Scripps Clinic and Research Foundation

As discussed in Chapter 3, the Scripps family had an enormous influence on the development of a number of early twentieth-century San Diego institutions, creating the foundation for many of today's research centers, among them the Scripps Institution of Oceanography, the Natural History Museum, the San Diego Zoo, and in 1924 the Scripps Memorial Hospital and Metabolic Clinic, which today is known as The Scripps Research Institute (TSRI). By the 1950s, the growth trajectory of the rapidly expanding Metabolic Clinic included recruiting top talent and capabilities in much the same way that General Atomic and the Salk Institute were doing at nearly the same time, which had also been the case in starting up UCSD.

According to Sarita Eastman's new history of TSRI, Ellen Browning Scripps's early interest in the hospital and clinic during the 1920s grew out of her awareness of the research breakthroughs then occurring elsewhere in diabetes treatment; she wished to contribute to those great events through her own philanthropy, just as she and her brother had done twenty years earlier with regard to marine biology. Her personal vision and the actions she took to realize it shaped the core culture of the institution for generations to come. In the period from 1928 to 1944 both the clinic and hospital remained small entities serving their local community. Then, as in later years, the organization had a clear recruitment philosophy—as an early Scripps physician noted, the clinic wanted "to start with a man who had secured Eastern recognition . . . that a man from the [West] Coast would not." At the same time, this physician rejoiced that the clinic's founding director James Sherrill "had been born in Texas and therefore [was] likely to have the Western spirit, rather than a spirit which you are likely to encounter in New England."[21]

During the postwar economic renewal of the 1950s a significant expansion began to take shape. Instrumental to the surge in growth was the leadership of James Copley, publisher of the San Diego *Union* and *Tribune* newspapers. His gifts and leadership helped establish the institution as a frontline center for research in immunology and later in many other fields. In 1955, the Scripps Metabolic Clinic and its aligned hospital recruited Dr. Edmund L. Keeney from Johns Hopkins to lead the institution into the new era. Keeney renamed it the Scripps Clinic and Research Foundation and embarked on an ambitious development plan using the renowned Rockefeller Institution for Medical Research in New York City as a model. The arrival of Frank Dixon and his considerable team from Pittsburgh in 1961, the construction of the privately funded Timkin-Sturgis Research Laboratory Building in 1966, and the addition of departments of neurology, hematology, radiology, and psychiatry in the late 1960s resulted in significant infusions of federal research grants. The research program achieved national prominence more rapidly than anticipated, outgrowing new labs as soon as they were built. Still located in downtown La Jolla on the Pacific Ocean, there was no further land available for growth in the immediate vicinity to accommodate the opportunities for expansion that emerged in the late 1960s.

Just as early naval and aviation research in San Diego led to essential collaborations in part responsible for the wholesale expansion of the research activities and interests at SIO, so too did the culture of medical research in the 1920s set the stage for major developments on the Torrey Pines Mesa after World War II. Dr. Eastman reminds her readers of another element crucial to the overall customs of the area, the extent to which the scientists, not only within the Scripps Research Foundation but among the emerging UCSD School of Medicine and the Salk Institute, throughout the 1960s had a highly collaborative, mutually supportive culture. Dr. Charles Cochrane, who came to Scripps in the 1950s with Frank Dixon, talked about these three institutions and the regular meetings they held in a conference room that was only about twelve by eighteen feet in area:

David Bonner (first chair of Biology at UCSD) was putting together the medical school up on the hill; Jonas Salk, whom we had known at Pittsburgh, came to work upstairs in our lab while he was building on Torrey Pines Mesa; and (the early UCSD people and Salk people) and our group of five met in one room. We should have had pictures taken because the group of 15 scientists then expanded into what is today the third largest complex of medical science and biotechnology in the country after San Francisco and Boston. You can imagine the germination of ideas that came from all this mixed talent during those meetings.[22]

Sarita Eastman's observations on the growth of SCRF also include the important role Pete Wilson played when TSRI moved onto the Torrey Pines Mesa. With the help of James Copley, the chair of the SCRF Board, aided by a high-powered development director from the East Coast, Dr. James Bowers, the Institute raised close to $12 million for a new building on the Mesa, which allowed its entire enterprise to relocate there in 1971, when Dow Chemical Corporation deeded its 13.2 acres of former pueblo lands on an exceptionally beautiful bluff to the foundation. Dow had obtained the property from the city, but local wags suggest that Dow's departing gesture was a result of its reconsolidation in reaction to the public outcry against their manufacturing napalm for the Vietnam War. Whatever the reason, the gift of land triggered a fund-raising campaign to build a new research campus, and by 1974 construction rapidly proceeded, thanks to more than $15 million in contributions from 1,140 donors, most of them former patients; $3.2 million from NIH for cancer research laboratories; and another $15 million secured through commercial financing.

The organization completed its move to the Mesa from downtown La Jolla in 1977, as soon as its new buildings were ready. However, the increased operating costs of the expanded research facilities now necessitated securing funds from increased patient volume. To this end, the board sought out and hired a new president and CEO, Dr. Charles C. Edwards, a former commissioner of the U.S. Food and Drug Administration as well as a previous assistant secretary of health in what was then the U.S. Department of Health, Education and Welfare. For the next sixteen years, Edwards led the organization, retiring in 1993. During this period he oversaw construction of additional research labs, establishment of a network of regional clinics, the forging of aggressive and lucrative research partnerships with industry (Eli Lilly, Johnson & Johnson, PPG) and in 1983 opening of the 164,000-square-foot Anderson Outpatient Clinic, thanks to a multimillion dollar gift from a family in Downey, California. The Institute at this time received no public support for its facilities or staff, so it aggressively pursued industry partnerships with companies such as Johnson & Johnson and Sandoz to assure cash flow while seeking big grants. This move, as Steven Caspar notes, contributed to an early involvement by industry and private investors in the life sciences in the region.[23]

By 1985, the Research Institute of Scripps Clinic had become the largest private medical research facility in the nation in terms of federal grant dollars received. By 1986, the research staff had grown to 400 members and fellows, and Scripps Research programs commanded worldwide respect.

Richard Ulevitch, a young PhD in biochemistry from the University of Pennsylvania who joined TSRI in 1972, might serve as a prototype of the individuals and the nature of the experience young scientists had when they joined the ambitious Dixon, Cochrane, and other early founders. Ulevitch was starting a postdoctoral fellowship in immunology at the University of Minnesota when the scientist for whom he worked—Robert C. Good—sent him to Scripps for three weeks to work with Charles Cochrane to learn some innovative procedures. Cochrane offered him a postdoc on the spot, but Ulevitch felt obligated to return to Minnesota. Serendipitously, his mentor left early in his postdoc for Sloan-Kettering, and Cochrane still had a job, so Ulevitch moved to La Jolla in 1972.

He was amazed at what he found there. On the roof of the research building was a squash court where Dixon and Cochrane (a champion squash player) regularly played, encouraging the other scientists to do likewise. The Institute at that time was awash in research funding, much of which had come from the major NIH grants secured by Dixon early in his career there. It was a totally "nonbureaucratic environment." It was built on "laboratory empires," with the young researchers and postdocs joining the labs of particular "superstars." If the young recruits were really good (which meant winning large federal grants), they eventually were able to create their own labs and grow their own empires. Otherwise, they were "out." Ulevitch managed over the years to build a large group, retiring from TSRI in 2008 to pursue his interest in venture capital.

Ulevitch was especially impressed with the ways in which TSRI in the early years managed to finance its operations in the absence of any guaranteed funding, which research universities, especially publicly funded ones, typically have. He described how, as early as the 1970s, the Institute was pioneering relationships with pharmaceutical companies to augment the NIH funding that the researchers were able to secure for their fundamental work. The Institute needed a continuous form of support, and pharmaceutical funding was a significant resource in providing that support. It allowed researchers to take chances on big new complex projects; it allowed the institution as a whole to put together handsome recruitment packages, and it enabled the purchase of equipment and development of facilities essential to competitiveness for federal grants. In Ulevitch's view, TSRI "paved the way intellectually and practically for how to work with pharma and the folks at UCSD were appalled. They saw what we were doing as compromising our research values. However, this funding was essential to TSRI, in the way that state funded faculty lines and facilities supported UCSD."[24] The research activities were not dictated by pharma, but rather the pharmaceutical companies with whom TSRI began working in the 1970s wanted rights of first refusal over all of the research coming out of the specific labs they supported. A successive number of partnerships were established over multiple years, beginning with an institute funded by Eli Lilly Pharmaceutical. Lilly pursued all their new biologics work in San Diego during the 1980s, in partnership with TSRI. Subsequently, many other large pharmaceuticals became involved with TSRI, including Johnson & Johnson, Sandoz, and most recently Merck.

Between the 1970s and mid-1990s, its pharmaceutical partnerships enabled the capacity of TSRI to grow significantly. At the time, as Ulevitch commented, they were seen as compromising and questionable by the researchers working at the nearby University of California San Diego campus. The business model that dominated UCSD was typical of most publicly funded research universities at that time. Professors' salaries, offices, facilities, and many graduate students were funded by the state. Professors then went on to secure major research grants from the NIH, NSF, or DOE, which allowed them to buy out some of their teaching time in exchange for research, support additional graduate students and postdoctoral fellows, and often purchase highly specialized pieces of equipment. Today, the ways in which publically funded research university faculty secure support is much more similar to what began at institutions such as TSRI in the 1970s. This occurred mainly as federal funds for basic research leveled off at the same time that the State of California reduced its support for the ongoing faculty and laboratory costs of public universities.

The Growth of the Sanford-Burnham Medical Research Institute

The history of what today is known as the Sanford-Burnham Medical Research Institute, founded in 1976, reads more like a story of an entrepreneurial start-up than that of a venerable research institution. Today the Institute has a staff of 1,200 (900 scientists) and an annual research budget of $150 million and is ranked number one worldwide among all organizations in biology and biochemistry for the impact of its publications, according to the Institute for Scientific Information.[25] Their website describes their chief product as "knowledge." Such achievements grew out of the unusual saga of a professor facing mandatory retirement from Tufts

University who wanted to continue doing cancer research. William Fishman, MD, PhD, and his wife Lillian one day got into their station wagon and drove across the country to California scouting where they might be able to set up shop to continue, postretirement, his developmental biology research on cancer. Dr. Fishman settled on La Jolla and the Torrey Pines Mesa thanks to a confluence of fortuitous events.

The Fishmans were determined to continue their research because of Dr. Fishman's groundbreaking work in the early 1970s, which confirmed that cancer cell development was inextricably linked with developmental biology. His work, as well as that of a number of other researchers across the country, defined a new field of cancer research, oncodevelopmental biology. It combined the study of cancer development with the development of normal cells. Dr. Fishman was a founding member of the International Society for Oncodevelopmental Biology and Medicine and was so engaged in his research that, instead of adapting to the age-mandated retirement requirements of Tufts University, he decided to continue his work in a more independent setting.

Thanks to a cancer conference in San Diego supported by the Kroc Foundation, the Fishmans were introduced to the burgeoning life sciences community on the Torrey Pines Mesa—the Salk Institute, the UCSD School of Medicine, and the Scripps Research Institute. They knew that the existence of these institutions represented a promising and fertile ground within which they could do work they wanted to do. In 1976 Fishman and his lifelong partner Lillian cofounded the La Jolla Cancer Research Foundation. They transferred a single grant with a budget of less than a $200,000 to this new foundation; within five years it grew to be designated as a National Cancer Institute.

The story behind the startup growth of the Institute is extraordinary. At a luncheon in her honor, Lillian Fishman shared how the welcoming and collaborative character of San Diego was the real key to their success. Early trustees were local businessmen such as George Ellis of La Jolla Bank and Trust and Dr. William Drell, founder of Calbiochem, an early biological company on the Torrey Pines Mesa. Clifford Grobstein, the dean of the UCSD School of Medicine at that time, served as the founding chair of their advisory board. Mrs. Fishman shared in a lengthy discussion with Walshok in the spring of 2006 that, as the Institute was setting up, its first major piece of equipment, an electron microscope, was personally loaned to them by Jonas Salk from the Salk Institute and used until the Friends Group, an auxiliary she had founded, was able to raise the money to purchase their own apparatus. Mrs. Fishman described how even small pieces of laboratory equipment were shared and borrowed from the UCSD School of Medicine and the Scripps Research Institute, so that they could get their work going full steam ahead. Within a decade they were attracting leading scientists and significant private philanthropy, most notably in the 1990s from the Burnham family and 2010 from philanthropist Denny Sanford.

These developments across the Torrey Pines Mesa throughout the 1960s and 1970s, initially only subtly, began to affect the regional economy. The political unrest of these years had distanced the once very tight relationship among UC, the military, and local business leaders, as noted earlier in this chapter. Nonetheless, the decidedly technocratic character of San Diego's civic culture persisted. Throughout the 1970s, for example, the growing UCSD campus began to offer free public events and lectures with leading lights from the literary, scientific, public policy, and arts communities, most of which were only very lightly attended. During this same period, lecture series offered in Balboa Park by NASA scientists in conjunction with the museums there, as well as the Leakey Foundation, drew thousands. At this time, the basic research thrust of the university, and the entire Torrey Pines Mesa for that matter, was rarely covered in the press or discussed in leadership groups such as the Chamber of Commerce or City Hall. However, in the early 1980s all that changed, and community leaders began to see new forms of economic promise in the now significant agglomeration of R&D institutions on the Mesa, which over a two- to four-year period led into San Diego's next reinvention.

THE CONSOLIDATION OF AN R&D INFRASTRUCTURE ON THE TORREY PINES MESA

Although the positive relationship between town and gown was greatly challenged in the late 1960s, taking nearly two decades to rebuild relations between the downtown business establishment and the institutions on the Mesa, the research community developing there took on a life of its own. It grew and flourished, however, not in ways originally expected by its civic boosters but most decidedly in ways compatible with those of its visionary scientific founders. This growth and the directions it took were greatly affected by the shifting research priorities of the federal government, especially from the 1970s onward when funding for the life sciences (in the form of health) rose rapidly while funding for engineering and the physical sciences remained flat. Undeterred by shrinkages in federal funding in the physical sciences, entrepreneurial scientists focused on the infusion of new funds for the health and life sciences; the UCSD campus as well as the other research institutes on the Mesa grew their talent pools to assure success in winning highly competitive research grants.

As early as 1969, these founding research institutions also served as incubators for entrepreneurial scientists, a handful of whom spun out companies that became the core of fully functional R&D clusters on the Mesa by the late 1980s. Most of the technology companies founded in the late 1960s and early 1970s were led by scientists and engineers who had initially been recruited to the region to work for GA, UCSD, TSRI, or Salk. The promise each of these institutions held to do groundbreaking, interdisciplinary research on topics directly related to national security and/or national health attracted visionary, restless, and entrepreneurial individuals, most of whom had a passionate belief in the power of technology to benefit humanity. According to sociologist Mark Jones, these institutions were the "magnets" that drew to the city its next generation of "bioscientific entrepreneurs." Their institutions "were the gateways through which these entrepreneurs passed on their way to founding new companies and a new kind of economic activity" in San Diego.[26] Thus, by the late 1960s a number of spin-off companies had formed whose founders were driven by opportunities to develop technologies or products of interest to the federal government and, in particular, the defense establishment. Nonetheless, in little more than a decade, many of these companies gave rise to new commercial enterprises, which eventually found their way into the market economy even though their early roots were in products of value to the U.S. Department of Defense or other federal agencies.

Between 1969 and 1984, the R&D platform established in the previous decade enlarged rapidly to include a wide variety of federal and foundation-funded research institutions. Combined, by the mid-1980s they came to represent a critical mass of R&D capacity and a strong attraction for international firms and venture investors seeking innovative products. In fact, by 1982, the UC–San Diego campus was ranked seventh in federal funding for research among the leading American research universities. Its research awards exceeded those of Berkeley, UCLA, and UC–San Francisco—all institutions with fully developed facilities and faculty and much longer histories. Such achievements started to put San Diego on the map in a whole new way, a preoccupation of civic leaders for more than a hundred years. However, San Diego now redrew the economic map entirely, creating one based on concentrations of world-class talent and innovative research and development for which the natural amenities and climate of the region took on a new meaning and value. Where once the hills and canyons and arid climate represented a barrier to economic development, in the "knowledge age" they had become highly tangible economic development assets. The city's leaders redrew the physical map of the city, too, in a wave of suburbanization deemed necessary to satisfy the demands imposed by the growth of high-tech enterprises.

The years from 1969 through 1984 represent a period of consolidation and expansion of R&D and attraction of talent to the Mesa as San Diego continued to navigate the rocks and shoals of a second-tier economy. Certain bedrock elements of the city's civic culture seemed not to have changed much from their well-established historical patterns, for example boosterism, which we have defined earlier as the concerted promotion of place by interested individuals and corporate entities, primarily through the commodification of undeveloped land for the sake of both personal profit and urban economic development; and dependence on the federal government, especially the military services and defense contractors as pillars of the local economy. The first few years of this period—into the early 1970s—was a time of sustained national, statewide, and local growth, which helped to empower the sudden expansion of the innovation ecology on the Torrey Pines Mesa. At the same time, however, San Diego experienced numerous crises that included corruption and corporate scandals such as the "Yellow Cab Conspiracy," which produced the indictment of the mayor and several members of the city council on charges of misfeasance; the decline of the tuna industry; and the implosion of the savings and loan industry across the Southwest, which triggered a precipitous slowdown in construction. And they included the inability of the downtown Economic Development Corporation to attract large companies or R&D consortia to the region.

The string of economic crises that civic leaders had to navigate throughout the late 1960s into the mid-1980s eventually turned their attention to finding a new path to regional prosperity. The research enterprise on the Mesa was becoming so robust that it represented hundreds of millions of dollars in external investments and thousands of new high-wage jobs just within the R&D companies themselves. There were also a few remarkable examples of local start-ups coming out of these R&D institutions, most notably Linkabit in wireless communication, ISSCO in computer graphics, and Hybritech, San Diego's first biotechnology company. These facts inspired exasperated civic leaders to turn their attention to how to accelerate the growth of local entrepreneurial technology companies as a strategy for creating new wealth and new jobs in the region. With that shift in focus, by the mid-1980s San Diego embarked on its third reinvention: the commercialization of products and services, which the R&D community was seeding as a strategy for growing locally based wealth and high-wage jobs. A variety of civic initiatives and new business collaboratives from the mid-1980s onward catalyzed and accelerated this process in ways that no one at the time could imagine. Especially significant was the founding of an organization based at UC San Diego called CONNECT whose focus was, and continues to be, networking the knowledge, skills, capital, marketing, and entrepreneurial know-how needed to commercialize promising technology into products whose manufacturing companies create wealth and jobs for the region.

In their bid for "instant greatness" as Nancy Scott Anderson characterized it,[27] the four anchor research institutions on the Torrey Pines Mesa, GA, UC San Diego incorporating Scripps Institution of Oceanography, the Salk Institute, and the Scripps Clinic and Research Foundation, were unequivocal throughout this period in their efforts to

- Attract exceptional, typically "cutting-edge" scientists and scholars to their institutions;
- Provide an atmosphere which facilitated interdisciplinary work in state-of-the-art facilities;
- Prepare the next generation of leading scientists, dramatically demonstrated by the fact that UCSD had departments such as applied physics and information sciences that produced PhDs, rather than engineering departments that awarded MSs, as well as a School of Medicine that produced more medical researchers than it did practicing doctors; and
- Position the research community in La Jolla as a force to be dealt with in Washington and around the globe.

And it worked.

By 1982 UCSD's annual federal research budget was seventh in the United States as Table 4.1 shows, and the largest in the UC system, qualifying the campus for membership in the venerable Association of American Research Universities after a mere twenty years.

GA by then had grown its annual budget substantially and spun out more than sixty defense R&D companies, most notably Science Applications International Corporation (SAIC) and Titan Systems. And, by 1977, with the arrival of a new director, Washington insider Charles Edwards, to the Scripps Clinic and Research Foundation, they too began a period of phenomenal growth. In addition, new anchor research institutions took root on the Mesa, most prominently, what are today the Sanford-Burnham Medical Research Institute, founded in 1976; the Neurosciences Institute, founded in 1962 by Nobel Laureate Gerald Edelman and moved to La Jolla in 1993; and the La Jolla Institute for Allergy and Immunology, founded in 1988. All of this growth was enabled by expanding budgets for science and technology agencies fueled by the national security interests of the Cold War, Sputnik, and the space race, which were a boon to aerospace, communications, and computing

TABLE 4.1

Top Ten total R&D expenditures: Universities and colleges, 1982.

Rank	Institution	Amount (in thousands of dollars)
1	Johns Hopkins University	$289,940
2	Massachusetts Institute of Technology	192,462
3	University of Wisconsin-Madison	157,520
4	Stanford University	147,941
5	University of Minnesota	146,466
6	Cornell University	145,769
7	University of California-San Diego	138,894
8	University of Washington	133,115
9	University of Michigan	119,973
10	Columbia University Main Division	115,734

Source: *Academic Science/Engineering: R&D Funds Fiscal Year 1982.* Surveys of Science Resource Series, NSF 84-308. Washington, DC: National Science Foundation, 1984.

companies within the region. They were further driven by President Nixon's declaration of a war on cancer, which combined with a nationwide expansion of medical schools and medical research to fuel the rapid growth of health and life sciences research in the region from 1971 onward. The growth stories of such institutions as the Scripps Clinic and Research Foundation and the Sanford-Burnham Institute for Medical Science are especially illustrative of what was occurring on the Mesa.

CONCLUSION

A few critical events occurred in the late 1970s and early 1980s that together began to represent a new path to economic prosperity in the eyes of a cadre of forward-looking civic leaders. Coincidental with the demise of the tuna industry (in the 1980s), a major savings and loan crisis (1990s) and with that a crash in the real estate industry, there were, as well, a succession of failed efforts to retain existing large industries or attract new ones to the region. A number of high-value-added companies employing diverse technologies were started up on the Torrey Pines Mesa. General Atomic, as noted earlier, had spun out sixty companies by the late 1960s, including Titan, founded by Gene Ray, and SAIC, founded by Robert Beyster; IVAC and IMED, led by Richard Cramer, an engineer who had worked on SIO research ships; ISSCO, one of the nation's first computer graphics companies, founded by Peter Preuss, a UCSD graduate student in mathematics; and Linkabit, a communications company founded by Irwin Jacobs, a UCSD professor along with Andrew Viterbi from USC and Leon Kleinrock. Hybritech, San Diego's first biotech company, founded in 1978 by Ivor Royston and Howard Birndorf from UCSD's Medical School, was about to be acquired for $500 million by Eli Lilly. All of these companies were growing rapidly, hiring lots of talent; with the exception of SAIC and Titan, they were purchased or merged with larger national enterprises, creating significant wealth for their founders and early investors.[28] In other words, while the industries on which the San Diego economy had thrived from the 1950s well into the 1970s were declining (housing and construction), even disappearing (aerospace manufacturing and tuna processing), examples of promising new industries were popping up on the Mesa.

Longtime editor of the *San Diego Union* newspaper, columnist, cobiographer of Roger Revelle, and San Diego historian Neil Morgan once commented that, with the birth of UCSD, San Diego had finally come of age. Morgan was certainly correct about the moment in time, but in this chapter we have argued that the city's growing up relied on a much larger complex of events and forces, shaped not only by history but by the expanding opportunities for research driven by national policy and funding strategies. Although Margaret Pugh O'Mara doesn't include San Diego among her "cities of knowledge" in her 2005 book of the same title, San Diego in fact became such a place, one of a number of regions across the United States that evolved into hubs of R&D. This occurred due to Cold War spending patterns; the advantages of preexisting research universities and institutes that became regional economic development resources; and local actions, including advocacy or land use decisions, that exploited the opportunity to grow their R&D core.[29]

In her detailed analysis of San Jose (the center of California's Silicon Valley, and close to Stanford University), Philadelphia, and Atlanta, O'Mara points out that, from the 1950s onward, high-tech growth represented a process of city building in many regions. Our argument throughout this book has been that San Diego has served as a model of such growth, with industries such as the military and, in particular, military-related R&D, at the center of San Diego's economic development strategy throughout the twentieth century. O'Mara presents this dynamic succinctly: "The government/university relationship that emerged as a result of Cold War politics did not simply affect the 'inside game'—the internal workings and research priorities of research universities—but transformed the 'outside game' of land management and economic development in the communities, in which these institutions were located." Moreover, "This relationship was a two-way street, in which federal programs influenced university choices and academic institutions and traditions had an important effect upon the design and implementation of public policy."[30]

O'Mara further notes the unavoidable intersection among policy, place, and the role universities play in forging the special "industrial geography of high technology" that persists through times of high-tech boom and bust. The high-tech environment flourishes alongside or in the midst of attractive suburban areas, "the world of office parks, freeway commutes, and proximity to residential subdivisions." The factory or downtown high-rise typically does not fit within these categories.[31] San Diego and its growth trajectory during the period in question fit O'Mara's formulation no less than do the particular cities she addresses in her book. The Cold War imperative at the heart of her discussion favored regions that possessed three characteristics, all features of San Diego's own landscape, economy, and civic culture:

1. *Tight links between researchers and the defense establishment.* This was certainly the case in San Diego beginning in the 1930s when Robert Gordon Sproul, as we noted in the previous chapter, designated Scripps Institution of Oceanography as the anchor for the University's Southern California Division of War Research. Roger Revelle, an academic and a naval officer, forged significant partnerships with naval research entities on Point Loma and was well known and well connected in Washington, D.C., across a variety of agencies.

2. *Awarding of R&D projects to regions that were favored due to their strategic importance to the security of the nation.* Here again, the growth of the Pacific Fleet and the expansion of aviation capabilities throughout the 1930s and 1940s combined to make San Diego's geographic position strategically important to the nation.

3. *Regions with available land on which to locate and expand research facilities.* Once again, San Diego, because of its abundant pueblo lands, was well positioned to expand the R&D infrastructure in the region, as we have described in this chapter vis-à-vis the growth of the not-for-profit research institutes on the University of California, San Diego campus.

In sum, O'Mara asserts that national policy, which favored certain geographies and certain kinds of institutional capabilities, all of which San Diego possessed by the mid-1950s, largely enabled local success. The disparities in growth of R&D capacities across regions of the United States, she goes on to argue, cannot be understood without awareness of the important role federal policies played in the 1950s and 1960s, not only in the awarding of funds but also in favoring geographic regions with special qualities including attractive places to live and work for scientific and high-tech professionals. San Diego met all those tests.

Even though San Diego benefited enormously and grew significantly during this period, especially its R&D sectors, the city continued to grapple with other kinds of economic challenges. By the summer of 1984, when unemployment in the city approached 10 percent and the economies of Europe and Asia were claiming more and more of the global market share of automobile, computer, and communications technologies, civic leaders began to create a new strategy for their future. A small group from the Economic Development Corporation, which had been created only a few years earlier by Mayor Pete Wilson for the purpose of finding new ways to attract high-tech companies and consortia to the region, attempted to challenge the conventional wisdom. They asked for a meeting with UCSD's new Chancellor Richard C. Atkinson and a few of his key staff. Their goal was to explore how the now remote UC San Diego campus could more actively reconnect to the economic future of the region by focusing on innovative efforts to commercialize technology and entrepreneurship in a manner that would significantly amplify the benefits generated by the early startups on the Mesa. One of this book's authors, a sociologist, and as of 1980 the dean of University Extension, was asked to do a series of interviews with both tech and business community leaders and come back to the chancellor with some ideas on how to proceed. Within three months, a small but inclusive leadership group gathered around the chancellor's table to evaluate and endorse and eventually finance a modest initiative to reconnect the science and business establishments in San Diego, the UCSD program in technology and entrepreneurship, which was quickly renamed UCSD CONNECT. By the spring of 1985 a new civic organization came to life to champion the growth of high-value-added commercially viable technology and life science clusters in San Diego. In barely fifteen years this catalyst would help change the face of San Diego's economy, the region's next reinvention and the subject of Chapter 5.

5 CONNECTING SCIENCE AND BUSINESS: SAN DIEGO'S NEXT REINVENTION

In this chapter, we discuss the period from 1982 to the present, during which most elements of San Diego's business community, economic profile, political economy, and civic culture experienced marked evolution. New organizations emerged to lead the city in new directions. Notable among these were the San Diego Economic Development Corporation (EDC), CONNECT, and the San Diego Military Affairs Council, whose efforts led to some gratifying successes as well as some stunning failures. Local and national actors also experimented with various new modalities such as public–private partnerships as they attempted to stimulate and manage the city's next wave of growth. Even in the face of such sweeping changes, however, we argue that the city maintained the long-term historical trends we have asserted throughout the book: San Diegans learned from their mistakes, capitalized their particular resources, and adapted well to local, national, and global events.

The next reinvention of the San Diego economy began in the mid-1980s, triggered by a variety of national and international developments that gave rise to new concerns about the competitiveness of the U.S. economy, especially the high-tech innovation economy. For decades in the post–World War II era, the United States had been the global leader in new technology development—electronics, semiconductors, televisions, medical equipment—and, as a result, had dominated world markets. Europe and Asia, however, over a forty-year period began to catch up with and on some fronts exceed the United States in terms of inventiveness, innovation, and quality of goods produced. European and Japanese automobiles, for example, entered the U.S. market and attained popular acceptance in unprecedented numbers. The Japanese in particular were making major gains in electronics and the computer industry. In response to these challenges many national initiatives emerged, including the founding of the U.S. Council on Competitiveness in 1986, led by the CEOs of twelve global technology companies and the presidents of a dozen of the largest American research universities; John Young, CEO of HP, initially chaired the council. The council's website notes that the impetus for its creation was not simply a need or desire to upgrade the nation's ability to compete in the tech field. Rather, it was motivated by the realization that the United States "had slid from being the world's largest creditor to the world's largest debtor, its position as a global leader in technology and innovation was declining and American industries were losing market share to international competitors."[1]

San Diego was clearly affected by these developments. And thus, on the heels of the Pete Wilson decade, the region pursued high-value industries aggressively. Private developers built industrial parks and lab space to accommodate science and technology enterprises they hoped would populate the region. The Economic Development Corporation established by Mayor Wilson actively pursued recruitment strategies targeting industries aligned with the diversifying R&D activities already in place. The private research institutions such as Salk and TSRI had begun to establish research partnerships with global pharmaceutical companies that included Lilly, Novartis, Johnson & Johnson, and others. And the Scripps Institution of Oceanography had added to its tight linkages with federal agencies such as the Office of Naval Research (ONR) and the Defense Advanced Research Projects Agency (DARPA), as well as close ties to global petroleum companies such as Shell. By 1982, UCSD was designing the first of what were to be many industry–university collaborative initiatives, the Center for Magnetic Recording, to advance the state of the art in information storage technology and to develop professionals for the data storage community. Companies such as 3M and Spin-Physics were founding partners, and the Center included a research library of timely books and journals as well as a staff person to translate relevant research reported in Japanese journals and trade publications.

Nonetheless, linkages among the research enterprises on the Torrey Pines Mesa, UCSD, and industry overall remained weak, largely because of the basic science focus of all the institutes as well as departments of UC San Diego. As noted earlier, at this time even the computer science and engineering departments at UCSD focused primarily on developing PhD students and rarely master's degrees or practice-oriented students, the opposite of what schools such as UCLA, Berkeley, and Stanford were doing. Similarly, most of the medical school graduates gravitated in large numbers to research careers rather than clinical medicine. Other than medicine, UCSD had no professional schools in fields such as business or management, public policy, or education. And at this time the campus had no technology transfer office, as the UC Office of the President had been providing such services in the pre–Bayh-Dole Act era. In other words, in the early 1980s, UCSD lacked the kinds of programs, departments, and infrastructure it needed if it were to act more decisively to support progressive change in the region's economic landscape. One way might have been to help local science- and technology-based startups to bring the products of their research to the marketplace, an issue that a new chancellor, Richard C. Atkinson, decided early in his tenure was a priority. He felt strongly that he had to do something.[2]

In effect, the various research institutions on the Torrey Pines Mesa focused on independent growth strategies, each seemingly in search of its own "instant greatness." The political strife of the 1960s had driven wedges between the San Diego business establishment, UCSD, and the R&D enterprises on the Mesa, wounds that healed but slowly. However, in 1982, a new opportunity appeared on San Diego's horizon that galvanized the community to come together as it had in the 1950s to create the new campus of the University of California and to secure regional economic benefits through R&D. San Diegans now developed a whole new way to bring new talent and new jobs to the region, indeed a new approach to innovation. With these events we open the chapter.

LEARNING FROM LOSING: THE MICROCOMPUTER CONSORTIUM STORY

In 1982, Admiral Bobby Inman, then recently retired from the Navy, undertook what *Fortune Magazine* called a "crazy idea" as leader of a research consortium whose main purpose was to develop an ultrafast supercomputer based on radical advanced technology intended "to beat anything coming out of Japan's 'fifth generation' effort." The companies joining the consortium included such fierce competitors as Control Data, Honeywell, NCR, RCA, Gould, and Allied-Signal, among others; ten in all. The resulting enterprise was called the Microelectronics and Computer Technology Corporation, MCC for short.[3]

At the time, Inman sat on the board of Science Applications International Corporation (SAIC), one of the most profitable of the companies that had spun out of General Atomic. Admiral Inman had enjoyed a remarkable career in the Navy; after he had a meteoric rise to the rank of full admiral (four stars) and served as director of naval intelligence, several postings followed high in the national security establishment. With personal and business ties to the San Diego community, he was a recognized talent who urged local civic leaders to make a bid to locate MCC on the Torrey Pines Mesa. In this effort, San Diego competed with fifty-six other cities from twenty-seven states. Inman was very familiar with the Mesa's attractions for such a company—the SR zoning, the proximity of the Salk and other top research institutions, and of course UCSD. According to Dan Pegg, then president of the Economic Development Corporation (EDC), Inman also appreciated the possibility of living in La Jolla and enjoying its comfortable and beautiful environment.[4]

San Diego's attractiveness to MCC was tempered by several issues. First, San Diego's economy was in a state of flux at the time: The city had recently lost Wickes Industries, a major furniture manufacturer; General Dynamics was on its way out; and the tuna business was on its last legs. In contrast, for the past several years, high-tech companies with UCSD as their focal point, especially biomedical and wireless communications R&D enterprises, had begun to take off. SAIC and other Cold War defense contractors were doing well, at least for the time being. Second, as much as San Diegans aspired to see a rendition of the Silicon Valley (in the form of a vast concentration of high-tech enterprises) take shape on the Torrey Pines Mesa, only bits and pieces of such an agglomeration existed at the time. As Dan Pegg noted, "The Mesa was composed of disparate talents still in great need to come together." Third, given San Diego's historic water and other infrastructural problems, real questions existed as to whether the city could support such a massive industrial enterprise. Fourth, Inman, as a native of Texas and an alumnus of the University of Texas at Austin, felt a strong connection to his roots and may have used San Diego as a decoy to inspire Austin to sweeten its bid. And finally, Austin offered MCC a package of inducements that San Diego simply could not have matched, including $35 million dollars worth of land, buildings, and endowed professorships at the University of Texas.

To win the bid, the city of Austin assembled an amazing partnership composed of top leaders in the state government, the state's flagship research university, and the local business community, all in support of the first-ever for-profit computer industry R&D consortium.[5] And, by all accounts, the gamble paid off handsomely. The university received thirty endowed professorships and a great boost to its computer and related engineering programs; for its part, the city of Austin then began thirty years of growth for its and the state's computer industries. As a recent article expressed it, the MCC deal "put Austin on the technology map, before Dell was a household name and the dot-com boom arrived." Moreover, it turned a wild idea—"that universities should play a leadership role in high tech economic development"—into "conventional wisdom."[6]

San Diego had convened a similar, equally remarkable statewide alliance in pursuit of its bid; although the Californians lost the competition, the city learned well the lessons that came from playing the game. Speaking from his experience as leader of the EDC's team, Dan Pegg noted that the bid caused the community, the UC system, and a host of other state agencies to come together—business and government in support of academia and vice versa. Pegg said that before MCC everyone in town was "pulling his own wagon as hard as he could, but the loss of MCC suggested the benefits of pooling their talents and pulling together." Another outcome from what Pegg called "these seminal events" was the new leadership role played by the EDC (and not the Chamber of Commerce, as in earlier times), which had succeeded in bringing San Diego's diverse and divided elements together. Above all, losing the MCC bid generated two enduring legacies for the region: It elevated the need for collaboration, and it established renewed interest in UCSD as an engine of regional economic growth.[7]

The moves by the Economic Development Corporation to pursue the MCC opportunity were significantly enhanced by the relatively new chancellor of the University of California campus, Richard C. Atkinson. A mathematician and cognitive psychologist, Atkinson had spent twenty-five years at Stanford prior to assuming the position of director of the National Science Foundation from 1975 to 1980. Atkinson had been hired in the 1960s to work at Stanford by the provost, Frederick Terman. Terman is a legend in higher education for the imaginative leadership he provided in helping to build Stanford University as one of America's great research universities simultaneously with supporting entrepreneurial and inventive young faculty and graduate students such as Donald Hewlett and David Packard. Terman also was the founder of the Stanford Research Park, which became a significant hub of innovative breakthroughs that shaped American technology throughout the 1950s and 1960s.

Atkinson was highly creative while in Washington as director of the NSF. He became a champion for closer ties between the basic research community and industry, largely influenced by his experiences in the Silicon Valley and at Stanford. He presided over the NSF when they first initiated the Small Business Industry Research Program (SBIR). The SBIR funded applied research activities if a principal investigator could bring a private sector company onto a project and that company would provide matching funds. Atkinson also worked closely with then senators Birch Bayh and Robert Dole in the development of a new national technology transfer strategy that became known as the Bayh-Dole Act. This bill allowed the institutions at which research was being conducted to take the leadership role in licensing and patenting activities that previously had resided with the funder.

The act is credited with unleashing enormous growth in innovation across the United States.

As a result of this experience and orientation, Atkinson became a dynamic leader and proponent of collaborative work and closer ties between industry and the basic research community on his arrival at UCSD in 1980. As a consequence, he immediately initiated a number of campus-based activities to enhance interaction with industry; he also became quite active on community organization boards focused on technology and economic development, in particular the EDC. Dan Pegg, the CEO of the EDC, looked to Atkinson for support and assistance in pulling together the proposal to MCC and his contributions were significant. Even though the region was unsuccessful in winning the bid for MCC, the relationship between Pegg and Atkinson continued; as of the summer of 1984, a number of new ideas began to emerge from their association.

UCSD CONNECT: A NEW BRIDGE BETWEEN THE ACADEMY AND THE BUSINESS COMMUNITY

Even before the final implosion of the savings-and-loan industry in the late 1980s or the reduction in defense spending throughout the 1990s, San Diego's business leaders were able to foretell a looming economic crisis. This led to a rethinking of economic development strategies in the region. As noted, by the early 1980s, it had become clear that traditional business development strategies were not working. Regional leaders realized that they needed to envisage San Diego's future beyond an economy based solely on real estate, defense, and tourism. And in a sense, they rediscovered the research institutions on the Mesa, which throughout the previous two decades had grown and prospered in parallel with the military/industrial establishment. The Economic Development Corporation's mobilization, a collaborative regionwide effort to compete not only for the Microelectronics and Computer Technology Corporation (MCC) in 1982, but also for SEMATECH (a semiconductor manufacturing consortium focused on R&D to advance techniques in chip manufacturing) in 1986, helped to crystallize this. San Diego was a finalist in both but lost both in the final round. Partly in reaction to these disappointments, San Diego's business community began looking for new ways to grow the regional economy.

In response to an overture in 1984 from the EDC's Executive Director Dan Pegg, the Chancellor's Office began to explore the possibilities. Atkinson talked with a small group of knowledgeable, forward-looking business leaders whose advice began to shape his next moves. The group included David Hale, the CEO of the growing biotech company Hybritech; Irwin Jacobs, who after the sale of his first company Linkabit was in the process of founding Qualcomm; and R. B. "Buzz" Woolley, an early San Diego investor with links to the Silicon Valley venture community. Wooley's experience with Pitch Johnson at Asset Management and Brook Byers at Kleiner Perkins proved especially useful.[8] Influential members of the downtown business community filled out the chancellor's advisors; prominent among them were Bob Weaver, managing partner of Price, Waterhouse, Coopers and Lybrand, and Dan Pegg himself. UCSD's team included the newly appointed Dean of the Division of Engineering Lea Rudee and the Dean of Extension Mary Walshok.

More and more San Diegans by the mid-1980s were heeding the call of global competitiveness; for some, that meant leveraging the R&D assets that had been incubating for twenty years on the Torrey Pines Mesa somewhat in isolation from the heart of the downtown economy. This small group of San Diego business and education leaders who met through the late summer and fall of 1984 determined there was a need to bridge this gap between science and business.

A series of interviews conducted by Walshok with potential stakeholders in science-based entrepreneurial activity soon revealed what it would take to create a program to accelerate innovation and entrepreneurship in the region. Among other key findings, they learned that San Diego faced two major challenges. The first, just described, was a research culture on the Mesa that was rich in both its quantity and quality of basic research but otherwise characterized by only limited interest in applied problems or technology transfer and commercialization. The second was a local business community, whose culture and capabilities remained firmly anchored in defense contracting, real estate development, tourism, and the hospitality industry. San Diego also had no resident venture capital funds, equity bankers, or major financial institutions, most likely due to its long and ongoing history of close economic ties to government and the defense establishment. San Diego's local technology business networks were less focused on for-profit business development than on government relations and procurement. Local capital had not fueled General Dynamics, General Atomic, Rohr, or National Steel and Ship-building, although all of these companies had local roots. More to the point, they had grown to be giants as a result of their successfully executed federal contracts. As a consequence, access to capital and entrepreneurial expertise proved difficult for early nondefense high-tech entrepreneurs in San Diego.

Although in the 1970s San Diego had no major banks or venture capital firms, it was home to powerful savings-and-loan establishments such as Home Federal Savings, U.S. National Bank, and Great American Savings (listed in *Fortune* in

1989 as one of the six most-admired savings institutions in the nation), among others. All owed their existence to the tremendous residential and retail expansion that began in the 1950s with California's exponential population growth. By the end of the 1980s however, most S&Ls across the Southwest—including San Diego's—were overleveraged and in crisis. Congress passed regulations that introduced new accounting rules and penalized S&Ls for owning and developing risky real estate projects, which many such as Great American had done.[9] In anticipation of a great boom in demand for leasable R&D "tech-flex" space, local savings-and-loans had underwritten development of numerous buildings—mostly on an entirely speculative basis—on the previously undeveloped Sorrento Mesa and adjacent Mira Mesa tracts. Many such companies soon went out of business even before their on-spec buildings found tenants; not until the end of the decade did absorption finally catch up with vacancies. In the meantime, some S&Ls such as Great American were acquired by much larger national banking institutions. By the 1990s San Diego was once again a branch-banking town. It still did not have pockets of local capital on which to draw, a condition that particularly hobbled the tech sector, which for decades had relied on defense-related contracting and procurement.

San Diego in the 1980s presented yet another obstacle to the growth of its high-tech industrial sector: At the time, few professional or business services existed to support science-based, commercially focused innovation companies. For example, among the top twenty-five law firms listed in the 1985 *San Diego Business Journal's* "Annual Book of Lists," not one mentioned intellectual property as a specialty. As Martin Kenney and others have pointed out, such services must be in place before innovative enterprises can begin to take off.[10] Early entrepreneurs thus had to rely on personal contacts, primarily outside the region, to obtain introductions to the resources they needed. And the local business service providers had few connections to the wider intellectual property, venture capital, and management consulting communities. They knew little about high-tech start-ups and did not know how to service the needs of these clients.[11]

Starting an entrepreneurial technology company in San Diego in the 1970s and early 1980s was a hit-or-miss process. For example, Hybritech's founders, Ivor Royston and Howard Birndorf, received venture funding from Kleiner Perkins Caufield & Byers, one of the Silicon Valley's top venture firms, through personal contacts going back to their Stanford days. The investors wanted the company to locate in the Silicon Valley, but Royston insisted that it remain in La Jolla. Kleiner Perkins approved the proposal and Royston's stipulation in part because Royston's research at the UCSD Medical School provided the underlying technology. They also approved the San Diego location because of a creative real estate development economy, which provided highly attractive land and industrial building costs for labs and offices, helping to significantly reduce the upfront risks (the University Mechanical development discussed in the previous chapter). Kleiner Perkins not only supplied financing; it also helped Hybritech hire experienced managers from large pharmaceutical firms outside San Diego to bring management know-how to the venture as well as linkages to the major players in the pharmaceutical industry. All of this was helped by the fact that Royston had spent time at Stanford before coming to UC San Diego. His spouse had at one time dated Brook Byers, who was still a friend. Byers began his venture career at Asset Management before joining Kleiner Perkins; he knew San Diegan Buzz Woolley because of an early tech company investment there.[12] If Royston had not had these personal connections to Silicon Valley, it is unclear whether his new firm would have received the funding and other help it needed.

San Diego's established business community remained unaware of Hybritech or its needs. One leading service provider in San Diego told us that he heard about Hybritech while he was working for his firm on another assignment in Brussels.[13] On returning to San Diego, this individual realized that young entrepreneurial companies needed assistance to break into European markets and that servicing San Diego start-ups might become a major growth area for his firm. He then devoted time and energy to learning more about these new companies, as did a few other pioneering business service providers in San Diego. There was, however, no formal mechanism for facilitating this process in a deliberate and high-impact way across the region throughout the 1970s and much of the 1980s. The group working with Chancellor Atkinson concluded that a formal mechanism was needed to facilitate connections and so created an initiative provisionally called the UCSD Program in Technology and Entrepreneurship, quickly renamed UCSD CONNECT.

In early 1985 they launched a program whose goal was to jump-start the technological innovation and entrepreneurship process. They understood the regional need for developing contacts, social networks, and business services of the type that had not been readily available to early entrepreneurs such as Irwin Jacobs in wireless or Ivor Royston in the biosciences. The rationale for launching this initiative—and the strong commitment people made to it—derived from the economic booms and busts San Diego had experienced throughout the 1980s. The initiative's form and character, however, mirrored a long history of civic efforts focused on adapting San Diego's regional economy to changing conditions. Using University Extension as an administrative platform, a collaborative civic initiative emerged, funded by local memberships and sponsorships and led by a tenacious and successful entrepreneur who had already made his mark and was ready to be a champion for the growing San Diego start-up community, William "Bill" Otterson.

The one-on-one interviews and roundtables leading up to the formation of CONNECT yielded a number of creative ideas. All focused on how the university and the community could collaborate on this issue as well as on ways to link academic researchers with entrepreneurs and to link both of these parties to venture capitalists and business service providers, to grow new companies that would create high-wage jobs and regional prosperity. Key early components of the program included such activities as:

- "Meet the Entrepreneur" and "Meet the Researcher" events;
- Financial forums;
- "Springboards for Technology Startups";
- "The Most Innovative New Products" award; and
- A variety of workshops intended to help scientists and businesspeople share insights and cultural practices, educating each other for the sake of more fruitful future relationships.

CONNECT from the beginning was fully funded by annual memberships. More than 1,000 companies and firms soon joined; the organization also generated substantial underwriting funds and fees for services. In the early years, it sponsored more than eighty annual events and continues today in its third decade to offer 300 events each year, assisting hundreds of startups annually. In addition to assisting technology startups CONNECT has been widely credited with helping to engender a critical mass of business service providers and local venture capitalists with the experience and connections needed to help technology entrepreneurs. It created a community through which a diverse array of professionals provided not only technical assistance but also access to valuable contacts, advisors, and capital. There is substantial anecdotal information about how the business culture changed, but it is hard to document empirically. We were able to obtain some comparative information on leading business service providers in the region between 1986 and 2011. It is suggestive although by no means conclusive.

Law firms provide an illuminating case. In 1986 the San Diego County Bar Directory listed 2,300 attorneys, a figure that had increased nearly sixfold by 2011, to 12,500. Among the top twenty-five firms in 1986, only two had more than fifty attorneys; by 2011 that number had increased to thirteen. In fact, eleven of the top firms in 1986 had twenty or fewer attorneys, while in 2011 none did. Most telling is the fact that sixteen of the top twenty-five firms in the 2011 list were started in San

Diego after 1980 and thirteen prior to the 1980s. By 2011, ten of the top firms listed intellectual property law as a specialty area. None did in 1986.[14] Other indications of the changing business environment in San Diego during this period relate to capital. In 1986 the *Business Journal* had no list for venture capital firms. In 2011 they reported eleven, all founded or locating there since the 1980s. Similarly, in 1986 the *Journal* did not report on wealth management firms, as there was only a handful in the region prior to that time. By 2011, the list of twenty-five top wealth management firms included nineteen established after 1980 and billions of dollars in managed funds.

Such snapshots suggest a major shift in the scale, character, and composition of business services that had taken place in the region. Many attribute a part of this transformation to the accelerated startup activity to which CONNECT contributed but also to the aggressive promotion of the region's promise that CONNECT's leadership pursued. Events to showcase San Diego's growing R&D capacity as well as its early company successes were organized not only within the region but across the country at venues such as the San Francisco Yacht Club in 1995, the Harvard Club in New York City in 1996, and at IC^2 in Austin, Texas, in 1990 to name but a few. And national media, such as *Wired* and *Forbes*, began to pick up on the buzz the local tech boosters were trying to create.

By becoming a vital regional resource that helped entrepreneurs in new and emerging science and technology fields, CONNECT became an important part of San Diego's regional innovation system. By 1990 the region was building significant momentum. Simultaneous with the growth of CONNECT in the late 1980s, a variety of related technology-focused regional organizations began to proliferate. They included the federally funded Defense Industries Consortium, the state-funded Regional Technology Alliance, and the research-community-based Science and Technology Council. All focused on the need to grow regional companies, in particular in response to the military reductions, and the defense sector downsizing of the 1990s. There were massive layoffs in the defense contracting industries across the nation with fully 60,000 in San Diego losing their well-paid jobs during a single eighteen-month period. In addition, by the 1990s a number of new civic initiatives to create support organizations for the growing technology-specific sectors began to take hold. These included organizations such as BIOCOM, founded in 1991; the Software Industrial Council, founded in 1994; and the San Diego Telecommunications Council, founded in 1998. Since 2000 new clusters and civic organizations advocating their interests have merged. Among the most important are CleanTECH San Diego, San Diego Sports Innovators, and, recently, the Wireless Health Network.

A timeline highlighting key civic activities and emerging organizations to serve San Diego's growing technology and life sciences clusters was prepared by CONNECT on the occasion of its twenty-fifth anniversary in 2010, highlights of which are shown in Figure 5.1.

THE EMERGENCE OF A CIVIC CULTURE FOCUSED ON INNOVATION

A lively civic culture was key to the coming success of the commercialization of high-tech in the region. From 1985 onward, just as the Chamber of Commerce had in prior decades, CONNECT became the civic platform through which San Diegans addressed their twenty-first-century aspirations for economic prosperity. A series of regional interviews conducted by a team led by Mary Walshok, in connection with Michael Porter's Monitor Group Cluster Study of San Diego (1994), uncovered a number of opinions about how San Diego was changing. Much of what follows sums up previously reported findings in a 2002 *Industry and Higher Education* issue on Innovation.[15] For example, a San Diego business leader commented that one feature of the region, not always understood by people from elsewhere, is that the relative geographical isolation of San Diego helped to build a sense of community and a need for partnerships. In addition, the defense downturn of the early 1990s further encouraged cooperation.

The leader of a defense contracting company spun out of General Atomic commented that "the immediate loss of an industry like defense manufacturing led to the need to focus on being more competitive and to seek out new industries." Other interviewees referred to the relatively compact geographical setting of San Diego's tech businesses, facilitating this cooperation. An executive with one of the region's early biotech companies praised the region's extraordinary social capital, referring to what might be the community's most "precious commodity"—trust.[16] There is, he said, a strong culture of mutual support in San Diego. There seems to be much more trust in the region than in Silicon Valley. "We do not walk around with nondisclosure agreements like in the Valley," he added.[17]

Another successful biotechnology executive called the region's business service providers "venture catalysts"—people who can help to put ventures together quickly and reliably. He said that San Diego had developed a critical mass of service providers, such as intellectual property attorneys and business planners. He noted, however, that these people were not in the region when the first biotechnology firms began. He went on to give CONNECT much of the credit for helping to build the pool of service providers needed by entrepreneurial technology

1985	1986	1988	1989	1991	1992	1993	1994	1996
CONNECT is founded, and Bill Otterson serves as first entrepreneur in residence and director.	"Meet the Researchers" and "Meet the Entrepreneur" programs are launched. The San Diego Venture Group (SDVG) is founded.	CONNECT publishes membership directory. The San Diego Technology Financial Forum is launched.	Athena San Diego is launched. The Biotechnology/Biomedical Corporate Partnership Forum is launched.	BIOCOM founded.	CONNECT launches the Defense Conversion Program.	The Springboard program is launched. The San Diego Software Industry Council is founded.	CONNECT is an early adopter of the Internet with the launch of CONNECTNET—an online database of investors and technology resources. Crossboarder CONNECT is launched.	Bill Otterson wins the national Ernst and Young Entrepreneur of the Year award. CFO CONNECT is launched.

1997	1998	2000	2001	2003	2005	2007	2009	2010
SDVG and CONNECT partner to hold the annual Technology Convergence Conference. CONNECT holds the AG BIO Conference. CONNECT Entrepreneurs Roundtable is launched.	San Diego Telecom Council (now CommNexus) launched.	Michael Porter's Cluster of Innovation report finds that San Diego outpaces the nations in job creation, productivity, and exports and VC funding.	CONNECT builds more alliances with tech transfer office on campus and across the Mesa.	Global CONNECT is formed due to growing interest in other regions.	Duane Roth becomes the next director of CONNECT. CONNECT spins out from the university to better serve the community.	CONNECT takes on program management of CEO Strategy Forum. CONNECT launches the Innovation Report. The board approves creation of CleanTECH San Diego.	CONNECT holds Innovation support for National Security Conference. CONNECT approves creation of San Diego Sport Innovators. La Jolla Research and Innovation Summit is launched.	The Biogen Idec Young Innovators Program starts. USD and CONNECT launch the Technology Entrepreneurship Law Clinic. SPAWAR and CONNECT partner to hold Wireless Health and EMR Conference. Roth coauthors Kauffman Paper on new model for drug discovery and development.

Figure 5.1 CONNECT's twenty-five years of innovation highlights.

Source: CONNECT.

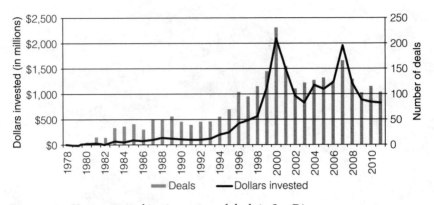

Figure 5.2   Venture capital investments and deals in San Diego.
Source: Thomson Reuters VentureXpert.

companies and for institutionalizing the "socialization of innovation." The head of an agricultural biotech company reinforced this remark by suggesting that the 1990s had witnessed a major expansion of venture capital funding in the region. This individual indicated that CONNECT had played an early role in convincing members of the venture capital community to regularly come down from the Bay Area. Since that beginning, San Diego had grown its own local venture capital and angel funding to supplement the outside sources. Figure 5.2 provides a snapshot of that growth over multiple years.

CONNECT's success signified the maturation of San Diego's business culture in terms of the city's emerging global competencies, in contrast to the more locally focused culture that had characterized prior decades. While still opportunistic, collaborative, and infused with boosterism, within a mere twenty years it had developed a highly vigorous, venturesome entrepreneurial business capacity. Local firms transformed or expanded their expertise, putting San Diego squarely on the map of the increasingly interconnected world of high technology. Equally important, however, throughout the 1990s was the influx of new investors, law firms, and global marketing firms with sophisticated management know-how. People and companies settled in the region because they perceived San Diego as an opportunity-rich community, built on a well-networked "new economy." And, as noted earlier in this chapter, the size, character and composition of business services in the region were changing substantially, to all appearances, developing a more entrepreneurial business culture with social dynamics characterized by cross-functional networking, collaboration, and high levels of pro bono involvement.

Above all, CONNECT served as a catalyst for San Diego's high-tech entrepreneurs, helping them to commercialize the fruits of their research. This resulted in substantial new regional capabilities. The commercialization of technology entails a journey from a promising idea or research result into production of useful products or processes that contribute to solutions of real problems in a manner that is scalable, affordable, and marketable. Thus commercialization extends beyond issues of patenting and knowledge transfer, which are regular activities of many research institutions. It requires testing, demonstrating, validating, and ultimately translating promising ideas into useful and marketable products, which is what entrepreneurial businesses do. Commercialization is a journey that Duane Roth, the late CEO of CONNECT, described as involving "four Ds": *discovery* research, *defining* a potential application, *developing* and validating the application, and *delivering* the solution to a market.[18] For this to occur, a number of conditions are necessary and a variety of competencies are essential, all of which the CONNECT model captured and developed through trial and error at UCSD Extension in the 1980s and 1990s. Such a proactive focus on technology commercialization is widely acknowledged as having enabled the rapid growth of strong science-based company clusters such as those established in IT, life science, and software in San Diego between 1985 and 2000.[19] The R&D output over the last decade in San Diego continues to support growth. Figures 5.3 through 5.5 document this clearly.

By 2010, its twenty-fifth anniversary year, CONNECT was receiving numerous accolades in the national press. In fact, Christine Quinn, the New York City council speaker commented in her "State of the City" address in February 2010: "In San Diego they have a great organization . . . called

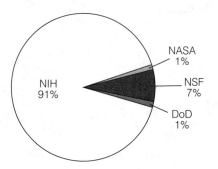

Figure 5.3   Percentage of total funding by agency, 2000–2010.
Source: USAspending.gov, National Institutes of Health.

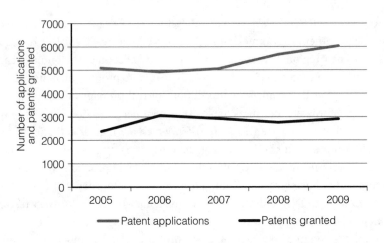

Figure 5.4   San Diego patent applications and patents granted, 2005–2009.
Source: U.S. Patent & Trademark Office.

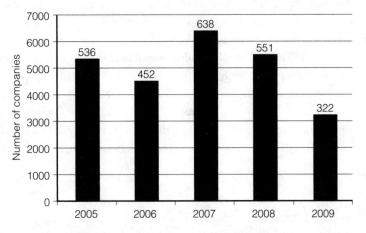

Figure 5.5   High-tech start-ups in San Diego, 2005–2009. *Note:* Uses definition for
high-tech developed by the U.S. Bureau of Labor Statistics; see www.bls
.gov/opub/mlr/2005/07/art6full.pdf.

Source: Dun & Bradstreet.

CONNECT. It literally connects the best talent, investors, workspace and the other
tools they need. This year, we will create the same thing right here in New York.
We're calling it NYC HIGH-TECH CONNECT." The map presented in Figure 5.6
indicates the extent to which the CONNECT idea has been emulated globally.

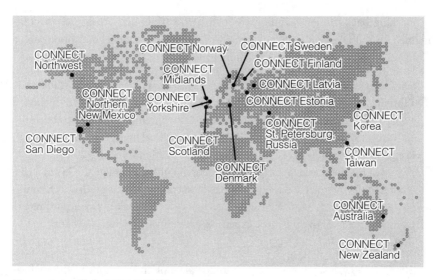

Figure 5.6   Global CONNECT network.
Source: CONNECT

This map in no way represents an empire built by CONNECT. Rather, it speaks to the important principles of practice adopted by many regions eager to create entrepreneurial business services while cultivating a civic culture and regional social dynamics that can enable the growth of an innovation ecosystem. In 2010, *Inc. Magazine* described it this way:

> CONNECT, one of the nation's first incubators, has been working with startups since 1985. The 2,000 ventures it has assisted have received more than $10 billion in funding. Participants get advice from mentors, as well as help with building prototypes, securing intellectual property, or performing preclinical trials. Who gets in: early-stage tech firms.[20]

Not only *Inc. Magazine* but national magazines targeted toward more general readers noted the "effects of CONNECT on San Diego's regional economy." As *Time Magazine* noted,

> In 1985 CONNECT sprang up to link the scientists and inventors at top research institutions . . . with investors, advisors and support services so their new ideas could become new products and companies. The inventive brew that CONNECT fermented has made San Diego home to a cluster of life sciences and technology companies such as Qualcomm, Biogen Idec, Life Technologies and Gen-Probe.[21]

Harking back to San Diego's early history, *US News and World Report* commented on San Diego's significant transformation from a martial metropolis and a Cold War economy into a globally competitive center of technology clusters:

> San Diego is home to the nostalgic Gaslamp Quarter, a picturesque coastline, and a thriving tech industry. Between UC San Diego, SDSU and USD, research plays a big role in the community, and researchers draw funding—which helps nurture further innovations according to CONNECT, a regional non-profit. CONNECT's President . . . says new data collected by the organization shows significant increases in the number of startups and the amount of VC funding. . . . City officials boast that the metro area has one of the highest concentrations of high tech companies in the nation. San Diego also ranks fourth for tech salary pay, according to Glassdoor data—above the more expensive cities of Washington, New York and Boston.[22]

The CONNECT story suggests the importance of civic culture to the realization of new economic outcomes. The core examples presented in earlier chapters of this book emphasized the vital role played by civic entrepreneurs, boosters, and business advocacy organizations in the invention and subsequent reinventions of San Diego's economy. The quest for clean industries led the city's founders to seize opportunities to build an economy fueled by the military. The early technology platforms associated with the needs of naval and aviation operations expanded significantly through two world wars and the Cold War. As a consequence, in San Diego there was a civic understanding of the importance of R&D to national security. That in turn animated a commitment to land use decisions that supported the establishment of research enterprises that were seen at the time as serving the nation's interests. From the 1980s onward, the collection of research institutions and the diversity of science and technology fields in which they were active enabled civic leaders to reimagine San Diego's economy once again in a new light—the struggle for global economic competitiveness.

The success of the CONNECT program exemplifies San Diego's most recent reimagination; in this instance a new organization served much as the Chamber of Commerce had at the turn of the prior century, as the hub for civic initiatives, as the city's chief lobbyist in Washington, and as the leading center of unabashed boosterism for San Diego as "technology's perfect climate." This indeed was the brand the Economic Development Corporation chose to promote at the turn of this century. To what extent do the facts about San Diego's transformation over the past twenty-five years match the boosterism so deeply embedded in the city's civic culture?

SAN DIEGO'S SCIENCE AND TECHNOLOGY CLUSTERS TODAY

On the occasion of its twenty-fifth anniversary in 2010, the leaders of CONNECT commissioned a comprehensive assessment of the regional innovation outcomes that had occurred since its founding. The report begins with a series of compelling maps and statistics. In the last two quarters of 2009 and the first two quarters of 2010, CONNECT reported that 319 innovation companies had been launched in the San Diego region. Over a twenty-five year period, 6,000 innovation companies employing 140,000 people had been created. Although these companies only numbered 6 percent of the employers in the region, they nonetheless produced 25 percent of the region's wages. The creation of high-wage jobs became a major strategy of civic leaders in the post–Cold War era. As we noted earlier, the loss of well-paid defense manufacturing jobs in the late 1980s and early 1990s motivated civic leaders to shift their focus to science- and technology-based companies creating innovative products of potential value to national and international commercial markets. San Diego leaders understood such companies as magnets to attract and retain the high-wage workers so important to regional prosperity. The results of these efforts proved impressive.

CONNECT reported in 2010 that the compensation for workers in the technology sector was 90 percent higher than the average wage in the region. Throughout this period little attention was paid to the growing discrepancy between the earnings and benefits within the high-tech sector and those in the other major industries in San Diego, in particular tourism, whose workers—mostly recent immigrants from Latin America and Asia—occupied the bottom of the pay scale. By 2010, researchers at SANDAG—the regional council of governments—noted with some alarm the slow deterioration of the middle class in the region and the need to rethink strategies for closing the growing gap between rich and poor. This phenomenon is not unique to San Diego but is an issue across America as more and more well-paid manufacturing and skilled jobs are being eliminated through technology-driven productivity gains and the globalization of production. SANDAG released a report in 2012 on the traded industry clusters in the region that sums up the overall employment picture (see Figure 5.7).

Time Magazine based its 2010 article, just quoted, about San Diego being the home to a cluster of life sciences and technology companies on a "major scale," on these data. The CONNECT report points out that, building on the early foundations established by the Scripps Institution of Oceanography and the Metabolic Institute at the Scripps Hospital, the region from the 1950s onward had incubated a sizable cluster of basic research enterprises; seventy-five distinct research institutes

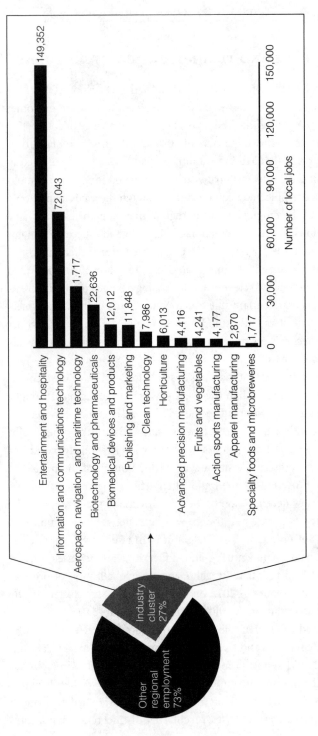

Figure 5.7 Traded industry cluster employment, 2010.
Source: California Employment Development Department.

with UC San Diego the anchor representing 50 percent of all R&D expenditures. Since the 1960s the San Diego Zoo had created an Institute for Conservation Research; the Navy had located its Space and Naval War Systems Command (SPAWAR) R&D contracting activity on the site formerly occupied by Consolidated Aircraft; and the region had attracted or incubated a variety of freestanding research institutes such as Salk, the La Jolla Institute for Immunology, Sanford-Burnham, and others, as we presented in the previous chapter.

Defense and transportation (for example, unmanned aerial vehicles, mag-lev public transit, and electric cars) represented the second cluster CONNECT identified in its 2010 report. Research and development in aviation as well as land and sea transportation continued their long significance for the San Diego economy. These never really diminished in importance the way aerospace manufacturing had, although their relative standing in the region's productivity has in fact declined. Defense research and manufacturing in San Diego had always pushed the limits of the technology of the time, and such certainly remains the case today.

Another cluster directly related to the region's evolving technology history is communications, security, and transportation. According to the Innovation Report in 2010, more than 260 companies occupy this cluster, the majority of which are defense contractors. One of the more notable contemporary clusters to evolve out of early military contracting has been in the field of IT, wireless, and communications/software, which in 2010 represented 3,000 companies in San Diego including companies such as Qualcomm, LG Electronics, Broadcom, Nokia, and Intuit. These companies, in fact, have created the largest share of the new high-wage employment created in the region since the mid-1980s. In January, 2013, the San Diego Workforce Partnership and San Diego Regional Economic Development Corporation published a comprehensive report, "Qualcomm & Telecommunications in San Diego." The document emphasizes the seminal role that Qualcomm—founded in 1985—has played in the growth of the sector, as demonstrated by the figures in Table 5.1. The company today employs more than 21,000 worldwide (of whom 11,775 are in San Diego) in 170 locations. The telecommunications and information industry as a whole encompasses 66,360 jobs in San Diego (direct employment), contributing $21.93 billion annually to the regional economy, while combined direct and indirect employment in the region totals 179,020, with an aggregate contribution to the economy that amounts to $38.1 billion, which represents 22 percent of the San Diego's gross regional product in 2010.[23]

By 2010 San Diego also had built a significant reputation as a center of biomedical and life sciences research and development institutions and successful business start-ups in related fields. The 2010 Innovation Report identifies 600 companies,

TABLE 5.1

Qualcomm telecommunications and information technology economic impact profile for San Diego County, 2010; economic output (in millions of dollars). *

	Direct output generated	Share of direct output generated	Total output generated**	Share of total output generated
Qualcomm	$2,351	1.3%	$4,528	2.6%
Telecommunications	$11,409	6.5%	$20,666	11.8%
Information technology and telecommunications	$21,926	12.5%	$38,111	21.8%
San Diego County output***	$175,068	100%	$175,068	100%

Source: "Qualcomm and Telecommunications in San Diego," 8.

*Analysis was completed using 2010 data with dollar amounts inflation adjusted to 2012.

**Total output generated includes direct, indirect, and induced output.

***Bureau of Economic Analysis (BEA), regional economic accounts, gross domestic product (GDP) by metropolitan area (millions of current dollars) (2010), updated September 29, 2011.

most of which are within a five-mile radius of the Torrey Pines Mesa. They include regional startups such as Life Technologies, Biogen Idec, Amgen, Genprobe, ResMed, and Synthetic Genomics. Over time, the innovations coming out of the start-ups have attracted global pharmaceutical companies, with Johnson & Johnson, Novartis, Eli Lilly, Pfizer, and Merck each establishing major R&D facilities in the region.

Steven Casper at the Keck Graduate Institute of Applied Life Sciences is one of the more comprehensive and systematic chroniclers of the growth of the life-science clusters across California since the 1980s, and in particular in San Francisco and San Diego. His work illuminates the different drivers of life science cluster growth in different regions. Casper characterizes San Diego's growth as a life science cluster from the late 1980s onward as "entrepreneur driven" due to the activities of a pool of managers and venture capitalists eager to start companies, many of whom came out of San Diego's first biotechnology company, Hybritech, acquired by Eli Lilly in 1986. Much like Qualcomm in telecommunications and information technology, Hybritech was key to the development of the cluster, which by the mid-1990s had developed into the third largest bioscience industry cluster in the world, trailing only San Francisco and Boston in size.[24]

CONNECT's Innovation Report for 2012 cites more than 40,000 direct jobs in the life sciences in San Diego (pharma, bio, medical devices, and renewable energy) with average wages exceeding $93,000 annually. In addition, NIH grant funding for basic research in the region exceeds $1.5 billion annually.

Finally, the report identified a grouping of companies that, while reflecting the prevailing image of San Diego as a "laid-back" beach community with extraordinary weather and an active lifestyle, had also evolved into a strong technology-based cluster—the action sports cluster, which by 2010 included 600 companies. In 1954 the first surfboard company in the region was established, Smith and Butterfield in La Jolla. Since then, fully in keeping with manifold advances in physics, chemistry, and synthetic materials at the core of the sporting goods and equipment industry, the region became home to major sports equipment companies such as Callaway, Ashworth, and Taylormade/Adidas, Underwater Kinetics—all well known for their cutting-edge gear. In addition to golf, a myriad of other sports-related product companies had developed, including surfboard, skateboard, cycling, scuba diving, recreational goods, and clothing companies.

The "clustering" of all these distinctive tech sectors across the Torrey Pines Mesa, as far as ten miles to the north in Carlsbad and six miles to the east on land that was once the Scripps family's Rancho Miramar, is dramatically visualized in the maps shown in Figures 5.8 to 5.14, prepared in 2012 by SANDAG for their report on San Diego's globally traded industry clusters.

These data demonstrate how diversified the San Diego economy had become by 2010. The SANDAG report includes additional nontechnology-based traded sectors such as hospitality, with 149,000 jobs averaging $21,800; publishing and marketing, with 12,000 jobs averaging $56,600; and horticulture and fruits and vegetables, with 10,000 jobs averaging $28,000. The regional employment total in all traded sectors represented just short of 332,000 jobs with the overall average wage at $55,900.[25]

THE MILITARY PRESENCE PERSISTS

In Chapters 1 and 2 we noted the pervasiveness of the military and defense contracting in the region and their historical impact on the local economy. As the present chapter has demonstrated so amply, the military is *not* San Diego's only cluster. In June 2012, the San Diego Military Advisory Council, an organization that established its independence from the Chamber of Commerce in 2004, released its most recent report on the local economic impact of Department of Defense activities. During the past year, $8 billion came to the region in the form of wages and salaries for active duty and civilian workers; $2.5 billion in retired veteran's benefits, and $10 billion in the form of major procurement contracts; in total, $20.5 billion in external investments. The ripple effect on such activities as construction, purchases, and services was not reported.

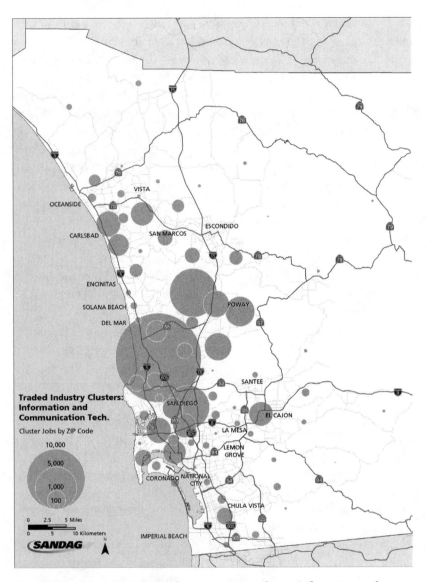

Figure 5.8   Cluster distribution by major statistical area: Information and communication technology.

Source: SANDAG.

San Diego has not lost its position as a major martial metropolis despite its impressive growth in globally traded technology clusters. Sixty percent of the U.S. Pacific Fleet and more than one-third of the combat power of the U.S. Marine

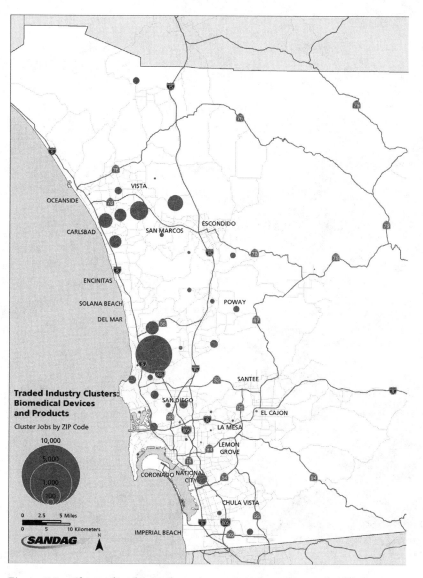

Figure 5.9   Cluster distribution by major statistical area: Biomedical devices
                   and products.
Source: SANDAG.

Corps resides in the county, figures that include 100,000 active duty personnel and
account for 311,000 civilian jobs (one in four in the county). Many of these are
high-paying jobs in health care, engineering, and financial services. The nation's

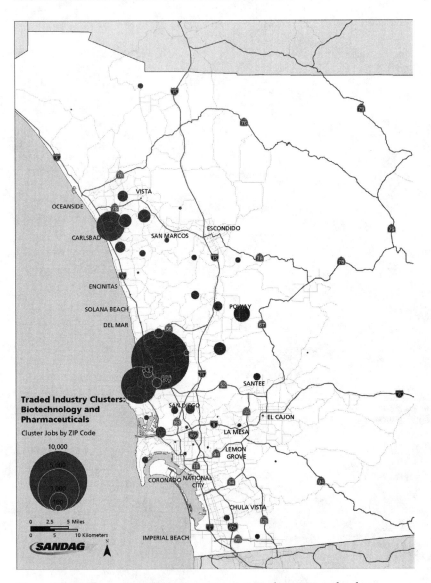

Figure 5.10   Cluster distribution by major statistical area: Biotechnology
and pharmaceuticals.

Source: SANDAG.

renewed focus on the Asia-Pacific world thus bodes well for the San Diego region's investment in advanced technologies, especially unmanned military aircraft and new weapons systems, even in the face of forthcoming cuts in military

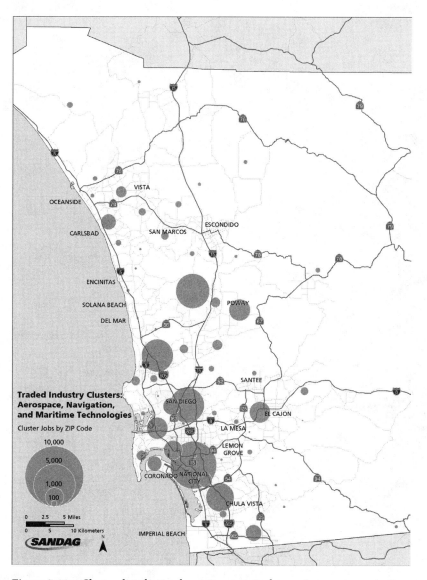

Figure 5.11   Cluster distribution by major statistical area: Aerospace, navigation, and maritime technologies.

Source: SANDAG.

spending. The synergies between R&D and the military, as well as their significant benefits to the San Diego economy established in the 1940s, clearly continue today, more than seventy years later.

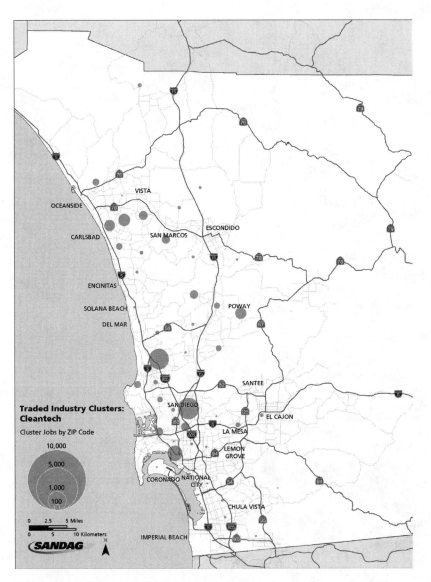

Figure 5.12   Cluster distribution by major statistical area: Clean technology.
Source: SANDAG.

DEFENSE SPENDING IN SAN DIEGO, 2010–2013

The armed services, especially the Navy and Marine Corps, remain central figures in San Diego's landscape and civic culture; the city is still very much a Navy

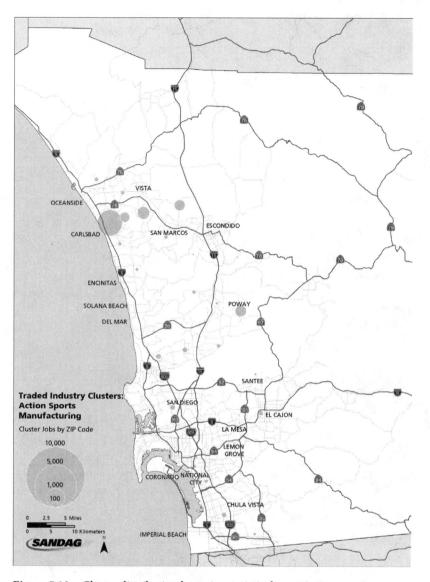

Figure 5.13   Cluster distribution by major statistical area: Action sports
                              manufacturing.

Source: SANDAG.

town as the statistics in Table 5.2 so clearly indicate. Numerous warships of all sizes
ply the harbor; military transport planes, helicopters, and fighter jets crisscross the
skies; and men and women in uniform are visible in many parts of the city. The

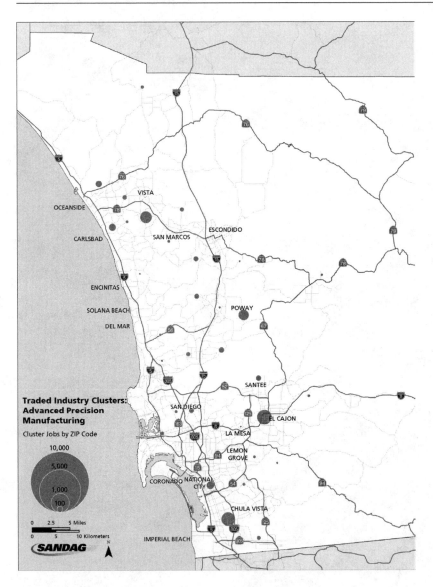

Figure 5.14   Cluster distribution by major statistical area: Advanced precision
manufacturing.

Source: SANDAG.

services still occupy huge tracts of the region's most valuable real estate, although
since 1989 several rounds of the Base Realignment and Closure (BRAC) process have
changed that situation at least to a degree. Most notably, Naval Training Center San

TABLE 5.2

Impact of defense spending in San Diego, 2010–2013.

	2010	2011	2012*	2013**
Direct spending (in billions of dollars)	$19.1	$20.3	$20.6	$20.7
Jobs (thousands)	309	319	311	306
Income (in billions of dollars)	$17.6	$17.8	$17.7	$17.7
Gross regional product (in billions of dollars)	$32.1	$32.2	$31.9	$32.3

*Estimate.
**Forecast.
Source: Fermanian Business & Economics Institute.

Diego—one of the great relics of San Diego's first reinvention, discussed in Chapter 2—was closed in 1997 and turned back to the city. The municipal government contracted with a private developer, the Corky McMillan Company, to transform 321 acres of the former base into a combined commercial-retail-residential-cultural-recreational complex, renamed "Liberty Station." The nearby Marine Corps Recruit Depot, whose acreage is coveted for much-needed expansion of the adjacent Lindbergh Field (San Diego International Airport) or other urban uses, will not revert to the city anytime soon, which is also the case for Marine Corps Air Station Miramar, a site the city could have purchased back from the Navy after World War II for $1; despite much heated debate and many unanswerable objections, some still say today that Miramar is the obvious place to establish a new regional international airport. Naval Air Station North Island, the several commands located on Point Loma, and Naval Base San Diego (also known as 32nd Street; at 977 acres, it is the largest naval base on the West Coast) continue to serve their original purposes. A short distance south of one of the area's most famous and historic resorts, the Hotel del Coronado, is Naval Amphibious Base Coronado, home to the Navy's special and expeditionary warfare training and the West Coast based SEAL teams—the same group that gained worldwide recognition for eliminating Osama bin Laden in 2011.[26]

Thus the close relationship between the Navy and the city endures, although not without some notable rough patches. A telling example emerged in the 1990s with the Navy's proposal to base three nuclear-powered aircraft carriers at North Island. Environmentalists and antinuclear activists expressed strong concerns over the possibility of the release of nuclear and other contaminants into the water or air and so generated an acrimonious debate. Navy officials (and the editors of the *Union-Tribune*) pointed to the service's near-spotless record of nuclear safety, but opponents cited a number of accidental releases of radioactive material into the bay, while deploring any increase in the stream of nuclear waste already emanating from San Diego. The Chamber of Commerce, the municipal governments, and the newspapers supported the nuclear carriers wholeheartedly, for all the old reasons—that each megaship pumped $100 million per year into the local economy.[27]

A related environmental issue materialized simultaneously with regard to the new dredging needed to deepen the harbor for the big ships. It had never been a secret that sailors in many different capacities dumped hazardous and toxic wastes into the harbor, including general shipboard trash, sewage, bilge oil, electrical components, fuel, and live ordnance. Such dumping had doubtless declined as Americans became more sensitive to environmental issues. (Sewage floating in the harbor helped Reuben Fleet convince federal officials in 1940 that the city needed big help from the national government, as discussed in Chapter 3.) And the Navy did after all help the city complete its first real sewage disposal system, during and after World War II. But the sediments and waters of the bay still contain many substances and objects extremely harmful to life and health. Since the last dredging of the carrier basin (1960–1961), a glutinous layer of silt and mud covered over many of the sins of the past, but stirring up or removing the naturally protective coating promised to expose the pollutants, releasing them back into open currents. The Navy again offered its long history of friendly and munificent reciprocity to skeptical San Diegans if they would permit the service to adapt the bay further to its future needs. This was serious business in the post–Cold War era, because congressional orders to close down "redundant" bases—the BRAC process—affected San Diego as well as many other martial metropolises.

Losing the carrier base to environmental concerns contradicted San Diego's civic tradition, so those who had any say in the matter eventually accepted the Navy's analysis of the purportedly minor impacts they might suffer by virtue of the new class of aircraft carriers coming to town. To sweeten the deal, the Navy offered to deposit the sand it dredged up on local beaches that had been hard hit by a recent series of severe storms. This worked well enough until live ammunition began appearing in the spoil, and the Navy halted the transfer of sand pending a solution to the not-unanticipated problem. Even protests over diesel exhaust from the dredging machines threatened to halt the dredging, until a federal judge threw that case out of court.[28] Thus environmental safety issues appear to have challenged the old consensus as no one and nothing had ever done in the past. The environmental permit applications—nuclear and otherwise—ultimately received approval, and the first of the "nukes," the *John C. Stennis*, made San Diego its home port in 1998; two others followed shortly thereafter.

The saga of the redevelopment of the Navy's Broadway Complex, formerly the Naval Supply Center, yet one more superprime property (sixteen acres at the foot of Broadway downtown, on the waterfront) provides a good look at the state of contemporary city–Navy relations. The Navy began to plan the site's renewal as early as 1980, when it moved the supply warehouses to a less valuable location. With federal approval, the Navy joined a multiagency public–private partnership in 1987, whose purpose was to build a giant new mixed-use project that included a hotel, commercial offices (3.25 million square feet of such space), plus 1,000,000 square feet of new office and administrative space for the Navy, all at "little or no cost" to the latter, according to the *Union-Tribune*. A federal judge dismissed challenges to the project's environmental impact statement, and all seemed in order to proceed, but concerns over BRAC combined with difficult economic conditions put the project on hold. As the grass grew, the BRAC Commission ordered the Navy to get it back on track or lose the property altogether. At this point (2006), developer Doug Manchester (introduced in Chapter 4) came on board to save it, in exchange for a ninety-nine-year lease on the land. Much political and legal wrangling ensued over Manchester's design for the "Pacific Gateway" as well as renewed environmental concerns. In 2011, the all-powerful California Coastal Commission ruled that Manchester's plan no longer conformed to state environmental law, and the Navy also had to fight a claim by an opposing coalition that the proposed complex was too easily exposed to terrorism; the project was back in court again. Only in October 2012 did the dust begin to settle with a victory in court for the Navy. Admiral Dixon Smith, then "naval mayor," was eager to go ahead, but a legal appeal and new objections by the Coastal Commission still stand in the way.[29]

CONVERGENCE: THE PATH FORWARD

San Diego's innovation economy since 2010 has continued to churn in terms of absolute R&D expenditures, patents and licensing activity, new company start-ups, and cluster growth. UC San Diego's research expenditure alone in 2011 exceeded $1 billion, as the figures in the NSF's ranking of the nation's top research institutions in Table 5.3 indicate.

Increasingly, growth occurs in what civic leaders refer to as convergent clusters and basic researchers refer to as interdisciplinary research programs. The convergence takes place at the intersection of engineering, life sciences, high-speed computing, and software development. Private donors have enabled many of these efforts by funding buildings, labs, equipment, and research talent to enhance the

TABLE 5.3

Top twenty institutions in research expenditures, 2011 (in millions of dollars).

Institution	Total research expenditures, 2011	Federally provided research funds, 2011
Johns Hopkins	2,145	1,884
University of Michigan	1,279	820
University of Washington	1,149	949
University of Wisconsin at Madison	1,112	594
Duke University	1,022	585
UC San Diego	1,009	637
UC San Francisco	995	570
UCLA	982	563
Stanford University	908	656
University of Pittsburgh, main campus	899	663
University of Pennsylvania	886	707
Columbia University	879	646
University of Minnesota-Twin Cities	847	489
Ohio State University	832	493
Penn State University	795	469
Cornell University	782	476
University of North Carolina, Chapel Hill	767	562
University of Florida	740	306
Washington University in St. Louis	725	469
MIT	724	489

Source: National Science Foundation.

region's competitive ability to secure external funding—Kavli, Skaggs, Jacobs, Waitt, Burnham, and Sanford are but a few of the philanthropists' names found on research buildings constructed across the Mesa over the last decade. Four dramatic examples of this are the Sanford Consortium for Regenerative Medicine founded in 2006, the J. Craig Venter Institute founded in the same year, UCSD Medical School's new Institute for Clinical and Translational Research founded in 2010, and the San Diego Center for Algae-Biotechnology founded in 2008, which are already having an impact on the San Diego economy.

Sanford Consortium for Regenerative Medicine

The Consortium was established in 2006 as an effort of UC San Diego, Sanford Burnham Medical Research Institute, Salk Institute, and The Scripps Research Institution to increase regional competitiveness for new research funding through collaborative work in stem cell research and its translation into clinical cures. When started it involved thirty-eight affiliated faculty who had secured more than $50 million in research funding from the California Institute for Regenerative Medicine (CIRM). Funding also included a $30 million gift from philanthropist and successful businessman T. Denny Sanford to create a shared research facility. The Sanford Consortium building was completed in 2011 and is located next to the iconic Salk Institute. It consists of a new $130 million, 130,000 square foot, research center, where the partners are able to work under one roof. The project received additional support from a $43 million grant from CIRM and is financed through "rents" (primarily from overhead on grants) paid by the researchers working there. In 2011 the La Jolla Institute for Allergy and Immunology became the fifth collaborating organization in the consortium.

Calling its self a "collaboratory," the Sanford Consortium engages in an active community outreach effort through partnerships with organizations such as BIOCOM, CONNECT, and an annual public symposium, the "Stem Cell Meeting on the Mesa." This event expresses San Diego's new high-tech civic culture all but perfectly as it attracts "hundreds of business, academic research and investor attendees to connect for one-on-one meetings and strategic partnering." These experiences have resulted in a cross-section of business community leaders who are knowledgeable about their work and, in fact, are on-going advocates for stem cell research in Sacramento and Washington, D.C., and among foundations. The former dean of the UCSD Medical School serves as their executive director after a number of years advising the government of Singapore on research strategies. Their board includes the CEOs of the five partner institutions as well as QUALCOMM founder Irwin Jacobs and Malin Burnham, a fourth-generation San Diegan whose family prospered from insurance and real estate holdings.

J. Craig Venter Institute (JCVI)

JCVI is a nonprofit research institute founded in 2006, with the merger of four research organizations and the J. Venter Foundation. It received more than $30 million from the Gordon Moore Foundation to get started. The Institute concentrates on advancing the science of genomics, while also seeking to understand its broader societal and ethical impacts. Approximately 400 scientists and staff work from facilities in San Diego and Rockville, Maryland, in the areas of genomic medicine, infectious diseases, microbial and environmental genomics, plant genomics, synthetic biology and bioenergy, bioinformatics, DNA sequencing, and public education in science and science policy. The Institute collaborates with many other organizations but especially UC San Diego, where in 2011 it broke ground on what will be one of the first "sustainable labs" in the world, designed to exceed the requirements for LEED Platinum Certification. When completed, the 45,000 square foot center will support 125 scientists and staff.

JCVI receives funding from both public and private sources. The Institute and its partners have made several important advances in sequencing new genomes, infectious diseases, and viruses. Researchers have also contributed large amounts of data on genes and proteins to shared scientific databases as an output of their projects, such as the Global Ocean Sampling Expedition, which identified more than 6,000,000 new genes from seawater samples.

Venter, the Institute's director, is a world-famous scientist who received his PhD in biology at UCSD in the 1970s. He went on to become one of the first to sequence the human genome through his company Celera Genomics, which put him on the cover of *Time Magazine*, and more recently his endeavors have led to the creation of the first cell with a synthetic genome. Like Jonas Salk in his day, Venter is a "rock star" scientist and has been featured on most television news magazine shows and in lengthy articles in publications such as the *New York Times Magazine*, *Men's Journal*, and *Time*, where he was identified as one of the 100 most influential people in America.

These two centers, while impressive, are not exceptional in the San Diego context. In spite of the "great recession" of 2008 and the considerable reduction in state support for the University of California, entrepreneurial scientists have been able to attract talent and funding to the region, using some sixty years later the same promise of freedom and support to do unconventional work offered by Hopkins, Revelle, and Salk in the 1950s and 1960s. Two other examples of convergent technologies further amplify this assertion.

UC San Diego Clinical and Translational Research Institute (CTRI)

Founded in 2010 by the UCSD School of Medicine, CTRI accelerates and improves the translation of research discoveries into practices that benefit human health through interdisciplinary interactions among basic scientists, clinical investigators, community physicians, and patients. It directs its efforts to six areas: education, clinical research design and operations, translational research technology, bioinformatics, collaborative alliances, and community engagement. The Institute also draws on a large base of expertise, with participants from numerous divisions of UC San Diego and San Diego State University, four research institutes (Salk, Sanford-Burnham, J. Craig Venter Institute, and the La Jolla Institute for Allergy and Immunology), hospitals (Palomar Pomerado, Rady Children's, and the San Diego VA Medical Center), trade associations such as BIOCOM and CONNECT, the University of California system through the BRAID consortium, and the national Clinical & Translational Science Awards (CTSA) consortium. CTRI is largely supported through grants from the National Center for Research Resources at the National Institutes of Health. Its scientists are exploring such new fields as biorepositories and a biomarker laboratory; it operates out of a large, new translational medicine building on the UCSD campus. Early projects undertaken by CTRI focus on studies that can elucidate the path to providing pharmaceuticals of value to diabetes and heart disease. For example, a major research study on the genetic underpinnings of type 2 diabetes is in progress, as are studies of the effects of flavonoid-rich cocoa on heart disease. In fact, the latter received significant national media attention because of early findings suggesting a positive relationship between cocoa and better heart function. Significant clinical trials on this topic are currently in progress.

San Diego Center for Algae Biotechnology (SD-CAB)

SD-CAB is a collaboration established in 2008 as a partnership among UC San Diego, The Scripps Research Institute, San Diego State University, and private industry. It is an especially good example of the synergies among basic and applied research, universities and businesses, venture capital and multinational corporations in new technology development. By bringing together strengths in biology, chemistry, and engineering, the Center aims to support the development of commercially viable algae-based solutions for renewable energy, green chemistry, bioproducts, water conservation, and carbon dioxide abatement. In addition to its research, SD-CAB also offers workforce education and training, community outreach, and facilitation with policy makers at the regional, state, and national levels. Interaction with the private sector includes a Commercial Partners Program and Advisory Board that counts companies such as Life Technologies, Carbon Capture Corporation (CCC), General Atomic, Sapphire Energy, LiveFuels, Neste Oil, and the Serenix Corporation as members. Close to 100 researchers were associated with these efforts as of 2012.

Green algae research is contributing to the growth of clusters of renewable energy and clean-tech activities, another example of how federal requirements and investments continue to stimulate new forms of economic activity in the region. A report on San Diego's life sciences clusters prepared by Global CONNECT at UCSD for the United States Studies Centre at the University of Sydney describes the evolution of green algae from a basic research topic into a potentially useful resource largely because of regulatory shifts and more stable funding since 2008. Increases in fuel prices and new societal concerns about climate change, conditions outside of the research lab, raised the perceived value of research on the potential applications of algae. Venture capital firms began investing significant amounts into new biofuel companies and the U.S. government increased the amount of funding devoted to energy research. Local scientists such as Stephen Mayfield, then at TSRI; Greg Mitchell at SIO; and Steve Briggs at UC San Diego, among others, who over the years had become experts on algae and related fields, were in a strong position to shift the focus of their work toward creating viable biofuels.

Along with the academic community, San Diego companies began to capitalize on the revived interest in renewable energy, often building on the business and scientific capabilities found in the region's biotechnology cluster. In 2005 J. Craig Venter also established a for-profit company, Synthetic Genomics in La Jolla, to develop several commercial applications using synthetic biology, including the creation of biofuels. In 2009 Exxon Mobil, one of the world's largest oil companies, announced a multiyear $300 million agreement with Synthetic Genomics to conduct research on algae-based biofuels. Another local algae biofuel company, Sapphire Energy, secured over $100 million dollars in venture capital financing during 2008, the lion's share of the $176 million awarded to San Diego's algae biofuels sector in that year. Sapphire's scientific advisors include Mike Mendez, Stephen Mayfield, and Steve Briggs. Given the location of the scientific talent, it was logical to establish the company in San Diego. The founding of other companies has quickly followed, including Kai BioEnergy and Biolight Harvesting, the former being founded by Steve Kay, a biologist who had originally worked at TSRI and at the time was dean of UC San Diego's Division of Biological Sciences.

There also has been an overlap with the local defense industry. General Atomic and SAIC both secured awards from the Defense Advanced Research Projects Agency (DARPA) to develop a JP-8 jet fuel equivalent from algae. In January 2009, DARPA announced contracts worth up to $43 million with General Atomic and $25 million with SAIC, assuming all milestones were met. According to the San Diego Association of Governments (SANDAG), as of 2008, the county's algae biofuels industry encompassed 513 jobs and over $63.5 million in economic output for the San Diego region. By 2009, research alone on algae employed 272 scientists in the region. By 2010 SANDAG reported that, overall, the Cleantech cluster had 7,986 jobs in the sector.[30]

Stephen Mayfield recently suggested that San Diego was the best place to move forward with research and development of algae biofuels because of two key factors: First, San Diego has a favorable environment for the growth of algae with abundant sunlight and warm temperatures; and, second, San Diego has a large quantity of biologists and a thriving biotech sector. Algae experts were already embedded in a community with a critical mass of biotech entrepreneurs. This meant that when the rest of the world was just beginning to develop an interest in alternative energy, San Diego already had the necessary infrastructure in place to quickly seize the new opportunity.

In 2007 CONNECT incubated CleanTECH San Diego, a nonprofit membership-based trade association, with support from the City of San Diego and local clean-tech companies. Now a freestanding entity, CleanTECH provides education, outreach, policy advocacy, and serves as a leader for further collaboration among the region's clean-tech companies in an effort to accelerate San Diego's position as a leader in clean energy. One such collaboration is with the Algal Biomass Organization, to advocate for the development and commercialization of algae biomass for biofuels and to provide networking and collaboration opportunities for researchers and companies in the field. CleanTECH helped to bring the annual Algae Biomass Summit in 2009 to San Diego and has partnered with a number of San Diego companies applying for federal stimulus funding for renewable energy offered by the Obama administration in 2008, helping various community members to connect and organize around this common cause. CleanTECH has also frequently partnered with CONNECT and BIOCOM to present networking events and seminars related to market opportunities in the clean-tech sector.

As more federal R&D grants became available for algae, members of the research community realized that, to make biofuels work, there needed to be a greater understanding of and ability to manipulate algae. They understood the need to get research out of the lab and into commercial sectors to test potentially favorable research outcomes upon the environment. This required interaction with all the other parties (engineers, biologists, and farmers) in the biofuels innovation system.

While there has been significant activity in San Diego's research and business communities around the algae biofuel opportunity, it is still early in this sector's development. Many science and engineering questions remain unanswered, which may be more effectively addressed by collaborative activities such as SD-CAB. However, several algae biofuel companies remain reluctant to share too many details for fear of compromising their competitive position. As the technology and industry mature, it is likely the firms will find precompetitive or noncompetitive issues on which to collaborate, such as standards and regulatory issues. Such an approach to growing this new industry cluster would mirror how other clusters have evolved in San Diego's recent history.

CONCLUSION

The story we have told in this chapter presents the journey a particular community took in developing its entrepreneurial economy. This lengthy discussion of the process and principles shaping San Diego's economic transformation into a leading center of globally competitive science-based clusters is critical to understanding how the city reinvented itself. Today cities across the Americas, Europe, and Asia struggle to unload the cumbersome baggage of the past while leveraging the assets and talents they still possess to reinvigorate their economies. Most think it is primarily a fiscal, a technical, and an educational problem. Only some recognize that it may also be a problem of civic culture, a civic culture that evolved in an older, more traditionally industrial time when identifying opportunities, assessing risks, securing partners, and implementing strategies called on very different approaches than the new global imperatives require.

In the 1980s, San Diegans accomplished a thorough refocusing of the city's business culture along with an infusion of significant new business competencies and capital resources, essential to the creation of an entrepreneurial startup community. This outcome enabled thousands of new products to see the light of day, hundreds of companies to start up and grow, and tens of thousands of new high-wage jobs to be created in the region, all over the past two decades. Knowing that San Diego embraced entrepreneurialism—a key attribute of what social scientists have identified with "new-economy" dynamics, as opposed to managerialism—the classic signifier of an "old economy"—is extremely useful to understanding why San Diego has been so successful. It also provides clues to what in the San Diego experience is relevant to other regions, the focus of Chapter 6.

6 INNOVATIVE, EVOLUTIONARY SAN DIEGO

Summing up the lessons from San Diego's 130-year journey of invention and reinvention is no simple task. It would be easy to dismiss the long history we have documented in the last four chapters as simply an idiosyncratic story of a single place. On the other hand, it might possibly represent a window into characteristics and principles of community reinvention relevant to other places grappling with how to adapt their economy to ever-changing circumstances. We clearly feel this is the case.

We started this book with the assertion that civic culture is essential to any understanding of the ways communities go about inventing their core economic platforms and the extent to which over time they are able to adapt those platforms to new external opportunities and challenges. We also underscored that San Diego's civic culture has been characterized by five durable key factors that have shaped evolving community initiatives over time and realization of new opportunities. These factors, which have been central to the stories we have told throughout this book, include:

1. *The natural advantages of place.* San Diegans chose early to exploit the advantages of climate and environment and were able to do so because of the availability of large plots of publicly owned pueblo lands that the city used successively for economic development opportunities.

2. *The core values of early settlers.* In the San Diego case, the health-seeking, anti-industrial values of the mature, reasonably well-educated early city

builders gave rise to a commitment that endures today to achieving economic growth through "clean industries."

3. *How communities organize to achieve economic promise.* In the absence of
   major industries or multigenerational family wealth, San Diegans relied
   on the talent and connections of key citizens and the pooled resources of
   multiple businesses and organizations when pursuing specific economic
   opportunities.

4. *What resources and talents a community cultivates.* Because of its early
   commitment to clean industry, the Navy, and R&D, San Diego has a long
   history of valuing and recruiting citizens who bring talent, expertise, and
   connections to the region.

5. *How citizens define and promote their place.* San Diego has a long history of
   promoting its beautiful environment as a functional setting for advanced
   technology industries, beginning with the Navy, then R&D, and continuing
   today with converging technologies such as health IT.

From the macrolevel we have told a story that documents how local actors establish particular paths to economic growth in a region by linking distinctive indigenous assets with specific external opportunities. Sometimes this process gels
but slowly, as it did in San Diego. However, once the momentum accelerates, as
it did with the Panama-California Exposition of 1915 in San Diego, a regional
economy begins to acquire unique technical and industrial capabilities as well
as a distinctive civic culture suited to those capabilities. And, as we have documented, over time leadership can shift and the character of talent needed can shift
to accommodate adaptive strategies. The 100-year-plus evolution of the San Diego
economy took shape around core technical and economic activities established
early in the twentieth century. We have attempted to show that a set of cultural
values and social dynamics took root a century ago that became part of the DNA
of the region and continue to be a part of its civic culture today.

In San Diego's case that civic culture was opportunistic and nimble, based on
shifting alliances among small business interests working to identify and secure
major economic development opportunities. The federal government turned out
to be the region's biggest customer, particularly the technologically advanced and
well-organized naval, aviation, and communications sectors of the military establishment. As we discussed in the previous chapters, land-use decisions involving
repeated gifts of land in response to the shifting needs of the military and the
federal government ended up favoring technology-based industries. As these new

industries gained footholds in the region, especially the defense industries, new civic institutions emerged to address their evolving needs over multiple decades. A new set of civic institutions emerged in the region yet again in the late 1980s and early 1990s to serve yet a new set of interests—this time, the commercialization of basic research.

Because the federal government for more than 100 years has been the region's biggest customer and benefactor, the character of the region's civic culture has not changed substantially. To retain a customer like the federal government over such a long period has required a civic culture continuously attuned to priorities in Washington, D.C., with particular regard to the demand for advancing technology. It has required the willingness and ability to offer local amenities, perhaps the most important of which is land, plus related concessions superior to those available in other places. And it has relied on multiple forms of regional boosterism, in terms of both advocating for the region and welcoming the talent required to serve the changing needs of diverse federal agencies.

With the wide array of federal contracting relationships San Diego began to develop more than a century ago, the region never experienced the consolidation of wealth and leadership so typical of more industrial cities whose primary wealth was built on natural resources, manufacturing, or agricultural commodities. Earlier chapters underscored how, in the absence of high concentrations of wealth, forms of collaboration and collective business action emerged in their place. These enabled the region to mobilize and refocus as needed to ensure its long and productive relationship with the federal government. San Diego's civic culture is of necessity opportunistic rather than deliberative. It has been fueled at times by excessive boosterism, which often resulted in false starts. Nonetheless, over time, the single-minded and tenacious attention to retaining and expanding federal investments in the region has underpinned its economy for more than a century.

The ever-increasing technological needs of the military from World War I through the Cold War also contributed to a civic culture that from the first grasped the growing significance of R&D to national security, the economic competitiveness of the nation, and most certainly the continued prosperity of San Diego. And because the appetite of the federal government was sufficiently diverse, fueling multiple forms of technology developments in the region, no one technology or industry sector dominated for too long. This had both positive and negative consequences. It surely made it difficult for an overconsolidation of power and influence by any one sector except for the military bases and payrolls. Over the years San Diego has had few Fortune 500 companies and a relatively small, not very stable "power elite." Nonetheless, as historians and political economists who have studied the region point out, there were "old boys" in San Diego, and they were not always good ones. These old boys were less the proverbial captains of industry than they were land developers, bankers, and providers of services largely paid for with federal payrolls and defense contracts. Nowhere in San Diego's history does one find the type of intergenerational concentrations of wealth and power that developed in more traditional industrial cities built on steel, automobiles, or agricultural commodities.

For more than 100 years the most important family names in San Diego were Scripps, Marston, Horton, and Spreckels. Edward and Ellen Browning Scripps had settled in the region in midlife after they had created their wealth in the industrial Midwest; John D. Spreckels came to town in his mid-thirties in possession of a substantial fortune earned from sugar and shipping; and George Marston arrived at age twenty and promptly began to build his own wealth in retail trade. The ideas about city building that emerged from their efforts contrasted vividly with the urban/industrial history of the Midwest. San Diego's economy as a consequence did not give rise to a Carnegie, a Rockefeller, a Mellon, a Ford, or a Danforth. Certainly, these San Diegans and other individuals created substantial wealth through land development and services, but high concentrations of wealth in a few families on the scale of other large American cities did not occur in the region until very recently, and then thanks to successes in the high-tech sector. For example, Irwin and Joan Jacobs, the founders of Qualcomm in 1985, have been identified by *Forbes* as one of the ten most philanthropic families in the United States. However, the bulk of their philanthropy has occurred in the new millennium.

In fact, as writers such as Mike Davis and Steve Erie have pointed out, apart from the pockets of sustained focus on the military, the defense establishment and more recently basic research, San Diego's civic affairs have been bedeviled by small-town politics, shady investment schemes, and discredited small-time tycoons.[1] Nonetheless, San Diego's long history of real estate development, Ponzi schemes, bankrupt enterprises, and fallen heroes has never seriously intruded on the focus of key civic organizations. The Chamber of Commerce, the powerful downtown Rotary Club, the promilitary city council, the congressional delegation, and economic development advocates have been unfailing in their efforts to ensure that the diverse agencies of the federal government continue to invest in the region. Even today, those investments cumulatively contribute up to approximately 50 percent of regional GDP. The discussion in previous chapters of the strategic actions taken by such groups starting at the close of the nineteenth century and continuing into contemporary times makes clear the extent to which the business community understood early and durably the importance of these federal investments to regional prosperity.

This history of shifting power relationships, of continuously rebundling local resources and realigning influence to sustain federal investments in the region created as a by-product a highly nimble, flexible, and open business culture. The contemporary literature on innovation and entrepreneurship suggests that the key components of successful innovation ecosystems contain many of the characteristics that we assert have been core to San Diego's civic culture for many decades. Add to that equation the interconnected technology trajectories that have evolved in the region since the early part of the twentieth century, and our story becomes one of a synergistic relationship between continuous shifts in technology with parallel shifts in civic culture and business practices to accommodate changing customer needs. That customer just happened to be the federal government rather than the American consumer; as a result, San Diego as a region was well positioned to be a big player in the "new economy." As David Audretsch argues, the twenty-first century represents a distinctive new economy driven by innovation and risk with far more localized and bottom-up strategies than were typically found in the old industrial economy.

Success in the new era requires entrepreneurial as opposed to managerial approaches to growth. San Diego has clearly been able to evolve an entrepreneurial culture over multiple decades because of this distinctive economic history. Thus, San Diego's contemporary success as an innovation economy may be partially attributable to its larger history of reaping economic benefit from federal R&D than has been the case in regions whose industries were more reliant on general consumers for their prosperity. That may have changed with the advent of Qualcomm and its globe-spanning consumer cell phone technology. In similar fashion, San Diego's biotech companies have begun in recent years to experience the emergence of their products into worldwide commercial markets. However, federal funding of San Diego's still-major military presence and the city's expanding research clusters on the Torrey Pines Mesa continue to grow.

SAN DIEGO'S CIVIC CULTURE TODAY: SOCIAL DYNAMICS ENABLING TWENTY-FIRST-CENTURY REINVENTION

Since early in the twentieth century, San Diego has built its economy and civic culture on a series of initiatives that focused on securing clean industries largely dependent on federal funds. Ever since, coalitions of small business and community leaders have driven successive waves of reinvention, causing the city's core economy and civic culture to evolve, perhaps most distinctively in the direction of innovation and entrepreneurship. In this regard we argue that San Diego has established an enviable record that *may* be replicable in other settings.

As San Diego has evolved its civic culture, it has created a capacity for nimbleness and reinvention that has given it significant comparative advantages in today's global knowledge economy. There are five features of San Diego's civic culture today that are particularly positive for the region's ability to continuously reinvent itself moving forward. These features include:

1. *A risk-oriented culture adept at managing uncertainty.* A central feature of San Diego's experimental history and prevalence of small industries is a civic culture and business community that has embraced risk.

2. *Entrepreneurial talent: Civic leaders, scientists, business professionals.* San Diego's long history of creating opportunities for people who want to challenge the status quo or create something new has resulted in an unusually large aggregation of entrepreneurial civic, business, and scientific leaders.

3. *Integrative civic platforms.* San Diego's civic culture is highly inclusive, cross-functional, and interdisciplinary. Institutions that span the boundaries between communities of ideas and practice have proliferated; in many other regions such entities continue to be siloed.

4. *Multiple gateways through which ideas and opportunities can be developed.* There is no one Establishment, Inc., in San Diego. There are actually many centers of gravity vis-á-vis leadership and access to resources. San Diego is characterized by an open innovation environment that allows people to easily move among social groups and within hierarchies.

5. *A culture of reinvestment: Time and money.* The absence of multinational corporations until recently, the century-long reliance on the federal government as a key customer, and the lack of accumulated family wealth have required a civic culture characterized by people investing significant amounts of personal time and resources to achieve civic goals. This is enhanced by the fact that those who come to San Diego stay because of their attachment to the place.

Each of these elements reflects a type of business culture that values personal involvement and shared responsibility enabled by collaborative projects and events. Throughout the earlier chapters we identified the types of activities that harnessed these qualities, enabling the city to overcome some of its most daunting obstacles and thus grow and prosper. And this culture persists as San Diego navigates the rise of global markets and competitors as well as the promising convergence of technologies in this, the twenty-first century.

A RISK-ORIENTED CULTURE ADEPT AT
MANAGING UNCERTAINTY

The risk orientation of San Diego's business culture has been a central feature throughout the city's economic evolution in large part because, rather than a stable industry, the region has had a stable customer for whose changing needs civic leaders have continuously adapted.[2] The twenty-first-century version of that adaptive civic culture has been to mobilize the region to support the translation and commercialization of federally funded research into products, industries and clusters. The CONNECT organization serves an especially useful example of the principles and practices of that civic culture, which is also manifest in a variety of other regional organizations such as BioCom, the Software Industry Council, CommNexus, the San Diego Economic Development Corporation, the San Diego Association of Government (SANDAG) and, continuing today, the influential Chamber of Commerce.

For generations, San Diego's business culture has embraced an orientation to risk as a central feature of its processes of economic evolution. We argue that the city's business leaders have undertaken such risk because the region, rather than hosting a stable industry, has served a stable customer—the federal government—for whose changing needs civic leaders have continuously adapted. In earlier years, San Diegans often promised more than they might actually be able to deliver to stimulate growth. During the World War I era, for example, the city expended enormous effort to secure a world's fair, ostensibly to honor the opening of the Panama Canal but more pointedly to show off the city to prospective investors and settlers; the Navy Department was a primary target. While the U.S. Congress awarded the official world's fair designation to the much more powerful San Francisco, San Diegans rich and poor strained their resources to contribute to the creation of their own more modest simulacrum, and they made it work, if only barely. While San Diego's Panama-California Exposition just broke even as an enterprise, the huge gamble nevertheless resulted in enormous long-term gains for the city.

Part of city leaders' risky approach to boosterism thereafter involved assuring the Navy Department an "unlimited supply of the purest mountain water" at preferential prices, as Chamber of Commerce documents frequently asserted. Having succeeded in its attempts to attract the Navy and Marine Corps to San Diego, the city then had to deliver on its promises, which went from difficult during the 1920s to impossible during World War II. Throughout that period, the city worked mightily to increase its water supply, but in the end the Navy solved the city's (and its own) problem for years to come by using its own resources to connect San Diego to the Metropolitan Water District's Colorado River Aqueduct.

The creation of UCSD, based on the audacious promise of establishing a world-class educational and research institution in a short period of time that would serve a multiplicity of diverse and demanding interests, was no less precarious an undertaking. In this case the city had not much more to offer than some beautiful tracts of land and enormous civic/political will. Key newcomers and outsiders, for example John Jay Hopkins and Governor Pat Brown, bought into the gamble; within a few short years, all parties to the undertaking basked in their success. Even when San Diego lost the gamble, as was the case with the Microelectronics and Computer Technology Corporation (MCC) in the early 1980s, the city learned powerful lessons from the experience, creating new institutions and ways and means of dealing with future opportunities. In recent years, the city's adaptive civic culture has mobilized the region to support the translation of federally funded research into goods, industries, and clusters that produce significant individual and regional benefits—yet another challenging enterprise.

The commercialization support efforts of the CONNECT program from the 1980s onward have resulted in large numbers of startup and early-stage companies securing venture capital. As of the late 1990s three times as many CONNECT-assisted companies were still in business five years after participating in CONNECT events than were other start-ups, according to CONNECT reports. The early programs to introduce successful entrepreneurs and their company stories to a broader community through the "Meet the Entrepreneur" series dramatized how distinctive the tech start-up process can be. Richard Cramer, who sold two medical device companies to Lilly (IMED and IVAC), described taking out second and third loans on his house and pawning his wife's wedding rings to meet expenses while validating their technology. Although such stories are common to all types of entrepreneurs, they were nonetheless especially appreciated by the tech community. Cramer also described how their intravenous technology was adapted during early testing and as well their understanding of the market's gatekeepers—hurdles to be overcome when putting a new device on the market. As a consequence their business strategy changed every six months.

Bill Otterson described how he had been turned down by thirty-one different lenders and investors for capital to meet payroll in his disc-drive company, Cipher Data Products, until a local investor with whom he played tennis came in at the eleventh hour. All became multimillionaires when the company sold. David Hale, CEO of the high-growth company Hybritech, shared how on some Saturdays, spouses and children would come in to the plant to package product to airfreight to customers. And the anchor companies for two of San Diego's most robust contemporary clusters were based on high-risk technologies that challenged the status quo—CDMA in the case of Qualcomm and monoclonal antibodies in the case of Hybritech.

The stories and personal encounters they shared helped the business community to understand and respect the wide range of risky cutting-edge research and development initiatives taking place on the Torrey Pines Mesa. As many of these early entrepreneurs were engineers and scientists, their interaction on a regular basis with the business community helped to build respect for their competencies and alerted the business community to what they needed in turn to bring to the highly uncertain, volatile, but potentially lucrative commercialization efforts.

ENTREPRENEURIAL TALENT: CIVIC LEADERS, SCIENTISTS AND BUSINESS PROFESSIONALS

The character of the research institutions across the Torrey Pines Mesa, not just the UCSD campus, proved propitious for an entrepreneurial civic culture. The twentieth-century founders of what have become world-class institutions today were enormous risk takers who pioneered entirely new disciplines: oceanography, immunology, radio and sonar, satellite communications, nuclear power, unmanned aerial vehicles, monoclonal antibodies, and algae biofuels. As the interviews quoted in Chapter 4 underscored, renegade scientists, full of "piss and vinegar," were drawn to the region's promise of addressing new questions in science as well as new ways "to do science." Having been shaped in the 1950s, 1960s, and 1970s by a culture of excellence and a commitment to "instant greatness," the scientists on the Mesa represented a unique pool of intellectual capital from which to harvest commercialization opportunities. The recruitment strategies for faculty and researchers that had focused on bringing people who were at the front end of knowledge development and involved in highly interdisciplinary endeavors also resulted in a diversity of science activities. The early and continuing emphasis placed on winning federal and foundation dollars, that quest for "instant greatness," attracted particularly tenacious and entrepreneurial scientists to the institutions on the Torrey Pines Mesa, large numbers of whom were able to secure resources in highly competitive sectors. This is an entrepreneurial skill that not all research scientists at all research universities possess; it may be one of the differentiating characteristics of the scientists at the highest-performing research institutions. San Diego's technologically literate business community understood early on that this was an unusual set of skills, and they developed a respect for this kind of science. It helped that many of the early companies, though not direct spin-offs from UCSD or Salk, involved faculty and researchers working in those institutions. The articulate leadership of UCSD's Chancellor Richard C. Atkinson throughout the 1980s helped greatly. The breadth of programs sponsored by UCSD CONNECT that celebrated in the wider community the importance of good science and fundamental research to health and prosperity also helped.

Simultaneously, the business community, including law, accounting, marketing firms, and real estate developers, was developing more sophisticated entrepreneurial skills and relationships. Within a decade of the founding of CONNECT, dozens of local law firms formed strategic partnerships with IP law firms from other parts of the country. Gray Cary Ames and Frye, a law firm founded in 1927, merged with a Palo Alto firm, Ware & Freiderich, in 1994, and in 2005 merged with DLA, Piper and Rudnick, a global law firm. Wilson Sonsini Goodrich & Rosati, the pioneering Silicon Valley law firm, opened offices in San Diego in 2004. The various venture forums sponsored by CONNECT in its early years resulted in many venture funds establishing offices in the San Diego region. Today San Diego has more than forty venture capital offices and funders, including Silicon Valley Bank. A number of national marketing firms with technology clients and experience in global markets opened offices or formed strategic alliances with local marketing firms. Within a decade, a genuinely risk-oriented culture adept at managing the uncertainties involved in managing R&D startups became firmly established in the region. By the mid-1990s growth in company formations, venture capital funding, and IP was accelerated significantly, as data in Chapter 5 indicated.

INTEGRATIVE CIVIC PLATFORMS

George Homans's assertion that frequent interaction between people and groups increases understanding and affection has become a fundamental concept of contemporary sociology, and it describes a key feature of San Diego's R&D community.[3] The Chamber of Commerce since its founding in 1870, the EDC as of the 1970s, and since the mid-1980s UCSD CONNECT became integrative mechanisms essential to cultivating the human relationships that generated shared activities and increased interactions between otherwise isolated communities.

If innovation occurs at the intersection of distinctive capabilities or in an ecosystem of complementary competencies, a community needs a place where diverse interests, knowledge bases, and resources can connect. This ecosystem evolved slowly in the Silicon Valley and along the Route 128 corridor in Massachusetts. Since the 1980s, however, in a number of places it has been enabled and facilitated by university-aligned or -located programs and civic initiatives such as IC^2 at the University of Texas, Austin; the Council for Entrepreneurial Development in the North Carolina Research Triangle Park; and UCSD CONNECT on the Torrey Pines Mesa in La Jolla.

Throughout the book, however, we have asserted that key features of San Diego's historical ability to marshal its social capital at critical moments—the several tipping points we have presented—to achieve positive economic outcomes may be of potential utility to other cities. Residing at the center of the city's social capital in earlier generations was the Chamber of Commerce (especially its directors and officers), a small and tightly knit group of booster-entrepreneurs who interacted with one another and the world at large on hundreds of different issues as they tried to improve their city's fortunes as well as their own. The Chamber's mistakes, missteps, and ineptitude on several important matters over the years should likewise be useful to others. Of special note, though, and another key argument we have attempted to offer, is the city's and the boosters' ability to expand their reach by constantly embracing new forms of talent including outsiders as well as evolving key social organizations. This has taken the form, at least since the 1970s, of creating new agencies, institutions, and modalities in seeking San Diego's progress and prosperity. The emergence of the Economic Development Corporation, CONNECT, and the San Diego Military Affairs Council—all quite separate from the Chamber of Commerce—have taken up many of the Chamber's old functions in promoting the city, representing perhaps a contemporary institutionalization of boosterism, although by new and more forward-looking, collaborative means. And yet the Chamber of Commerce continues to serve the city well, advocating effectively for San Diego's growth and prosperity through numerous initiatives and programs, some venerable and others entirely new.

These platforms—today's boosters—represent more than just a collection of networking activities and events. They involve stakeholders in a variety of meaningful interactions that produce three sets of benefits:

1. They organize activities that harvest experience and knowledge in the region in a manner that can truly help the scientist seeking validation for an idea or the entrepreneur seeking input on a business plan or the civic leader concerned about public policy.

2. They occur in a setting that is pretransactional and completely open. Ideas and plans can be discussed, criticized, and adapted in a highly collegial manner in advance of an "official" presentation, be it for angel capital, the development of a business plan for venture capital, corporate partnering, or to state agencies or ordinary citizens. To this end, as Homans has suggested, a culture emerges in which technology's economic value is broadly understood, ideas are not stolen, and side deals are not made; as a consequence, people feel free to share their knowledge in an open and collegial manner.

3. The nature of the interaction is such that people learn not only about specific technologies or businesses but also about one another. That is how a community of innovation and culture of shared risk can evolve.

In surveying members who contribute endless hours to various CONNECT mentoring, evaluation, and education programs, for example, one hears again and again, "I participate in these programs as much for what I learn about my colleagues as because of the exposure to new ideas and new business plans. Getting familiar with the 'personalities' as well as the capabilities and client lists of my peers in the business community helps me put together teams in the future that work for the companies I'm supporting."[4] The events and activities sponsored by a commercializing platform need to have these key characteristics.

The result is a civic culture that supports an enormous amount of information- and resource-sharing among a large and diverse community of interests and competencies. The comment one often hears at various CONNECT or Software Industry Council events is, "I can't personally help you, but I have a friend or a colleague who's very good at this." Or, "There's no one in San Diego who's working in this particular space, but I have a good friend in Seattle who is supporting a company of this nature. Let me get his name to you immediately." This spirit of not just knowledge sharing but resource and relationship sharing is absolutely essential in an entrepreneurial community.

Finally, the community benefits from the platforms that are focused on science-based enterprise. For example, on many occasions, scientists and engineers navigating through the various CONNECT programs to explore the potential for commercialization of an idea or application have yet to resolve whether they should try to patent or license their technology. The close interactions between CONNECT and the technology transfer offices at the various research institutions on the Torrey Pines Mesa help mitigate the potential dangers of sharing an idea before it is patented. The other benefit of the platform is that it can be a receptor community for many of the promising patents and licensing arrangements coming out of the various technology transfer offices across the research institutions on the Mesa. Protection of intellectual property is absolutely critical once an idea or application is defined as having real promise. The journey through the testing and validation of the idea or application and the exploration of its viability in terms of production, marketing, and pricing, however, is a longer one. It is this lengthier commercialization process for which platforms such as CONNECT have proven so valuable. Even today the technology transfer offices across the Mesa work closely and effectively with CONNECT.

MULTIPLE GATEWAYS THROUGH WHICH IDEAS AND OPPORTUNITIES CAN BE DEVELOPED

Since the expansion of basic science in the 1950s and the growth of adventurous research institutions on the Mesa, the need for multiple forms of testing, validation, and, more recently, commercialization resources has grown. Above and beyond the existence of CONNECT and CONNECT-like programs providing integrative platforms that draw in the knowledge and resources of both the entrepreneurial science community and the entrepreneurial business community, there is enormous value in having multiple gateways through which science and business can interact. The San Diego community, especially the Chamber and EDC, and later UCSD CONNECT, learned early that they did not need to be the gatekeeper, the central door through which all industry interactions including business creation occurred, but rather that this function could be fulfilled by one of many honest brokers in the ecosystem. Once again, recent research bears out the value of multiple points of entry in a knowledge-creating community.[5]

The frequency and diversity of interactions through community intermediaries, industrial affiliate programs, technology commercialization initiatives, entrepreneurship education in schools of engineering, and nimble offices of technology transfer result in knowledge flowing in many directions, leading to faster and more effective application, development, and commercialization of promising research initiatives. Universities such as UC San Diego and Stanford have dozens of offices located in multiple departments and schools through which industry interactions occur, as do the dozens of not-for-profit research institutes on the Torrey Pines Mesa such as Salk and Sanford-Burnham. These represent an important part of the innovation equation because of the ease with which people can have access to the knowledge that ultimately produces products, companies, jobs, and wealth that can accelerate the rate of start-ups.

The UCSD example is instructive. CONNECT was founded before there was an office of technology transfer at UCSD and simultaneously with the establishment of the school's first industrial affiliates program. At the time CONNECT was founded in 1985, there were no technology industry groups in the San Diego region except for the American Electronics Association, whose members were engineers drawn primarily from defense contracting businesses. The venerable Chamber of Commerce included few technology companies and had lost its earlier connections to the technology sectors it had so aggressively promoted in the early 1960s. The EDC, formed in the 1970s, also wished to focus on business attraction rather than incubations and start-ups. CONNECT in its first decade became the platform through which a variety of campus-based industrial affiliates programs were formed and from which a number of industry-specific advocacy groups spun out, in particular and the Regional Technology Alliance. CONNECT was a strategic partner in the development of the Von Liebig Center for Entrepreneurial Studies within the School of Engineering, the clinical research initiatives in the School of Medicine, and a variety of other independent but aligned activities. It also was the source of much of the wealth and leadership that led to the establishment of a business school at UC San Diego in 2005.

Multiple gateways matter. A commercialization platform is critical, but it is also essential to engage all of the various paths to knowledge development and technology connections. The CONNECT program differed from many other commercialization efforts throughout the United States and the world by being part of a larger ecosystem, contributing to its growth as a hub and convener, and not by running it or acting as the exclusive gateway to it. Thus, the region benefits enormously from lots of good ideas and business development opportunities flowing into its offices from multiple sources. The 2012 Innovation report from CONNECT indicated that a new high-tech company is started every twenty-four hours. This is one sign that the highly fluid ecosystem of innovation is working effectively.

A CULTURE OF REINVESTMENT: TIME AND MONEY

A final characteristic of the region's entrepreneurial civic culture is a culture of reinvestment. This has developed because successful entrepreneurs, whether they were scientists or businesspeople, have shared their know-how, have supported others attempting to replicate their efforts or success, and have made substantial commitments of time and resources to growing the innovation culture of which they are a part. This element of San Diego's identity also has deep historical roots, extending back to the city's earliest days. Of special interest in this regard is the way newcomers, at least since the time of Alonzo Horton and ever after, have in short order come to love San Diego and its potential and thus invested heavily their time and assets to make the place even better. In a relatively short period of time, such recent arrivals weave themselves into the very fabric of the community. Names such as Scripps, Spreckels, Marston, Fleet, and Fletcher from years past come quickly to mind, and their gifts to the city have endured. More recently, Revelle, Hopkins, Salk, Wilson, Burnham and other scientists and businesspeople too numerous to list have undertaken tremendous commitments to move the city forward, each in his or her own way. And, in recent decades, successful entrepreneurs engaged in technology development have invested significantly in the region: Irwin Jacobs, Gary and Mary West, and Ted Waitt, to name a few.

Based on the extraordinary involvement of hundreds of scientists and businesspeople from the San Diego region in CONNECT's various programs and the panoply of technology specific networking and advocacy groups that developed in San Diego throughout the 1990s, it is possible to describe the ways in which this culture of reinvestment is expressed today. It begins with a sharing of knowledge and relationships that can be mobilized to support the work of relatively unknown and untried individuals and ideas. Through mentoring, seminars, workshops, and interactive roundtables, more experienced professionals and scientists share their knowledge with less experienced people and are generous in their efforts to help make connections that contribute to success. This type of sharing involves significant contributions of personal time by a wide range of individuals, not unlike the tireless efforts of the Chamber in securing the Navy, of civic leaders in obtaining a UC campus, or of the EDC with the bid for MCC. Typically, these individuals are not simply established leaders or successful entrepreneurs with discretionary time and money to mentor and support new business ventures. Participants include large numbers of well-educated, highly seasoned professionals whose typical billable hour represents hundreds of dollars. Through programs like CONNECT, individuals contribute their time, wisdom, and experience on a pro bono basis. In 2012 CONNECT reported 300-plus events using approximately 1,000 volunteers to help start and grow science- and technology-based companies in the region.

Reinvestment also involves cash. CONNECT was the incubator for the formation of an angel investment group known as the Tech Coast Angels that today numbers more than 300 individuals. Using the offices of CONNECT and sharing support staff, the Tech Coast Angels meet at the University Faculty Club once a month for briefings on exciting new developments in which angel investment could make a difference. This group includes a wide array of individuals with diverse business backgrounds (retired attorneys and bankers, successful real estate developers, and tech entrepreneurs knowledgeable in business and science). Just as important as the involvement of early-stage angel investors in the commercialization process is access to institutional sources of capital, such as venture capital and corporate partnering. Successful entrepreneurs and experienced, well-connected business service providers in the region are often bridges to major sources of capital for new companies. Through these individuals, doors are constantly opening for the young, the unknown, or a spin-off team from an established company.

Finally, one of the most noteworthy characteristics of the San Diego region is the impressive growth in local philanthropy between 1985 and 2010. While philanthropy was essential to the establishment of pivotal institutions such as SIO, TSRI, and Salk, its role has enlarged significantly in recent decades. The vast majority of new philanthropic funds are in personal foundations, family foundations, and advised fund mechanisms such as community foundations and the Jewish Family Foundation. These come from the wealth created by successful science and technology entrepreneurs in the region. Billions of dollars have been placed in new funds established since 1985. Much of this new wealth has been contributed to the university and research institutions on the Mesa in the form of endowed chairs, fellowships, and financial support for promising graduate students as well as for buildings and labs. Organizations such as CONNECT are often partners in the development of the prosperous companies from which these resources have come. Successful entrepreneurs have also taken on leadership roles in assuring the growth of wholly new enterprises such as the establishment of UCSD's new graduate school of business, or the formation of the Sanford Consortium for Regenerative Medicine and West Health on the Torrey Pines Mesa. Support extends to K–12 charter schools focused on developing the pipeline of math and science talent as well as museums, the San Diego Symphony, and public libraries. San Diego has come of age since the 1950s thanks to hundreds of millions of dollars in new philanthropy.

San Diego's spirit of philanthropy and culture of reinvestment have been especially critical for the university's continued success as a leading research institution as well as the growth of robust clusters of innovative science-based companies in the San Diego region. It harkens back to San Diego's earliest roots when families such as Scripps and Spreckels contributed to health, research, and cultural institutions; civic leaders such as George Marston commissioned reports on the city's future promise, and organizations such as the Chamber of Commerce collected contributions to support community improvements and new research centers such as the Marine Biological Institute.

Surveys of the pro bono participants and investors in many of these technology-focused activities reveal that people are looking for two kinds of return on investment. Clearly, business development motivates participation; however, as important as financial return is the return on involvement and participation. Because the commercialization strategies embedded in the business culture of San Diego involve meaningful tasks with visible outcomes that benefit the region as well as the individual participants, not simply their economic interests, there is a sense of contributing to civic well-being as well. The commercialization efforts instigated in the 1980s were clearly enhanced by the membership fees and program underwriting support so generously provided by a variety of businesses across the region, but they also required the personal involvement of hundreds of professionals and scientists. That may be one of the reasons San Diego's reinvention process was so effective through the 1980s and 1990s.

These features of San Diego's contemporary civic culture are not that common in many other parts of the United States, much less Europe or Asia. And these cultural and social dynamics may be a key reason many places with similar, even superior assets to those in San Diego have been slower to reinvent themselves in spite of compelling externalities.

WHY AN ENTREPRENEURIAL CIVIC CULTURE MATTERS

The stories we have told and the data we have shared in the course of the book have led us to conclude that San Diego has continuously redefined itself over the years, demonstrating a nimbleness and capacity for renewal that was essential to more than just the city's growth—in fact, to its very survival. All urban economies need to be entrepreneurial; San Diego has enjoyed particular advantages because its leaders, whether in business, the sciences, academics, or today the knowledge industries, have been able to find and harness the ability to put risk, capital of several varieties, ideas, and hard work together in search of prosperity.

David Audretsch and A. Roy Thurik assert that organizational characteristics and social dynamics of communities and firms differentiate old from new economy practices, not simply a region's hard assets.[6] Drawing on their argument, the evolution of San Diego's civic culture and social dynamics (in the absence of major industrial development, particularly in traditional manufacturing) likely predisposed it to success in the new, more entrepreneurial economy. In a seminal piece published in 2002, just as the dot-com bubble was bursting and thousands became unemployed or stuck with worthless stock, Audretsch and Thurik developed an evocative characterization of the distinctive elements of what they described as the "new economy," one that captures many of the features we have argued are central to San Diego's civic culture. They assert a shift is taking place between "two polar worlds," old and new, and provide a detailed analysis of what it means to move from an industrial or "managed" economy to a knowledge or an "entrepreneurial" economy. The heart of their argument focuses on what sorts of organizational strategies, public policies, and cultural values drive economic growth and competitiveness.

Their argument, like that of Paul Krugman and Richard Florida among others, is that conventional models of economic growth were built out of the industrial experience where the focus was on economic inputs such as land, labor, capital, equipment, and facilities.[7] Economies of scale, corporate management, and command-and-control forms of organization served them well. In contrast, in the new economy, knowledge, information, ideas, and investment emerge as the most important ingredients for growth. Such inputs are favored by highly open flexible forms of organization, in what they call the "entrepreneurial economy." When industries build their products and profitability on inventions, ideas, and information, knowledge becomes a critical growth asset, a resource that can be shared and enlarged on rapidly and in multiple settings. Thus, it cannot be easily controlled, organized, or managed in the way that natural resources, labor, and facilities can.

According to Audretsch, most of the new economic theorists assert that knowledge differs inherently from traditional factors of production and cannot be transferred across geographic space without cost. In fact, knowledge is best developed and exploited in the context of localized production networks embedded in innovative clusters.[8] This is because knowledge resides within the people and organizational practices set in specific geographic regions and can be shared more quickly and accurately through continuous face-to-face interactions. As Michael Porter at Harvard University has observed, "The paradox of globalization is that location still matters."[9] Audretsch and Thurik argue that it actually matters more.

San Diego exemplifies a community that early on had to rely on close collaborative networks, nimble strategies and attention to technology development to assure its continuing relationships with the military. The larger business community always placed a higher premium on knowledge and talent than did many communities such as Detroit, for example. The evolution from a military economy into a Cold War economy and eventually into an economy that thrives on globally traded products and services necessitated embracing new forms of talent and a willingness to adapt systems and incentives. San Diego always relied on coalitions of smaller enterprises. It never developed large industrial firms that innovated within the boundaries of particular core technologies and markets to sustain and grow markets. San Diego, much as Audretsch and Krugman describe, has for the most part been characterized by many small firms with a greater diversity of technologies and, with that, variable approaches to decision making and community life than in more typical industrial economies.

The small number of supplier firms who provided the construction, health services, insurance, entertainment, and education services required by the military in the 1920s through the 1950s, expanded into networks of suppliers feeding the enlarging defense contracting industry throughout the 1960s to the 1980s. Today, added to these are large numbers of small R&D firms in a contiguous geographic area. San Diego's jobs and wealth have typically been a function of the clustering of these sorts of smaller companies, rather than the concentration of one or two major employers or a leading national company. San Diego has throughout its history been an economy of small businesses, many of which provided services to military bases (that is, construction) or otherwise benefit from military payrolls (such as retail, autos, restaurants). Even today, Qualcomm, the global communications Fortune 500 company, with tens of thousands of employees globally, supports only 11,775 jobs in San Diego. Sempra Energy, also a Fortune 500 company now based in San Diego, employs more than half of it 17,500 workers locally. The largest pockets of employment are within the hundreds of industries clustered in the sectors described in Chapter 5 of this book and, of course, the military.

The long-held assumption in the economic development community, that without large, stable, anchor firms a community is at economic risk, is less and less true. Audretsch argues that entrepreneurial economies achieve their stability through overall employment within the clusters of hundreds of small firms. Chapter 5 detailed the extent to which San Diego has developed seven distinct clusters over the last fifty years. Job security is a function of the skill sets that aggregate within these clusters, which facilitate significant mobility between firms within the cluster. Here again, the San Diego story suggests a long history of smaller firms within key economic clusters. An additional characteristic of the San Diego economy, which has enabled much of its innovation and prosperity, is the diversity of technologies and organizational practices within the region. One could argue that San Diego has been a one-customer town. However, it is hard to argue that San Diego has been a one-industry town because of the parallel growth of the communications, life sciences, health sciences, and aviation sectors.

Over multiple decades, San Diego has benefited from a variety of technologies that in the modern era are converging into new and promising capabilities, as was noted in Chapter 5. This diversity of technologies and clusters of small firms has enabled the kind of permeable boundaries, interfirm mobility, cross-professional associations, formal collaborations, and strategic alliances such as those described in Chapter 5. These are core to the success of entrepreneurial economies.

The new economy as characterized by Audretsch ultimately depends on "flexibility" as the organizing principle for economic growth as opposed to "scalability," the engine for growth in more traditional economies.[10] Flexibility implies freedom and incentives rather than regulation, a focus on outputs rather than inputs, local control more than national policy, and, most certainly, a system of finance based on risk including multiple forms of return on investments. This contrasts vividly with the types of financial institutions, markets, and practices that characterize industrial economies, where, as Audretsch points out, the focus is on "picking winners." In entrepreneurial economies, market makers prosper. Numerous interviews with some of the early entrepreneurs who built the platforms from which San Diego's current globally traded clusters developed suggest that the operating principles in their industry reflect the qualities elucidated in Audretsch's work. Over time San Diego has evolved into a business community with the cultural values and business practices that are highly suited to the uncertainties and continuous adaptation required by entrepreneurial technology companies.

A high tolerance for uncertainty as well as failure is also an essential part of that culture. The ability to take large risks, manage failure, and learn from it is core to more dynamic entrepreneurial enterprises. As Audretsch points out,

> An externality of failure is learning. In the entrepreneurial economy, failure of companies is a process of searching for new ideas. It similarly follows that the positive virtues of long term relationships, stability and continuity under the managed economy give way to flexibility, change and turbulence in the entrepreneurial economy. What is a liability in the managed economy is, in some cases, a virtue in the entrepreneurial economy.[11]

The data that we have provided on San Diego's continuous adaptation to changing external circumstances suggest that its core culture has been more entrepreneurial than managerial for many decades. This entrepreneurial capacity is further reinforced by the kinds of associations and civic institutions—the civic culture—that have shaped how people behave once they move to the region. The population of the region continues to grow as Table 6.1 shows.

San Diego's entrepreneurial culture has been reinforced by the character of what could be called the intermediary or boundary-spanning institutions that have been catalysts for this entrepreneurial economic growth over multiple decades, starting with the Chamber of Commerce more than 100 years ago and most certainly in the activities of the CONNECT program today. These institutional mechanisms

TABLE 6.1
*City of San Diego and San Diego County
population, 1860–2010.*

Date	City	County*
1850	650	
1860	731	
1870	2,300	
1880	2,637	
1890	16,159	
1900	17,700	
1910	39,578	61,665
1920	74,361	112,248
1930	147,995	209,659
1940	192,486	289,348
1950	334,387	556,808
1960	573,224	1,033,011
1970	696,769	1,357,854
1980	875,538	1,861,846
1990	1,110,549	2,498,016
2000	1,223,400	2,813,833
2010	1,307,402	3,095,313

*The contemporary borders of San Diego County were
established in 1907; thus population statistics for the
county earlier than that do not compare accurately to later
figures.

Source: U.S. Census.

and social networks provide diverse integrative activities that have enabled a civic culture that is nimble and astute at evaluating new opportunities, can mobilize appropriate teams to help translate ideas and opportunities into viable enterprises, and values knowledgeable and varied forms of talent investment, networking, and evaluating performance. Additionally, these types of regionally anchored, boundary-spanning organizations are prominently involved in advocacy on behalf of specific sectors at the local, state, and national level. Just as William Kettner and Colonel Joseph Pendleton in the World War I era were powerful voices in Washington, D.C., for the importance of San Diego to the federal government's national security agenda, today the Chamber of Commerce, EDC, and CONNECT continue to play that role on behalf of the nation's economic competitiveness agenda.

THE DYNAMICS OF REINVENTION

America's history of westward expansion features numerous instances of pioneers who leveraged natural assets as a formidable tool in the city-building process and who became dedicated "entrepreneurs of place," as so aptly defined by Daniel Boorstin.[12] The major enterprises on which America's economic leadership was built—agriculture, steel, coal, oil, automobiles, industrial products, computers, and phones—were all begun by individual entrepreneurs operating in distinctive geographic and civic places that enabled their inventiveness. All succeeded because of their ability to scale production and distribution to compete successfully in national and international markets. With that scaling process came organizational processes (such as assembly lines) management systems (including layers of review, approval, and controls), and corporate organizations (that is, formal and bureaucratic systems). Thus, most early innovative enterprises were quickly transformed into managed as opposed to entrepreneurial organizations to grow both productivity and markets. And, typically, the civic cultures of these initially enterprising places—Detroit, Rochester, Philadelphia—developed in a manner (values, practices, decisions criteria, and relationship to government) that not only reflected but sustained the core industries.

Over time nimbleness and comfort with risk were replaced by caution and attention to sustaining the rewarding and predictable status quo. To sustain or rediscover the early entrepreneurial spirit and capabilities that initially built America's great industries, cities, and social organizations is no mean feat. Some places, like San Diego, have remained quite entrepreneurial and opportunistic, not necessarily consciously but because they needed to in order to thrive. Thus, there may be features of their civic culture that provide clues to places interested in reclaiming their entrepreneurial roots. The San Diego story suggests a variety of features that could potentially be replicated in other regions committed to reengineering or reinventing their economies. These relate to four features of any place that can be analyzed and understood.

The San Diego case elucidates the interplay between these various features throughout its epochs of invention and reinvention. As we discussed in Chapter 1, places are shaped by the particular geographic assets and limitations as well as the industrial legacies that develop over time. The demographics of early settlers and successive waves of immigrants—their religious traditions, education and skill levels, their views of government—invariably shaped the ways in which they developed their human capital. Risk, money, success or failure, and talent are valued differently in different places. How a community comes together to solve problems or make decisions, how it organizes its core civic, cultural, and volunteer activities, is affected by what becomes embedded cultural values and social dynamics. The "features of place" vary enormously from one city or region to another. And we hypothesize that how a place recognizes and understands new economic threats and opportunities is filtered through these lenses. These features all come into play as communities mobilize to respond to new economic imperatives. Precisely how and with what tools this mobilization occurs, for example, tax policies, marketing campaigns, or new forms of local investment, again vary by place.

The current national conversation about how to renew and reenergize the American economy in response to unprecedented global challenges and opportunities has focused attention squarely on innovation as the driver of growth and entrepreneurship as the key to unlocking America's creative capacity. That is why previously understudied regions such as San Diego have become so compelling to scholars, policy makers, and politicians. They are the places where this convergence of innovation and entrepreneurship take place. And they are often places with few of the traditional assets that until recently were associated with global competiveness. Our argument has been that they *do* have a civic culture characterized by opportunism, openness, and the ability to simultaneously mobilize their traditional hard assets as well as diverse civic interests when it is important to address new economic realities. It is what some have characterized as absorptive capacity. Having lived with successive eras of economic uncertainty, such places become less settled, less self-satisfied, less reliant on large stable employers and established hierarchies. As a consequence, they often appear less sophisticated, less well-organized, more naïve, more characterized by boosterism. Nonetheless, this openness and flexibility may be what enables them to absorb new realities more quickly and mobilize to address those realities.

Clearly there is a dynamic process in which communities must engage when confronting challenging new economic realities. In many more traditional economies, elites have been quick to see new realities and with the best of intentions to lead from the top with expert reports and large philanthropic investments. However, an entrepreneurial economy needs communitywide buy-in and systemic change. San Diego had not only to alter its highly public land use and water policies but also to undergo a much more intimate social revolution as well, perhaps the most outstanding example of which occurred through much of the 1950s and into the 1960s. Then Roger and Ellen Revelle informed the citizens of La Jolla that they would have to embrace ethnic diversity and eliminate restrictive covenants against renting or selling homes to Jews if they wanted the University of California to locate there.[13] Moreover, the city had to offer an enthusiastic welcome to newcomers into society, as it did so well with the military in the 1920s and 1930s, the Cold War engineers and physicists in the 1950s and 1960s, and the famed scientists such as Salk, Urey, and Grobstein who migrated to San Diego thereafter. It gave seats to talented newcomers on prestigious boards, and, in the absence of a stable elite, entrepreneurs and new residents were quickly integrated into leadership roles, understanding that both time and money were expected from them for important civic initiatives. Other cities have addressed their challenges and opportunities very differently, once again, we would assert, because of how historical, economic, and sociocultural factors interact and become embedded over time.

What values, leadership, and organizational strategies are used when communities mobilize for change may be a more critical differentiator of success than many realize. Why some regions are more efficient and adapt earlier to changes in technology and global imperatives is likely affected by the ways in which the civic culture enables both an assessment and analysis of the interplay between what has come before with what is possible moving forward. This is a function of how the community's public policies, local organizations, and government agencies address the rebalancing of these dynamic factors. Once communities realize there is a substantial need for change, mobilization effects kick in. However, we argue that, in different regions with differing economic histories, there may be characteristics of embedded social and cultural dynamics that deter the ability of communities to recognize, much less absorb and eventually act on new realities.

We have argued throughout this book that the absorptive capacity of any community to recognize new realities, assess what must be done to change, and ultimately develop the capacity to reinvent itself results from the interplay between the industrial legacies and the physical, capital and intellectual assets of the region, as well as the extent to which regional social organizations are open to new knowledge, new information, and new forms of talent. The conventional wisdom on clusters rarely takes the more cultural, social/psychological, and social structural issues into account when attempting to tease out the differences among regions that are more or less adaptive.

There is a significant body of research and theory that reinforces the conclusions we have come to about the distinctive character of the San Diego economy and its evolution over time. Michael Porter's work on clusters and the importance of agglomerations of multiple capabilities in specific industrial clusters is seminal to our understanding of San Diego's evolution.[14] The importance of talent to regional economic development is at the heart of the very significant work of Richard Florida,[15] as well as that of Lynne Zucker, who has studied talent dynamics in the life sciences.[16] The importance of capital for experimentation and the development of new enterprises have been well-documented in the work of Alessandro Grandi and Rosa Grimaldi[17] as well as that of Tallman and Phene.[18] Most especially, the significance of collaborative networks and open systems productive of knowledge sharing is central to the work of thinkers such as AnnaLee Saxenian.[19] Finally, as noted in Chapter 1, a growing number of scholars have emphasized the significance of geographic agglomeration to the growth of innovation economies.

Nobel Laureate Paul Krugman in 1991 wrote about this topic,[20] and, more recently, Steven Casper's work addresses the significance of triggering events in particular geographies as catalytic to creating momentum for change and entrepreneurial successes.[21]

The San Diego story suggests that many of these factors are in play. The topography, climate, and natural resources of the region affected the kinds of economic opportunities of which the region was capable. However, the types of people who early migrated to the region, in search of an alternative to the gritty industrial Midwest cities, brought with them social and cultural values that shaped the kinds of economic opportunities that were pursued. Externalities clearly affected how the geographic and sociological characteristics of the place converged into the development of a concrete set of economic opportunities, when those opportunities become clear, as they did in the case of the military at the turn of the twentieth century for San Diego. Local talent mobilized to find the capital and the incentives to bring the Navy to town. In so doing, the city's leaders also seeded a long-term relationship with a very good customer with an early need for advanced technology and one whose priorities shifted constantly and expanded over time, to which San Diegans repeatedly adapted. The result in San Diego's case is what we find today, an innovation economy characterized by a civic culture that is quite distinctive, not a mirror of the past but one that is built on the past.

CAN A COMMUNITY REINVENT ITS CIVIC CULTURE?

In an entrepreneurial age where innovation increasingly drives growth and economic competiveness, community assets and capabilities different from those of the industrial age may matter. Communities across America are grappling with how to engage new global realities and reinvigorate their regional economies. Change is imperative. Civic culture profoundly affects how communities not only recognize the need to change but have the cultural and sociological wherewithal to change and adapt. The cultural and social dynamics of a community shape how individuals and organizations gain access to and use new kinds of information to identify opportunities and challenges. They affect how much information and what kinds of resources people are willing to share and mobilize in addressing new community challenges and opportunities. They affect where people look for leadership to catalyze and guide new initiatives. They affect how communities think about the role of government—local, state, and federal—in addressing new economic challenges. Unless communities dissect the character of their civic culture—simultaneous with assessing their technological, fiscal, and geographic assets and gaps—they are unlikely to be able to mobilize quickly to respond to new realities. The central lesson of the San Diego experience is that a community with putatively fewer assets than many early American cities was able to recognize and create new economic opportunities, in large part, because of its civic culture. And it has continuously adapted and reinvented itself in the face of shifting external threats and opportunities because of that civic culture.

Thus, the question becomes, How does a community go about analyzing and interpreting the character of its civic culture? What does it need to understand about the historical roots and contemporary dynamics of its civic culture to engage it or change productively? Adapting to new economic realities often requires a different outlook, mentality, or set of goals, changes in individual behavior and social dynamics. In their book, economic historians Douglass North and Robert Thomas make two observations critical to this point. The first is, "Before wealth can be created, human beings have to learn to work together and, if there is to be subsequent progress, new forms of association have to be developed." The other is, "While we associate economic growth with technological development, organizational innovation has played an equal, if not more important role since the beginning of the industrial revolution."[22]

The San Diego case suggests at least six ways in which a community can begin the journey to better understand the nature of its regional civic culture. If communities do a serious analysis of (a) their physical and social assets and gaps; (b) their distinctive industrial and economic legacies; (c) their sources of civic leadership; (d) their pockets of entrepreneurial practice and success; (e) how socially inclusive they are; and (f) the character and quality of intermediary institutions in the region, they will go a long way to understanding their own culture and social dynamics. With this understanding, a process of reinvention can occur. A little more detail on each of these may be useful.

The first of these requires a clear understanding of the key characteristics and values of the region's early settlers and how this, in turn, may have shaped the character of the economic and business activities that developed in the region. The contrast between skilled furniture makers migrating to western Michigan and the gritty early industrial assembly-line workers in Detroit comes to mind. Additionally, the religious backgrounds, ethnic values, social positions, and education levels of early settlers can affect how the opportunities of a place are defined. San Diego's growth trajectory was in no small way affected by the anti-industrial values of its early, educated, midwestern city migrants.

Second, it is also important to understand the effects that particular kinds of economic activity can have on civic behavior. A community that is made up of a few large enterprises in contrast to a collection of small businesses may end up having a more managed approach to problem solving in the civic sphere, as opposed to a more collective pooled approach. How a region thinks about and pursues economic growth is a second factor helpful to understanding civic culture. In an economy that for decades or centuries has been built by companies for which scale is the driver, the approach to civic problems likely will mirror the analytical, hierarchical division of labor strategies with which local leaders are comfortable. In contrast, communities where diversification and forms of innovation and adaptation have been core to economic growth may yield leadership in the civic space that relies on different tools and problem solving strategies.

Third, communities need to understand the origins and motivations of their civic leadership. Are their leaders captains of industry—a small, elite powerful group—because of their wealth and influence, or does leadership arise from collaboration among small business leaders? One thinks of the difference between agribusiness and small family farms and how this shapes the civic culture in communities that are characterized by one or the other.

A fourth important dynamic has to do with entrepreneurial attitudes and behavior patterns. The United States has a long history as one of the more entrepreneurial countries in the world—it is truly a history of entrepreneurs of place and industries. Nonetheless, some regions of the country and some metropolitan areas appear to be more or less entrepreneurial in their attitudes and behaviors. Understanding how citizens perceive and assess risk through interviews, by looking at the kinds of enabling social networks, educational programs, and intermediary organizations that exist to support entrepreneurial enterprises and emerging technologies may be one way to differentiate places. Analyzing the character of the supportive business culture is another. The example we provided, of shifts in the legal and financial community within San Diego over a twenty-five-year period, suggest a move toward more and more entrepreneurial enterprises in the local economy.

A fifth characteristic has to do with how open or closed a community is. This is highly nuanced, and it brings to light the markers of competence, authority, and social acceptability in any given community. Some communities place very high barriers to entry and thus make it difficult for new residents to secure jobs, qualify for loans, join clubs, sit on a for-profit or not-for-profit board, or serve as advisors to the mayor or university president. Other communities reach into a much more diverse array of educational, social, and ethnic backgrounds for participants in these kinds of activities. In many communities people can quickly identify the gatekeepers, what schools matter, and with whom to talk to get anything done. In other communities, this is less the case—newcomers are embraced quickly with less concern about high-status credentials, and one finds high levels of participation across multiple social groups. This becomes important because permeable social boundaries and readiness to include outsiders, especially those with economically relevant talent or resources, can enrich the amount of knowledge and information sharing that occurs, thus thickening the web of relationships that can be mobilized for social action. It also allows people to build familiarity and mutual trust within the community across social, economic, and functional boundaries. In less nimble communities people may be very well networked within a group or class of citizens but not as well connected across groups and classes of citizens. These are things that can be identified and addressed.

Finally, a sixth factor is the extent to which a community has organizations that actively enable knowledge sharing, socializing, and trust building across multiple social and knowledge boundaries, which may contribute in significant ways to the absorptive capacity of that community. Forums in which new economic realities, trends, and world affairs are shared, breakthroughs in science and technology are introduced, among not only a small elite but a larger public, can create the kind of civic intelligence that is supportive of innovative and entrepreneurial initiatives.

The San Diego case suggests that on these six dimensions, San Diego's position on a continuum would fall toward openness, collaborative, nonhierarchical, risk taking, inclusive, and trust building. The question is: Where would a St. Louis, an Indianapolis, a Rochester, an Austin, or a Miami fall on a continuum related to these social and cultural dynamics? The San Diego case raises some interesting hypotheses about how to understand differences between regions and their innovation outcomes. It is quite possible that the San Diego story is idiosyncratic, a one-time instance of a number of factors converging to enable continuous reinvention and expansion of regional prosperity even in very challenging times. However, it is equally likely that analyses of the innovation capabilities of other regions would benefit significantly from the development and inclusion of measures that would capture some of these less easily measured characteristics of place.

Clearly, place matters in profound and complicated ways. Civic culture is likely as important to a place as is its industrial legacy, its access to capital, its intellectual assets, and its geographic advantages. How these are transformed into economic growth opportunities is shaped by the character of that regional civic culture. Without understanding that character, we cannot understand why places with very similar hard assets are so different in terms of their innovation outcomes and economic performance. San Diego, a second-tier city, would not have been predicted to fare as well as it has moving into the twenty-first century based on any traditional economic forecasting models. Its civic culture allowed it to bundle limited assets and address significant gaps in a manner that has resulted in recurrent reinventions of its economy.

NOTES

PREFACE

1. James Fallows, *More Like Us* (Boston: Houghton Mifflin), 1989.

CHAPTER 1

1. John D. Spreckels, speech at a testimonial dinner in his honor, June 13, 1923. Ed Fletcher Papers, Mandeville Department of Special Collections, University of California at San Diego Library, MSS 81, Box 27 (hereafter cited as Fletcher Papers, UCSD).

2. U.S. Department of Commerce Bureau of Economic Analysis data, as reported in the National University System Institute for Policy Research's *San Diego Economic Ledger*, November 2009, 3(5), 1.

3. Ibid., 2–3.

4. According to the San Diego Convention and Visitors Bureau (ConVis), 31,100,000 visitors came to town during 2011, more than half of whom stayed overnight; "San Diego County 2012 Visitor Industry General Facts," retrieved on May 3, 2012, from www.sandiego .org/downloads/1336073008.02374500_bd104b1b9c/2012%20General%20Facts.pdf.

5. For an exhaustive discussion of this issue, see Abraham Shragge, "Boosters and Blue-jackets: The Civic Culture of Militarism in San Diego, California, 1900–1945," PhD dissertation, UCSD, 1998.

6. *San Diego Economic Ledger*, November 2009 3(5), 4.

7. Ibid., 5.

8. "San Diego High-Tech Economy Dynamics," *San Diego Economic Ledger*, October 2011 6(2), 1–3.

9. "Dynamics of San Diego's Economic Recovery," *San Diego Economic Ledger*, November 2011 6(3), 3–4.

10. Ibid., 5.

11. "Health Care Working in San Diego," *San Diego Economic Ledger*, August 2007 1(4), 2–3.

12. Political scientists G. A. Almond and Sidney Verba gave *civic culture* a drier but still effective definition: "the ways in which political elites make decisions, their norms and attitudes, as well as the norms and attitudes of the ordinary citizen, his [or her] relation to government and to his [or her] fellow citizens." See *The Civic Culture: Political Attitudes and Democracy in Five Nations* (Newbury Park, CA: Sage Publications, 1989), 3–4.

13. Daniel Boorstin posited the most useful definition of this term: Boosters were a class of entrepreneur who first acquired large tracts of relatively remote raw land they suspected to lie within the path of future development, "commodified" that land by subdividing it and otherwise preparing it for future development, and then sold it off piece by piece to "the next greater fools" whom they had to convince of the likelihood of the property's future appreciation in value. Boosters were thus speculative and very energetic "entrepreneurs of place" whose efforts resulted in dozens of "upstart cities" across the American landscape during the era of Manifest Destiny and thereafter. See Boorstin, *The Americans: The National Experience* (New York: Random House, 1965), 49, 113–168.

14. Robert G. Spinney, *City of Big Shoulders: A History of Chicago* (DeKalb: Northern Illinois University Press, 2000), 26.

15. Howard P. Chudacoff and Judith E. Smith, *The Evolution of American Urban Society*, sixth edition (Upper Saddle River, NJ: Pearson/Prentice Hall, 2005), 40.

16. Quoted in Spinney, 10.

17. Ibid., 23.

18. William Cronon, *Nature's Metropolis: Chicago and the Great West* (New York: W. W. Norton and Co., 1991), 60–65, 372.

19. Ibid., 377.

20. Eric Sandweiss, *St. Louis: The Evolution of an American Urban Landscape* (Philadelphia: Temple University Press, 2001), 28–37, 201.

21. Ibid., 39, 156.

22. Ibid., 207.

23. Ibid., 233–234.

24. "Detroit History"; retrieved in August 2010 from www.historydetroit.com/stats.asp.

25. Frank B. Woodford and Arthur M. Woodford. *All Our Yesterdays: A Brief History of Detroit.* (Detroit: Wayne State University Press, 1969), 13, 133.

26. Ibid., 134.

27. For discussion of the significance of break-points in American urban history, see Charles Horton Cooley, "The Theory of Transportation," in *Sociological Theory and Sociological Research: Being Selected Papers of Charles Horton Cooley* (1894; rpt. New York: Augustus M. Kelley, 1969), 67; A. F. Weber, *The Growth of Cities in the Nineteenth Century*, 172; Blake McKelvey, *The Urbanization of America, 1860–1915* (New Brunswick, NJ: Rutgers University Press, 1963), viii; McKelvey, *The City in American History* (London: George Allen and Unwin Ltd., 1969), 46–47; Paul W. Gates, "The Role of the Land Speculator in Western Development," in *The Public Lands: Studies in the History of the Public Domain*, ed. Vernon Carstensen (Madison: University of Wisconsin Press, 1963), 361–362; and Eric Monkkonen, *America Becomes Urban: The Development of U.S. Cities and Towns, 1780–1980* (Berkeley: University of California Press, 1988), 81.

28. Don Lochbiler. *Detroit's Coming of Age: 1873 to 1973.* (Detroit: Detroit News, 1973), vii.

29. Woodford and Woodford, 189–191.

30. Lochbiler, vii.

31. As will be explained in greater detail in later chapters, a great deal of San Diego's publicly owned land came to the city as part of its Spanish and later Mexican colonial heritage. These particular tracts, of tremendous importance to the city's development, were first delineated in the late eighteenth century as part of San Diego's "pueblo," or colonially mandated commercial establishment.

32. M. L. Walshok (Principal Investigator), Evaluation of Generation I of the Workforce Investment Regional Economic Development (WIRED) Initiative, interim report prepared for the U.S. Department of Labor, Employment and Training Administration, Office of Policy Development, Evaluation and Research, Washington, DC, 2009.

33. Molly McClain, "The Scripps Family's San Diego Experiment," *Journal of San Diego History*, 56 (1) 2010, 1.

34. Edward Bellamy, *Looking Backward from 2000 to 1887* (Boston: Houghton Mifflin, 1889), Chapter 21.

35. McClain, 22.

36. R. DeVol, P. Wong, et al., *America's Biotech and Life Science Clusters: San Diego's Position and Economic Contributions* (Santa Monica, CA: Milken Institute, 2004); and M. Porter (2001), "Clusters of Innovation Initiative: San Diego," US Council on Competitiveness, May 2001; available at www.compete.org/images/uploads/File/PDF%20Files/CoC_sandiego_cluster.pdf.

CHAPTER 2

1. We are indebted to Roger Lotchin, who coined this term in his landmark works, *The Martial Metropolis in War and Peace* (New York: Praeger, 1984), and for his most comprehensive analysis, *Fortress California, 1910–1961: From Warfare to Welfare* (New York: Oxford University Press, 1992).

2. Quoted in John W. Reps, *Cities of the American West: A History of Frontier Urban Planning* (Princeton, NJ: Princeton University Press, 1979), 243; also in Clarence Alan McGrew, *City of San Diego and San Diego County: The Birthplace of California, Vol. I* (Chicago: The American Historical Society, 1922), 70–71.

3. Edward S. Miller, *War Plan ORANGE: The U.S. Strategy to Defeat Japan, 1897–1945* (Annapolis, MD: Naval Institute Press, 1991), 9–25. The plan formed the foundation of the nation's Pacific strategy during World War II and made no mention whatsoever of San Diego in its early iterations.

4. San Diego Chamber of Commerce (hereafter cited as COC) to U.S. Representative J. C. Needham, n.d. Minutes of the Regular Weekly Meetings of the San Diego Chamber of Commerce Board of Directors (hereafter cited as SDCOCBOD) 1900, 21–24.

5. "The Pacific Ocean and Its Shores Are Destined to Be the Theatre of the World's Greatest Commercial Activity" [sic], August 3, 1904. SDCOCBOD 1904, 221–223.

6. "Fleet Will Not Enter Harbor while Here," San Diego *Union*, March 17, 1908, p. 2.

7. "Cheering Thousands Greet the Greatest Naval Parade On Record," *Union*, April 16, 1908, p. 3.

8. SDCOCBOD, April 29, 1908, 1. Ralston Realty Company had donated $500, and George Marston and several banks had each given $250, as had the San Diego Gas and Electric Company; many others had given from $1 to $25.

9. E. W. Scripps to C. E. Groesbeck, O. W. Cotton, L. S. McClure, and SDCOC, May 11, 1908. SDCOCBOD 1908 (2).

10. "Business Men Approve of Exposition," *Union*, September 7, 1909, 1.

11. "A Vote for Prosperity and Commercial Prestige," Editorial, *Union*, August 8, 1910, 4.

12. Secretary of the Navy George von L. Meyer to Senator John D. Works, February 7, 1912. USNA-DC RG80, Correspondence Files of the Secretary of the Navy (hereafter cited as SecNavGenCor) file 10924-62, box 484.

13. "Second Endorsement," from General Bixby to the Secretary of War, February 10, 1912. A "Third Endorsement" is attached, routing the communication to the Secretary of the Navy. Secretary of the Navy George von L. Meyer to Senator John D. Works, February 14, 1912. Senator John D. Works to Secretary of the Navy George von L. Meyer, February 15, 1912. All in USNA-DC RG80, SecNavGenCor file 10924-63, box 484.

14. "3rd Endorsement." General Board No. 439, December 19, 1912. USNA-DC RG80, SecNavGenCor file 10924-71, box 485.

15. California's vast Eleventh Congressional District at this time comprised San Diego, Orange, Riverside, Imperial, San Bernardino, and Kern Counties.

16. William Kettner, *Why It Was Done and How* (San Diego: Frye & Smith, 1923), 10.

17. President General Board (Dewey) to Secretary of the Navy. Second Endorsement, General Board No. 414-1, March 15, 1913. USNA-DC RG80 SecNavGenCor, file 10924-75, box 485.

18. "President's Annual Report, 1912," 6. SDCOCBOD 1912.

19. Kettner, *Why It Was Done and How*, 47.

20. This quotation comes for an untitled document, perhaps a press release, found in Chamber of Commerce records, dated 1914.

21. This expression appeared in the city's 1904 memorial to the federal government, "The Pacific Ocean and Its Shores Are Destined to Be the Theatre of the World's Greatest Commercial Activity," noted earlier.

22. McGrew, *City of San Diego*, Vol. 1, 210–213.

23. "Congress Members Arrive to Inspect Harbor of the Sun," *Union*, August 7, 1915, 1.

24. "San Diego Selected Base for Subs," San Diego *Union* (hereafter cited as *Union*), January 2, 1919, 1.

25. "San Diego Naval Base," Editorial, *Union*, January 3, 1919, 4.

26. "Committee in Charge Prepares Resume of Facts Concerning Proposed Plans of Government," *Union*, September 7, 1919, 7.

27. "Naval Secretary Coming to Coast to Inspect Work," *Union*, January 15, 1919, 1.

28. "Naval Authorities Favor Large Training Camp on Shores of San Diego Bay," *Union*, January 12, 1919, 4. Some months later, when these events had come to pass, the newspaper gave all the credit to Kettner, who had initiated the idea, sold it to the Navy Department and Congress, and otherwise set the processes in motion. See "Committee in Charge Prepares Resume of Facts Concerning Proposed Plans of Government," *Union*, September 7, 1919, 7.

29. "Kettner Shows Benefit to City of Naval Camp." *Union*, August 4, 1919, 5. According to the newspaper, it was necessary to make a gift of these lands because "the house of representatives . . . had . . . prohibited the army and navy from acquiring any real estate by purchase" that they would then have to develop. But the Navy could, on the other hand, develop land that it already owned, or that was given to the Department free of charge. See

"Committee in Charge Prepares Resume of Facts Concerning Proposed Plans of Government," op. cit.

30. Roger Lotchin, "The City and the Sword in Metropolitan California, 1919–1941," *Urbanism Past and Present* 7:2 (Summer/Fall 1982): 1–16; "Introduction: The Martial Metropolis," in Lotchin, ed., *The Martial Metropolis*, xii–xiii; and Lotchin, *Fortress California, 1910–1961*, esp. chs. 1, 2, 5, 6, and 9.

31. T. N. Faulconer, Executive Secretary, San Diego Board of Park Commissioners, to William Kettner, August 30, 1919. USNA-DC RG80 SecNavGenCor, file 5303–559:31/2, box 212; and B. F. Hutchinson, Senior Member, Planning Board, to Chief of Naval Operations, December 11, 1919. USNA-DC RG45 Naval Records Collection of the Office of Naval Records and Library, Subject Files 1911–1923, file PN-12, Box 531, folder 5.

32. "Building a Seaport," Editorial, *Union*, August 2, 1920, 4; "Navy Items Carried in Record Vote," August 4, 1920, 1; and "San Diego Will Be Made the 'Hampton Roads of the Pacific' If City Votes on Tuesday for Navy Items, Says Admiral Parks," August 1, 1920, 1.

33. "Prosperity Here Declared Due to City's Advertising," *Union*, July 14, 1920, 5.

34. "Welcome to the Fleet," Editorial, *Union*, 7 August 1919, 4.

35. "San Diego Taxpayer Presents Array of Facts and Figures Proving That Naval Site Is Business Investment," *Union*, September 17, 1919, 4.

36. Captain B. F. Hutchison, Senior Member, Planning Board, to CNO, December 11, 1919. USNA-DC RG45 Naval Records Collection of the Office of Naval Records and Library, Subject Files 1911–1923, file PN-12, Box 531, folder 5.

37. John Nolen, "City Plan for San Diego California, prepared for the City Planning Commission, the Harbor Commission, the Park Commission of San Diego, 1926," 24, 30. Mandeville Department of Special Collections, Geisel Library, UCSD. The cost of Nolen's plan of 1908, $10,000, had been paid for by George Marston, but the plan had been largely ignored by the rest of the Chamber directors and the citizenry.

38. Ibid., 29–30. With regard to San Diego's tuna business, small communities of Japanese, Italian, and Portuguese fishermen had begun to establish the commercial viability of tuna on a limited scale only after 1911, but the exigencies of World War I provided a sudden demand for protein that enabled local fishermen and canners to greatly expand their activities. From then until the early 1950s, tuna was an important pillar of San Diego's economy, but it declined rapidly thereafter as both the fishing and packing moved overseas in response to labor costs, tariff regimes, and environmental concerns. See Andrew F. Smith, *American Tuna: The Rise and Fall of an Improbable Food* (Berkeley: University of California Press, 2012).

39. According to Secretary Denby, "The Naval Establishment has larger shop equipment than any other Government activity or any privately owned plant in the United States. The total value of shop and tool equipment, exclusive of drydocks, building ways, and buildings for industrial work under all bureaus of the Navy Department is approximately $63,000,000"; *Annual Report of the Secretary of the Navy, 1926* Washington: USGPO, 1927), 31.

40. Clarence H. Matson, *Building a World Gateway: The Story of Los Angeles Harbor* (Los Angeles: Pacific Era, 1945), 82. How petty the San Diegans must have appeared to a real *macher* like Matson, who surely knew that they admired the human made as much as anyone else, as was obviously the case with the Panama Canal!

41. San Diego's Congressman Phil Swing noted in 1931 that since he had become their representative in 1920, "San Diego has received more consideration at the hands of the government than any city in the United States"; SDCOCBOD October 1, 1931, 1.

42. SDCOCBOD Executive committee meeting (hereafter cited as Ecm), July 18, 1935, 5. The same document compared these figures to naval expenditures in the San Francisco Bay Area, including the Mare Island Navy Yard, ammunition depot, and naval hospital, as well as the operating base at San Francisco and the air station at Sunnyvale. These added up to $166.7 million. It must be noted, however, that the Navy had established its Mare Island bases in 1853, Naval Base San Francisco in 1864, and Sunnyvale in 1930.

43. Pensacola, Florida, was at least San Diego's equal with regard to naval aviation, and Los Angeles was home to several major aircraft manufacturers long before San Diego landed its first large airplane company. See Lotchin, *Fortress California*, ch. 4.

44. Ivor D. Spencer, "U.S. Naval Air Bases from 1914 to 1939," *United States Naval Institute Proceedings*, November 1949, 1953. Spencer was considerably less valedictory about North Island's worth to the Navy than were civic leaders and naval aviators.

45. Other Navy-related environmental problems included significant pollution of the bay and offshore kelp beds from untreated naval sewage, trash, and the discharge of oil-laced bilgewater.

46. William Wagner, *Ryan, the Aviator: Being the Adventures and Ventures of Pioneer Airman and Businessman T. Claude Ryan* (New York: McGraw-Hill, 1971), 3–155.

47. William Wagner, *Reuben Fleet and the Story of Consolidated Aircraft* (Fallbrook, CA: Aero Publishers, 1976), 3–39.

48. Ibid., 175.

49. Ibid., 176–177; SDCOCBOD May 4, 1933, 2–3; and "New $1,500,000 Air Investment Promised Here in Coming Year," *Union*, July 25, 1934, 1–3.

50. Wagner, 177; and SDCOC August 9, 1934, 2. Fleet decided that this time he did not need the government's money, and so the company paid for the move itself.

51. SDCOC Ecm, August 1, 1935, 2; December 26, 1935, 1; March 12, 1936, 3; September 3, 1936, 1; and June 10, 1937, 4.

52. SDCOCBOD December 10, 1936, 1; and December 17, 1936, 2–3.

53. SDCOCBOD December 10, 1936, 1.

54. SDCOC Ecm, July 5, 1937, 3.

55. Gerald Nash, *The American West Transformed: The Impact of the Second World War* (Bloomington: Indiana University Press, 1985), vii, 17; see also Lotchin, *Fortress California*, 171.

56. James O. Goldsborough, "Bottom Falls out of San Diego's Cul-de-Sac," *Union*, September 21, 1993, A-2. According to Goldsborough, "San Diegans cherish the cul-de-sac, and some have come here because of it. . . . New San Diegans replicated much of what had been dear to them in the South and Midwest. Part of that was the sense of being sheltered and safe among their own. The cul-de-sac felt safe."

57. "FDR Orders 100,000 Army-Navy Boost," *Union*, September 9, 1939, 1.

58. "Annual Report of the President—1938–1939," published in the Chamber's monthly magazine, *San Diego Business*, November 1939.

59. "Forrestal Visits Consair Plant in Brief S.D. Stop," *Union*, October 5, 1940, B:8.

60. E. H. Foley, "Public Improvements Necessitated by the National Defense Program at San Diego, California," October 8, 1940. USNA-DC RG71, file ND11/A1-1, box 1352.

61. Wagner, *Reuben H. Fleet*, 223–224.

62. Steven Erie, Vladimir Kogan, and Scott A. MacKenzie, *Paradise Plundered: Fiscal Crisis and Governance Failures in San Diego* (Stanford, CA: Stanford University Press, 2011).

63. SDCOCBOD, June 18, 1942, 1.

64. Laurence Hewes, *Intergroup Relations in San Diego* (San Francisco: American Council on Race Relations, 1946), 12–13.

65. "Half a Million Workers," *Fortune*, March, 1943, quoted and cited in Herbert Northrup, *The Negro in the Aerospace Industry* (Philadelphia: Industrial Research Unit, Wharton School of Finance and Commerce, University of Pennsylvania; distributed by University of Pennsylvania Press, 1968), 17.

66. Leroy Harris, "The Other Side of the Freeway: A Study of Settlement Patterns of Negroes and Mexican Americans in San Diego, California," PhD dissertation (Carnegie-Mellon University, 1974), 59; and *San Diego Union*, June 30, 1942.

67. The "Ringle Report," by Lieutenant K. D. Ringle, USN, and its companion "Munson Report," by C. B. Munson of the U.S. State Department, provide fascinating and sobering pre–Pearl Harbor assessments of the Japanese communities in Southern California. Both investigators conclude that there was "no Japanese problem" in California; that people of Japanese descent were, with few exceptions, "pathetically patriotic to the United States"; that they were thus "underutilized patriotic assets" to the nation; and so that they should *not* be interned in the event of war with Japan. Ringle's report may be found at the Navy Department Library, Navy Yard, Washington, DC, file BIO/ND11/EF37/A8-5'; and Munson's report, dated November 24, 1941, in the U.S. National Archives, Records of the Department of State. The language quoted about the suspected perfidy of Japanese farmers in San Diego may be found in SCBOD rwm, February 26, 1942, and February 4, 1943. See also Donald H. Estes and Matthew Estes, "Further and Further Away: The Relocation of San Diego's Nikkei Community," *Journal of San Diego History XXXIX* (1993), 1–32.

68. U.S. Congress Select Committee Investigating National Defense Migration, *Hearings*, 77th Congress, 1st sess. (Washington, DC: GPO, 1941), Part 12; and U.S. Congress, Subcommittee of the Committee on Naval Affairs, *Hearings*, 78th Congress, 1st sess. (Washington, DC: GPO, 1943), Part 2. Hereafter, these publications are cited as *Hearings*, National Defense Migration; and *Hearings*, Congested Areas, respectively.

69. *Hearings*, National Defense Migration, 4823–4841.

70. Day & Zimmermann, *Summary of Industrial and Commercial Survey, City and County of San Diego* [hereafter cited D-Z] Vol. 1 (San Diego, 1945), 47–48.

71. D-Z, Vol. 1, 45, 119.

72. D-Z, Vol. 1, 26–21.

73. D-Z, Vol. 1, 89, 95.

74. Ibid., 151–152.

75. San Diego Chamber of Commerce, *San Diego Business,* March 11, 1946, 1.

76. SDCOC, "1950 Annual Business Survey," n.p.

77. SDCOC, *San Diego Business*, April 1, 1947, 1.

CHAPTER 3

1. Andrew F. Smith, *American Tuna: The Rise and Fall of an Improbable Food* (Berkeley: University of California Press, 2012), 55.

2. Gary E. Weir, *An Ocean in Common: American Naval Officers, Scientists, and the Ocean Environment* (College Station: Texas A&M University Press, 2001), 4–5.

3. E. H. Foley, "Public Improvements Necessitated by the National Defense Program at San Diego, California," October 8, 1940. USNA-DC RG71, file ND11/A1-1, box 1352.

4. Deborah Day, "Roger Randall Dougan Revelle Biography," Scripps Institution of Oceanography Archives, n.d., 7; retrieved in December 2002 from http://scilib.ucsd.edu/sio/biogr/Revelle_Biogr.pdf.

5. Helen Raitt and Beatrice Moulton, *Scripps Institution of Oceanography: The First Fifty Years* (Los Angeles: The Ward Ritchie Press, 1967), 13.

6. Patricia A. Schaelchlin, *La Jolla: The Story of a Community* (La Jolla, CA: Friends of the La Jolla Library, 1988), 126–128.

7. Judith Morgan and Neil Morgan, *Roger: A Biography of Roger Revelle* (La Jolla, CA: Scripps Institution of Oceanography, 1996), 22.

8. Ibid.

9. Ibid., 28.

10. Bruce Linder, *San Diego's Navy* (Annapolis, MD: Naval Institute Press, 2001), 129.

11. Weir, *An Ocean in Common*, 4–5.

12. Naval Ocean Systems Center (NOSC), "Fifty Years of Research and Development on Point Loma: 1940–1990," (San Diego, CA: Author, 1990), 2; retrieved in September 2011 from www.spawar.navy.mil/sti/publications/pubs/td/1940/index.html.

13. Morgan and Morgan, *Roger*, 5–7.

14. Quoted in Day, "Revelle Biography," 8.

15. Naval Ocean Systems Center (NOSC), "Fifty Years of Research and Development on Point Loma: 1940–1990," (San Diego, CA: Author, 1990), 23; retrieved in September 2011 from www.spawar.navy.mil/sti/publications/pubs/td/1940/index.html.

16. Nancy Scott Anderson, *An Improbable Venture: A History of the University of California, San Diego* (San Diego: UCSD Press, 1993), 29.

17. Raitt and Moulton, *Scripps Institution of Oceanography*, 143.

18. Quoted in Raitt and Moulton, *Scripps Institution of Oceanography*, 145.

19. Ibid., 146.

20. Anderson, *An Improbable Venture*, 37. According to the NOSC report, this partnership was in fact the foundation of a national collaboration that supported "an integrated and economical program of defense research and development."

21. Ibid., 5–7.

22. Henry Luce, in an editorial in *Life* magazine in February 1941 entitled "The American Century," saw American participation and victory in the coming war as a great opportunity for the nation to spread prosperity, the values of American-style democracy, and American political hegemony around the world. Henry Wallace, then FDR's vice president, expressed similar optimism, although from a rather different philosophical point of view, in his best-known speech, "The Century of the Common Man," delivered to the Free World Association in May 1942.

23. Most of the Catalinas and Coronados and 8,600 B-24s were built in San Diego; the rest were built at Consolidated's Fort Worth plant and at Ford Motor Company's factory at Willow Run, Michigan.

24. John Niven, Courtlandt Canby, and Vernon Welsh, eds., *Dynamic America: A History of General Dynamics Corporation and its Predecessor Companies* (New York: General Dynamics Corporation and Doubleday & Company, 1960), 264, 273, 331.

25. Roger Franklin, *The Defender: The Story of General Dynamics* (New York: Harper & Row, 1986), 137.

26. Niven, Canby, and Welsh, *Dynamic America*, 331.

27. Ibid.

28. Ibid., 374.

29. "University Branch Vital, Hopkins says," *San Diego Union*, December 17, 1955, A2.

30. James Britton, "Corporation with a Soul." *San Diego Magazine*, June 1956, 22.

31. Copley to Edwin Pauley, August 9, 1957. Copley in this letter stated his argument in favor of locating the new UC campus in La Jolla to UC regent Pauley, who adamantly opposed the idea.

32. Anderson, *An Improbable Venture*, 38.

33. San Diego Chamber of Commerce, "Proposed Statement Regarding 'University of California Community,'" December 7, 1959, 2, in MS-0040, Records of the San Diego Chamber of Commerce, Box 73, folder 7, San Diego State University Library Department of Special Collections. Also, San Diego *Union*, "Convair Supports Drive for State University Here," October 19, 1955.

34. Ibid., 40, 41.

35. Roger Revelle, interview, May 15, 1985, UC San Diego Library Archives.

36. Sproul to Regent Edward L. Harbach, June 18, 1956.

37. Pat Hyndman, speech given to the San Diego Executive Association, attended by the authors, December 17, 2012.

38. Clark Kerr's and Governor Brown's interviews were conducted in 1983 and 1985, respectively; transcripts in the UC San Diego Library Archives.

39. Copley to Regent Edwin W. Pauley, August 9, 1957.

40. "Statement of the San Diego *Tribune* by Clark Kerr," June 6, 1959. In MC 0040, Records of the San Diego Chamber of Commerce, Box 73, folder 1.

41. San Diego County Planning Department, "Objectives and Policies: Preliminary Statement of Alternates, Second Confidential Draft," August 19, 1960, 3–6. This report presented both the "Geraniums," or anti-industrialization argument, *and* the "Smokestacks" position in starkly negative terms, while clearly favoring the "Selected Industry" alternative—as a most suitable third way.

42. Quoted in Anderson, *An Improbable Venture*, 39, 51.

43. Revelle interview, op. cit.

44. Ibid., 69, 134. Also, Morgan and Morgan, *Roger*, 62.

45. Jim Arnold interview, October 5, 1985, UC San Diego Library Archives.

46. Morgan and Morgan, *Roger*, 63. Regent Ed Harbach complained to his colleague Jim Archer that Revelle was either unwilling or unable "to plan, document, budget and in general supervise or start the supervision of the expansion of the La Jolla campus." Harbach to Archer, October 16, 1957. Also, Herbert F. York, *Making Weapons, Talking Peace: A Physicist's Odyssey from Hiroshima to Geneva* (New York: Basic Books, 1987), 207–208.

47. Anderson, *An Improbable Venture*, 84–85.

48. Ibid., 86, 87, 90.
49. Ibid., 139.
50. Ibid., 142–143.
51. Ibid., 143.
52. Ibid., 144–145. Booker later recruited Irwin Jacobs to UCSD.
53. Ibid., 116.
54. Ibid., 128–129.
55. Ibid., 131.
56. Ibid., 157.
57. SDCOC, "Resources of the San Diego Area as Related to the Size, Use, and Need for Medical Education Facilities," 1960, 16.
58. Anderson, *An Improbable Venture*, 155–156.
59. Ibid., 158–162.
60. Ibid., 162–163.
61. Interview with Peter Salk, January 9, 2012.

CHAPTER 4

1. *Washington Post* journalist Joel Garreau coined this term and defined it in his book, *Edge City: Life on the New Frontier* (New York: Doubleday, 1991). According to Howard Chudacoff and Judith Smith's interpretation,

> Outside metropolitan borders, "exurbs," "out-towns," and "mall towns" had grown into major residential and commercial centers, providing residents with amenities of urban life while making it unnecessary to travel to a nearby city except for special occasions. Communities with full services of shopping, entertainment, banks, schools, water, and police and fire protection" characterized such places.

(Chudacoff and Smith, *The Evolution of American Urban Society,* 6th edition, Pearson Upper Saddle River, NJ: Prentice Hall, 2005, 302–304). Moreover, residents of the nearby city *commute to* the Edge City to work, shop, and play. University City and North City West, later renamed Del Mar Heights, differ from this description in that they are both within San Diego's extended city limits and pay their property taxes to the city; their water, schools, and public safety are all part of the municipal system.

2. Sol Penner, interview, May 5, 1999, UC San Diego Library Archives.
3. Paul Saltman, interview, May 10, 1999, UC San Diego Library Archives.
4. The Soviet H-bomb test in 1953 caused the Atlas project to attain the "highest national priority" thereafter. Successful full-range test flights occurred in 1958, with deployment both as an ICBM and a launch vehicle for satellites and manned spacecraft a year later. Although the H-bomb-tipped Atlas was replaced by the Minuteman in 1965, its use as a satellite launcher continued until 1995. See "SM-65 Atlas"; retrieved in August 2012 from http://en.wikipedia.org/wiki/SM-65_Atlas.
5. Mike Davis, "The Next Little Dollar," in *Under the Perfect Sun: The San Diego Tourists Never See* (New York: The New Press, 2003), 64–67, 78. Also, "Bust Town?" *Time* Magazine, August 17, 1962, 30.
6. Economic Research Bureau of San Diego, *San Diego Economic Bulletin*, annual "year in review" issues, January 1965–January 1973.

7. No one has compiled or told this story better or in more excruciating detail than Mike Davis in "The Next Little Dollar," 77–133.

8. Ibid., 91–92.

9. John Davies, interview with Mary Walshok and Abraham Shragge, spring 2009.

10. Ibid., 79, 85.

11. Pete Wilson, "The State of the City of San Diego," January 12, 1972, 2–6.

12. Pete Wilson, "A Report to the People of San Diego," January 8, 1974, 5.

13. Ibid., 4, 12, 14. Irvine Reynolds was employed by the Copley International Corporation, a subsidiary of San Diego's Union-Tribune Publishing Company.

14. Steven P. Erie, Vladimir Kogan, and Scott Mackenzie, *Paradise Plundered: Fiscal Crisis and Governance Failures in San Diego* (Stanford, CA: Stanford University Press, 2011), 50–51.

15. "Master Plan for the University of California Community," Planning Department, City of San Diego, March 1959, 23.

16. Bob Dorn, "Property and Greed," *San Diego Reader*, July 22, 1982.

17. Larry Remer, "The Selling of Torrey Pines," *San Diego Newsline*, June 17–24, 1981. Also, Anthony Perry, "Sell or Lease? Council Must Decide How to Manage City Land," *San Diego Union*, July 21, 1981, B-1.

18. Interview with Mike Madigan, fall 2010.

19. Interview with Pete Garcia, spring 2011.

20. Richard A. Rettig, *Cancer Crusade: The Story of the National Cancer Act of 1971* (New York: Authors Choice Press, 1977), 2–3, 8.

21. Sarita Eastman, *Good Company: The Story of Scripps Health and Its People* (San Diego: Scripps Health, 2012), 59.

22. Ibid., 85.

23. Steven Casper (2009), *Social Structure and Marketplace Formation within California Biotechnology* (Industry Studies Working Paper: 2009-02). (Claremont, CA: Keck Graduate Institute, Claremont College.

24. Richard Ulevitch, interview, February 29, 2012.

25. "Sanford-Burnham Medical Research Institute"; retrieved in January 2013 from www.sanfordburnham.org/ourmission/about/Pages/Home.aspx.

26. Mark Peter Jones, "Biotech's Perfect Climate: the Hybritech Story." PhD dissertation, University of California San Diego, 2005, 260.

27. Nancy Scott Anderson, *An Improbable Venture: A History of the University of California, San Diego* (San Diego, CA: UCSD Press, 1993).

28. IVAC and IMED were both acquired by Eli Lilly; ISSCO was acquired by Computer Associates International; Linkabit was acquired by MA/Com (which later became Qualcomm).

29. Margaret Pugh O'Mara, *Cities of Knowledge: Cold War Science and the Search for the Next Silicon Valley (Politics and Society in Twentieth-Century America)* (Princeton, NJ: Princeton University Press, 2005).

30. Ibid., 58–60.

31. Ibid., 2.

CHAPTER 5

Portions of this chapter come from a previously published essay, "The Invention of San Diego's Innovation Economy," in *The Strategic Management of Place* by David Audretsch and Mary Walshok (Cheltenham, UK: Edward Elgar, 2013).

1. "Council on Competitiveness, History," December 2012; available at www.compete .org/about-us/history/.

2. Patricia A. Pelfrey. *Entrepreneurial President Richard Atkinson and the University of California 1995–2003* (Berkeley: University of California Press, 2012).

3. Brian O'Reilly and Lorraine Carson, "What's So Great about Admiral Bobby Inman?" *Fortune*, November 10, 1986; available at http://money.cnn.com/magazines/fortune/fortune_archive/1986/11/10/68258/index.htm.

4. Dan O. Pegg, interview, December 17, 2012.

5. "Austin Icons Revisit MCC," March 8, 2012; available at www.pecanstreet.org/2012/03/austin-icons-revisit-mcc/.

6. Ibid.

7. Dan Pegg, interview, December 17, 2012.

8. R. B. Wooley, interview, March 26, 2012.

9. Iris Engstrand, *San Diego: California's Cornerstone* (Tulsa, OK: Continental Heritage Press, 1980), 207.

10. Donald Patton and Martin Kenney, "The Spatial Configuration of the Entrepreneurial Support Network for the Semiconductor Industry," *R&D Management*, Vol. 35, Issue 1 (2005).

11. Authors' interviews with Ivor Royston, 2008; Harvey White, 2008; and R. B. Wooley, February 2012.

12. R. B. Wooley interview, March 26, 2012.

13. M. Porter, *Clusters of Innovation Initiative: San Diego* (Washington, DC: U.S. Council on Competitiveness, 2001); available at www.compete.org/images/uploads/File/PDF%20 Files/CoC_sandiego_cluster.pdf.

14. *San Diego Business Journal Annual Book of Lists* for 1986–2011.

15. M. L. Walshok, E. Furtek, C. W. B. Lee, P. H. Windham, "Building Regional Innovation Capacity: The San Diego Experience," *Industry & Higher Education* 16.1 (2002): 27–42.

16. According to Robert Putnam, in his landmark work, *Bowling Alone* (New York: Simon and Schuster, 2000), social capital includes

> . . . features of social organization, such as networks, norms, and trust that facilitate coordination and cooperation for mutual benefit. Social capital enhances the benefits of investment in physical and human capital. . . . [Social capital consists of] relationships based in patterns of reciprocal, enforceable trust that enable people and institutions to gain access to resources like social services, volunteers, or funding.

Bob Edwards and Michael Foley suggest that such qualities represent a key element of the "'civic culture' argument," with "deep roots in American political science." They comprise the glue that holds a community together and keeps it functioning. See "Civil Society and Social Capital" in Bob Edwards, Michael W. Foley and Mario S. Dani, eds., *Beyond Tocqueville: Civil Society and the Social Capital Debate in Comparative Perspective* (Hanover, NH: University Press of New England, 2001), 7.

17. M. Porter, *Clusters of Innovation Initiative: San Diego* (U.S. Council on Competitiveness, 2001); available at www.compete.org/images/uploads/File/PDF%20Files/CoC_sandiego_cluster.pdf.

18. Duane Roth and Pedro Cuatrecasas, "The Distributed Partnering Model for Drug Discovery and Development," 2010, the Ewing Marion Kauffman Foundation; available at www.kauffman.org/uploadedFiles/distributed-partnership-model_12510.pdf.

19. R. DeVol, P. Wong, et al., "America's Biotech and Life Science Clusters: San Diego's Position and Economic Contributions" (Milken Institute, 2004); available at www.milkeninstitute.org/pdf/biotech_clusters.pdf.

20. Nitasha Tiku and April Joyner, "Incubation Nation: Where Great Ideas Are Born," *Inc.*, May 1, 2010.

21. Bruce Katz, "City Centered," *Time Magazine*, October, 21 2010.

22. Liz Wolgemuth,"10 Best Places for Tech Jobs," *US News & World Report*, September 15, 2009.

23. San Diego Workforce Partnership and San Diego Regional Economic Development Corporation, "Qualcomm & Telecommunications in San Diego: An Economic and Workforce Needs Assessment," January 11, 2013; available at www.sandiegobusiness.org/sites/default/files/011113-TelecomReport.pdf.

24. Steven Casper, "How Do Technology Clusters Emerge and Become Sustainable? Social Network Formation and Inter-firm Mobility within the San Diego Biotechnology Cluster," *Research Policy 36*: 438–455.

25. We would have liked to compare such contemporary data with those from 1985, the year of CONNECT's creation, but numbers on overall globally traded employment were not being collected by regional economic development agencies at that time.

26. According to the Naval Amphibious Base Coronado's official website, "NABC supports over 30 tenant commands, including Amphibious Construction Battalion One, Naval Special Warfare Group One, and Tactical Air Control Group One. The on base population is 5,000 military personnel and 7,000 students and reservists"; retrieved on December 17, 2012, from www.military.com/base-guide/naval-amphibious-base-coronado.

27. See *San Diego Union*, January 7 and 17, 1990, pp. 1 and B-7, respectively; September 1, 1990, p. B-1; January 4, 1996, p. B-2; May 30, 1996, p. B-3; February 26, 1997, p. B-9 (a letter to the editor from two physicians at UCSD School of Medicine, claiming that contrary to information from the Navy and the *Union*, nuclear radiation is *not* good for the human organism); and September 24, 1997, p. B-9.

28. See, for example, *San Diego Union Tribune*, "Making a Place for Castles in the Sand," March 16, 1995, p. B-11; "Dredging on Deck for Larger Carriers," December 15, 1995, p. 1; "Coronado Wants New Look at Navy Plan for Carriers," January 4, 1996, p. B-2; "Napa Firm to Dredge Bay—Sand Goes to Beaches," April 5, 1996, p. B-3; "Navy Granted Right to Resume Sand-Dumping, but Coastal Panel Could Intervene Soon," December 13, 1997, p. B-1; and "Judge Rejects Plan to Halt Navy Dredging," March 26, 1998, p. B-4.

29. See *San Diego Union-Tribune*, "Navy Broadway Complex: A History," November 4, 2011, available at www.utsandiego.com/news/2011/nov/04/navy-broadway-complex-history/; and "Navy Wins Federal Judgment on Broadway Complex," October 17, 2012, available at www.utsandiego.com/news/2012/oct/17/navy-wins-federal-judgement-broadway-

complex/. In the interest of full disclosure: Douglas Manchester has recently acquired ownership of the *Union-Tribune* newspaper.

30. "Traded Industry Clusters in the San Diego Region," *SANDAG Info*, December 2012, 6.

CHAPTER 6

1. Mike Davis, "The Next Little Dollar: The Private Governments of San Diego," in Mike Davis et al., *Under the Perfect Sun: The San Diego Tourists Never See* (New York: The New Press, 2003); and Steve Erie et al., *Paradise Plundered: Fiscal Crisis and Governance Failures in San Diego* (Stanford, CA: Stanford University Press, 2011).

2. The five characteristics of the civic culture enabling commercialization in San Diego originally appeared in M. L. Walshok, "Connecting Science and Business," in R. Miller and B. J. Le Boeuf, eds., *Developing University-Industry Relations: Pathways to Innovation from the West Coast* (San Francisco: Jossey- Bass, 2009).

3. George Homans, *The Human Group* (New York: Harcourt Brace, 1950).

4. M. L. Walshok, *(MOD) Metrics for Capturing Crucial Social Dynamics of Innovative Regions: Implications for S&T Policy*. Final Report to the National Science Foundation, NSF Award #0914793 (2012).

5. Henry Chesborough, *Open Business Models: How to Thrive in the New Innovation Landscape* (Boston: Harvard Business School Press, 2006).

6. D. B. Audretsch and R. Thurik, "What's New about the New Economy? Sources of Growth in the Managed and Entrepreneurial Economies," *Industrial and Corporate Change* 10(1) (2001): 267–315.

7. R. Florida, *Rise of the Creative Class* (New York: Basic Books, 2002); and P. R. Krugman, *Geography and Trade* (Leuven, Belgium, and Cambridge, MA: Leuven University Press and MIT Press, 1991).

8. Audretsch and Thurik, "What's New about the New Economy?"

9. "Q&A with Michael Porter"; retrieved in January 2013 from www.businessweek .com/magazine/content/06_34/b3998460.htm.

10. Audretsch and Thurik, "What's New about the New Economy?" 267–315.

11. Ibid., 307.

12. Daniel Boorstin, *The Americans: The National Experience* (New York: Random House, 1965), 113–116.

13. Mary Ellen Stratthaus, "Flaw in the Jewel: Housing Discrimination against Jews in La Jolla, California," *American Jewish History* 84.3 (1996): 189–219.

14. M. Porter, *Clusters of Innovation Initiative: San Diego*, (U.S. Council on Competitiveness, 2001).

15. R. Florida, *Rise of the Creative Class* (New York: Basic Books, 2002).

16. L. G. Zucker, M. R. Darby, et al. "Geographically Localized Knowledge: Spillovers or Markets?" *Economic Inquiry* 36(1) (1998): 65–86.

17. A. Grandi and R. Grimaldi. "Exploring the Networking Characteristics of New Venture Founding Teams." *Small Business Economics* 21 (2003): 329–341.

18. S. Tallman and A. Phene. "Leveraging Knowledge Across Geographic Boundaries." *Organization Science* 18(2) (2007): 252–260.

19. A. Saxenian, *Regional Advantage: Culture and Competition in Silicon Valley and Route 128* (Cambridge, MA: Harvard University Press, 1996).

20. P. R. Krugman, *Geography and Trade* (Leuven, Belgium, and Cambridge, MA: Leuven University Press and MIT Press, 1991).

21. S. Casper, (2007). How Do Technology Clusters Emerge and Become Sustainable? Social Network Formation and Inter-Firm Mobility within the San Diego Biotechnology Cluster. *Research Policy* 36 (2007): 438–455.

22. Douglass C. North and Robert Paul Thomas, *The Rise of the Western World* (Cambridge, UK: Cambridge University Press, 1973), 1.

INDEX